Simple Fare

REDISCOVERING THE PLEASURES OF REAL FOOD

RONALD JOHNSON

ILLUSTRATIONS BY ROBBIN GOURLEY

SIMON AND SCHUSTER

NEW YORK   LONDON   TORONTO   SYDNEY   TOKYO

SIMON AND SCHUSTER

SIMON & SCHUSTER BUILDING

ROCKEFELLER CENTER

1230 AVENUE OF THE AMERICAS

NEW YORK, NEW YORK 10020

DESIGNED BY EVE METZ
MANUFACTURED IN THE UNITED STATES OF AMERICA

10   9   8   7   6   5   4   3   2   1

LIBRARY OF CONGRESS CATALOGING-IN-PUBLICATION DATA

JOHNSON, RONALD
   SIMPLE FARE : REDISCOVERING THE PLEASURES OF HUMBLE FOOD / RONALD
JOHNSON : ILLUSTRATIONS BY ROBBIN GOURLEY.
      P.   CM.
   INCLUDES INDEX.
   1. COOKERY.   I. TITLE.
TX714.J64   1989
641.5—DC20

89-6140
CIP

ISBN 0-671-66585-5

TO MY FATHER, ALSO A FINE COOK

Contents

Introduction

Samuel Johnson, never at a loss for an opinion, once remarked: "I look upon it, that he who does not mind his belly will hardly mind anything else." That he probably had in mind his pint of beer with a chop and brussels sprouts, rather than Socrates toasting wine over a rude wood table set with bread, rank cheese, sliced onion, and a bowl of olives, is only an accident of place and time. Either philosopher would have as happily, I like to think, sat down with us today to an herb omelet, tossed salad, and peeled fragrant tangerine. Well fed, over an exotic cup of hot coffee, they would proceed the same to make sense of a wayward universe.

Unfortunately, these kinds of honest, frugal feasts are hard come by these days. As inflation shrinks the dollar, serving a family becomes more and more that Alice in Wonderland dilemma of running faster to stay in place. Instead of a butcher, a baker, and a backyard garden, a shopper has to spread his budget over a supermarket stuffed to bursting with a thousand beckoning items.

An ordinary citizen there will spend more on manufactured breakfast items alone than the rest of the world can afford for daily fare (with most of the cost going toward packaging, dehydration, reconstitution, additives for shelf life, flavor enhancers, advertisement, and distribution from handler to handler). And this shopper will still not eat as well and healthily as a French peasant with a filling daily bowl of soup and plate of fruit the land around provides, the Egyptian with his scoop of chickpeas and lentils topped with spicy condiments, the pasta with garlic and tomatoes of Italy, all Mexico hale and hearty on tortillas filled with chile beans, or in China a heap of rice topped with well-seasoned vegetables and shreds of fish or meat.

This book is about how to feed friends and family from a modern supermarket, at least possible expense, with most joy. Being a writer of course I must do both, since I have little cash to spend even when a celebrity knocks on the door. And when they do knock and then dine, from anywhere and everywhere, I ask them to share their own gastronomical economies. The one question I always ask is "What is the best simple dish

11

you know and like to eat again and again?" Here are some of the answers, dishes we can all turn out to general praise, I think.

For my part, even if I could afford lobster and truffles, oysters and prime rib, caviar and champagne, if lark's tongues were a staple and trout lept from my streams, these dishes I would still take comfort from, and share at my table.

San Francisco, 1989

Simple Fare

Beautiful Soups

Soups are synonymous with basic thrift and sustenance. Brimful of vitamins, constructed in one pot from what is gleaned from local produce, from Eden onward, they were our ancestors' daily fare. Soup can also be the modern answer to how someone on a budget can feed a family well on a dib of this and a dab of that—and day to day, too. Anyone close to the soil knows to keep a pot on the fire, to wring essence from scraps and jellies from roasts, a stew of sweetest vegetables, so why not we?

Granted, soups must be coaxed and sniffed and tasted, and they must be stirred and well herbed, and kept gently bubbling sometimes until the last spoonful. Most honest, hearty soups grow even friendlier for this. But no one can feel stinted (at least no one truly hungry) with a steaming bowl, a loaf of bread, a glass of humble wine . . . .

ONION SOUP, WITH ITS TOP OF CRUSTY TOAST AND CHEESE, IS A CLASSIC OF ECONOMY WITH GUSTO, A MEAL IN ITSELF. FORTUNATELY, IT CAN ALSO BE TRANSLATED FROM ITS ORIGINAL SETTING AS A DAWN MEAL, AFTER A NIGHT ON PARIS, IN THE NOW-DESTROYED URBAN PRODUCE MARKET, LES HALLES. ROUGH AND READY, HOT AND STEAMING, WITH A LAST GLASS OF WINE, IT SEEMED SUSTENANCE ENOUGH FOR A LONG TRAMP HOME OVER THE SHINY STREETS AND THEN TO SLEEP.

Onion Soup Mapie

IF THE CLASSIC REQUIRES FOR ITS BASE AN EXCELLENT BEEF STOCK (A LONG, LABORIOUS, AND FAIRLY EXPENSIVE PROCESS) FOR ITS RATHER HASTY PRODUCTION, WE WITH PINCHED POCKETS ARE GIVEN TWO WAYS OUT. ONE, YOU CAN TRY FOR A LONG, SLOW INFUSION OF ONIONS INTO A CANNED STOCK, OR USE THIS RECIPE FROM MAPIE, THE COUNTESS DE TOULOUSE-LAUTREC (YES, OF *THOSE* TOULOUSE-LAUTRECS), WITH ITS BASE OF WHITE WINE.

WITH BRED DETERMINATION, AND FROM HER PHOTOGRAPHS A FLAIR FOR IMPOSING HATS AND ROPES OF PEARLS, SHE BECAME A KIND OF JULIA CHILD FOR FRANCE IN THE AFTERMATH OF WORLD WAR II. HER IMMENSE *LA CUISINE DE FRANCE*, THOUGH OFTEN MAGAZINISH, HOLDS REAL SECRETS AND TRUSTWORTHY TREASURES. ONE CHEF I KNOW USES HER SIDE BY SIDE WITH THE *JOY OF COOKING*.

EVEN AN INEXPENSIVE WHITE WINE OF THE JUGGED CALIFORNIA KIND GIVES THIS SOUP A FINE TART FLAVOR TO BALANCE THE SWEETISH ONIONS, AND IT IS PREPARED IN A TRICE OR TWO.

SERVES 4

- 4 *medium onions, thinly sliced*
- 3 *tablespoons butter*
- 8 *thin slices French bread (or 4 slices white bread, cut in half)*
- 4 *teaspoons flour*
- 1½ *cups dry white wine, heated*
- 3 *cups water, heated*
- *salt and freshly ground pepper*
- *grated Parmesan cheese (or Gruyère)*

Sauté onions in butter in a soup pot over medium heat. Stir now and again, and adjust heat if necessary, to make sure onions color evenly. In about 15 minutes they will be golden. (This should be a gentle, easy process, for you don't want onions to burn through haste.) While onions cook, dry out bread slices in a medium oven. They should be pale gold in color. Remove bread from the oven, turn off heat, and put soup bowls in to warm.

Stir flour into onions and cook 3–4 minutes. Add wine and water, then salt and pepper to taste. When the soup boils up, lower heat and simmer, uncovered, 30 minutes. Place bread slices in the bottom of soup bowls, sprinkle with a generous amount of Parmesan cheese, and ladle hot soup over. Serve at once.

Italian Spinach Soup

A DELICIOUS, EASY, LIGHT SOUP, AND PRETTY TO LOOK AT, TOO. I ONCE HAD A TERRIBLE VERSION OF IT IN ROME WHEN A PARTY OF US WERE INVITED BY AN AMERICAN POET ON A PRIX DE ROME WHO INSISTED WE SHOULD SAMPLE "HOW THE ITALIANS REALLY ATE." WE HATED TO GIVE UP EVEN ONE NIGHT OF ROME'S GREAT RESTAURANTS, BUT WE AGREED TO GO FOR WHAT TURNED OUT TO BE ONE OF THE MOST AWFUL AND ECCENTRIC MEALS EVER SERVED. IT COMMENCED WITH THIS SEEMINGLY INFALLIBLE SOUP (WHICH I HAD COOKED FOR YEARS). UNFORTUNATELY, THE POET HAD NOT UNDERSTOOD THAT SPINACH MUST BE WELL WASHED, AND THERE WERE COLOSSEUMS OF AUTHENTIC ITALIAN DIRT AND GRIT IN EACH SPOONFUL. WHILE THE POET WAS IN THE KITCHEN TURNING THE VEAL GRAY, WE ALL SMILED AND, AS ONE, POURED OUR SOUPS BACK INTO THE TUREEN. BUT NO—HE INSISTED WE EACH HAVE ANOTHER SERVING. SO HE WATCHED US CONSUME IT TO THE LAST, CAREFUL OF OUR TEETH.

SERVES 4

1 *pound fresh spinach (or 1 package frozen)*
3 *tablespoons olive oil*
½ *cup finely chopped onion*
4 *fresh mint leaves, finely chopped (or 1 teaspoon dried)*
3¾ *cups chicken stock*
1¼ *cups milk*
salt and freshly ground pepper
freshly grated nutmeg

Wash spinach well in several waters. Drain in a colander, remove stems, then chop into large shreds. (Frozen spinach has only to be thawed and chopped.)

Add olive oil to a soup pot and cook onion over medium heat until soft. Stir in mint, add spinach, and cook, stirring, until wilted. Add stock and milk, and season to taste with salt, pepper, and nutmeg. Not *too* much nutmeg—only a suggestion.

Simmer, uncovered, 10 minutes. The soup can be served hot or cold.

I PICKED UP THIS TREASURE OF THRIFT NOT FROM A NOTORIOUSLY TIGHT-PURSED SUCCESSFUL HOSTESS BUT FROM HER COMPLAINING LONGTIME COOK. AS I COMPLIMENTED AT THE STOVE, SPOON IN HAND FROM HER OFFERING, SHE MADE A SHRUG AND SAID, "MA'AM, SHE SAY WE GOT TO STRETCH."

Pea Pod and Lettuce Soup

SERVES 4

½ *pound pea pods* (*without peas*)
salt
water
 4 *outer lettuce leaves*
 2 *tablespoons butter*
½ *cup chopped onion*
½ *cup milk*
½ *cup heavy cream*
 1 *tablespoon minced parsley*
 1 *teaspoon minced fresh mint* (*or* ½ *teaspoon dried*)
freshly ground pepper
 1 *cup finely shredded lettuce*

Put pea pods in a kettle with salted water to cover. Bring to a boil, lower heat, and simmer, uncovered, 20 minutes. Add lettuce leaves the last 5 minutes of cooking. Place in a blender with ½ cup of cooking water and puree, going from slow to fast speed. Put through a food mill to remove tough portions of pods and scrape back into blender.

Sauté onion in butter until tender, puree with pea and lettuce mixture. Return to the kettle, add milk, cream, parsley, mint, and salt and pepper to taste. Thin, if necessary, with more milk. Simmer 5 minutes, add shredded lettuce, and cook another 3–4 minutes, or until lettuce is barely done. Serve hot.

WHEN YOU ARE PREPARING ASPARAGUS (AT THE HEIGHT OF ITS SEASON, WHEN INEXPENSIVE, AND YOU CAN'T WAIT ANYMORE) REMEMBER THIS SOUP AT THE SAME TIME FOR A DELIGHTFUL LUNCH

Asparagus Stalk Soup

OR DINNER COURSE THE NEXT DAY. AFTER WRINGING ALL THAT FLAVOR OUT OF THE ASPARAGUS, THIS IS DEFINITELY A CHIN-UP DISH, AND YOU ARE TO BE FORGIVEN IF YOU CALL IT BLANCHED ASPARAGUS SOUP WITH PRIDE.

SERVES 4

2 *tablespoons butter*
1 *small onion, chopped*
2 *cups asparagus stem ends,*
   cut in 1-inch lengths
4 *cups milk*
salt and freshly ground
   pepper
pinch of sugar
a few drops of lemon

Melt butter in a soup pot and sauté onion and asparagus 5 minutes over medium heat. Add milk, bring to a simmer, and cook, uncovered, 15 minutes over low heat. Puree in a blender, then put through a food mill to remove any strings of the stalks. Return to the pot and add salt and pepper to taste, sugar, and enough lemon to perk up taste.

Refrigerate overnight to gather flavor. The soup can be eaten either hot or cold. If hot, top each serving with a pat of butter.

Triple Celery Soup

SERVES 4

CELERY ROOT MAKES A FINE VEGETABLE WHEN IT IS AVAILABLE IN THE MARKET, PARTICULARLY AS A PUREE TO ACCOMPANY MEATS RATHER THAN THE USUAL MASHED POTATOES. HERE IT IS A SPLENDID WAY TO USE THE OUTER COARSE STALKS OF CELERY THAT MIGHT OTHERWISE BE THROWN AWAY. THIS SOUP IS A KIND OF ESSENCE-OF-CELERY—VERY DELICATE, ESPECIALLY COLD.

2 *tablespoons butter*
1 *cup chopped onion*
2 *cups chopped celery, with leaves*
½ *pound celery root, peeled and diced*
4 *cups water*
¼ *teaspoon celery seeds*
salt and freshly ground pepper
1½ *cups milk*
lemon juice

Melt butter in a soup pot and sauté onion until soft. Stir in celery and celery root, and cook gently about 5 minutes over low heat. Add water, celery seeds, and salt and pepper to taste. Cover and simmer 30 minutes. Put through a food mill to remove celery fibers, then puree thoroughly in a blender—going from slow to fast speed.

Place puree back into the pot, add milk, and simmer 5 minutes. Taste for seasoning and add a few drops of lemon juice to perk up the whole thing. Serve hot or chilled.

I'VE TRUSTED THIS SOUP FOR YEARS TO START OFF A COMPANY DINNER WITH *ÉCLAT*, AS WELL AS TO PROVE THAT EVEN BROWSING YOUR JULIA CHILD MIGHT TURN UP INEXPENSIVE DELIGHTS. THOUGH NOW WE OCCASIONALLY GET YOUNG TURNIPS STILL ATTACHED TO THEIR EQUALLY SAVORY GREENS, ANY WITHOUT WILL FIND THIS SOUP STILL IN RANGE SUBSTITUTING OTHER TONIC GARDEN OR SUPERMAR-KET GREENS. MRS. CHILD SUGGESTS SPINACH, BUT I PREFER MUSTARD GREENS—EVEN YOUNG DANDELIONS OFF THE LAWN, BEFORE FLOWER, MIGHT LEND CLASS TO THE GREENY MYSTERY OF THIS SOUP.

Green Turnip Soup

SERVES 4–6

1½ *pounds turnips*
5 *tablespoons butter*
1 *teaspoon sugar*
salt and freshly ground
    pepper
1½ *cups water*
4 *cups packed turnip*
    greens (or mustard
    greens)
3 *cups chicken stock*
1 *cup milk*
1 *tablespoon lemon juice*

Pare and quarter turnips. Place with 3 tablespoons of butter, sugar, a little salt and pepper, and water in a soup kettle. Simmer, covered, 15–20 minutes, or until turnips are soft. Uncover, turn up heat, and boil until liquid evaporates. Turn heat down to medium and toss turnips in the buttery remainder for several minutes to glaze slightly. Scrape turnips into a blender.

Wash greens through several waters and cut out tough stems. Add remaining 2 tablespoons of butter to the kettle and toss greens until they wilt. (Turnip greens take only about 5 minutes, but the rougher mustard greens will take more like 15.)

Add greens to blender with turnips and puree, going from a slow to a fast speed. Return to kettle. Add stock and simmer 10 minutes, then add milk. If you wish a thinner soup, put in a little more milk. Add lemon juice and taste for seasoning, adding more salt, pepper, or sugar as necessary.

For a richer soup, a little more butter can be stirred in just before serving.

Peter's Welsh Soup

THIS STURDY SOUP COMES FROM COMPOSER AND THEATER ENTRE-PRENEUR PETER HARTMAN, WHO TOOK UP RESIDENCE FOR A TIME IN A MISTY WELSH CASTLE. HE MIGHT BE CASTLED, BUT ECONOMY WAS AS NECESSARY THERE AS IT WAS FOR HIS NEIGH-BORS IN COTTAGES, FROM WHOM HE LEARNED THIS CUPBOARD SOUP. THE SECRET IS, OF COURSE, TO WRING THE VERY LAST OF FLAVOR FROM THE VEGETABLES BY MAKING A STOCK FROM THE PEELS, A USEFUL TRICK TO REMEMBER WHEN YOU ARE THROWING OUT THAT SORT OF THING AND DON'T HAVE PIGS OR RABBITS TO FATTEN. THE FRENCH USE EVEN THE PAPERY ONION SKINS IN STOCKS TO GIVE THEM A SLIGHTLY DARKER COLOR, AND ALMOST ANY VEGETABLE TRIMMINGS CAN BE BOILED UP AND THEN REDUCED TO AN ESSENCE, TO BE KEPT IN THE REFRIGER-ATOR FOR ANY KIND OF VEGETABLE SOUP—NOTHING LOST.

SERVES 4–6

2 *medium potatoes*
2 *medium turnips*
2 *medium carrots*
2 *medium onions*
6 *cups water*
salt
2 *tablespoons butter*
freshly ground pepper
pinch of dried thyme (or
summer savory)
1 *bay leaf*
¼ *cup heavy cream*
(optional)
paprika (or minced
parsley or minced chives)

Peel all vegetables and place peelings in a soup pot with water and salt to taste. Bring to a boil, let bubble several minutes, then skim off any scum from the top. Lower heat and simmer, uncovered, 45 minutes.

While this vegetable stock is cooking, cut potatoes, turnips, and carrots into ¼-inch dice. Chop onions coarsely. Heat butter in a large frying pan and cook onions until limp, then add diced vegetables and cook 10 minutes over low heat.

When stock is cooked, strain it through a colander and reserve. Discard peelings and return broth to the pot with vegetables. Add salt and pepper to taste, thyme, and bay leaf. Simmer, uncovered, 30 minutes, or until vegetables are tender.

The soup can be served as is, but it is better, I think, pureed with a little heavy cream added for body. Serve sprinkled with paprika, parsley, or chives.

Plains Chowder

CHOWDERS ARE ALWAYS THOUGHT OF AS CONSTRUCTED AROUND FISH OR CLAMS, BUT THEIR VARIETY DEPENDS ON LOCALE AND INGREDIENTS AT HAND. IT COULD BE CHICKEN, SAY, OR AS IN THIS MIDWEST VARIATION, SIMPLY GREEN BEANS. PRACTICALLY THE ONLY CONSTANTS IN THE WORLD OF CHOWDERS ARE MILK, POTATOES, AND SALT PORK (BACON WILL DO), SO THINK OF CHOWDER AS A FLEXIBLE SIMPLE MEAL MADE WITH INGREDIENTS AVAILABLE AT THE MOMENT.

SERVES 4–6

¼ *pound salt pork, cut in*
   ¼-inch cubes
1 *cup chopped onion*
1 *pound green beans,*
   trimmed and cut in
   1-inch pieces
1 *cup light beef stock*
1 *bay leaf*
2 *tablespoons minced*
   parsley
2 *cups peeled and cubed*
   potatoes
3 *cups milk*
1 *cup heavy cream*
salt and freshly ground
   pepper
paprika

Sauté pork in a soup pot over medium heat. When cubes are golden, lift out with a slotted spoon and reserve. Add onion to fat and cook until soft, then add beans and cook another 5 minutes. Add stock, bay leaf, parsley, and potatoes.

Cover pot and cook 15 minutes over low heat, or until vegetables are tender. Add milk, cream, and salt and pepper to taste, and bring to a simmer. Cover and simmer 10 minutes.

Serve sprinkled with crisp salt pork and paprika.

Swiss Cheese Soup

THE DIFFERENCE BETWEEN THIS—WITH ITS CHEESE, NUTMEG, AND BROWNED BUTTER—AND ORDINARY "MILK TOAST" IS THE DIFFERENCE BETWEEN TWO WORLDS. IT NEEDN'T HAVE ONLY SWISS CHEESE, EITHER, AS IT IS EXCELLENT WITH CHEDDAR OR PARMESAN, AND I ONCE CONSTRUCTED IT WITH PUMPERNICKEL, WHICH WAS SPLENDID. IT HAS THE KIND OF SOUL-SATISFYING SIMPLICITY THAT ONE SITS DOWN TO ALONE ON A CHILLY NIGHT WHEN YOU DON'T REALLY WANT TO COOK. IN SPAIN, THERE IS ANOTHER OF THESE ONE-DISH MEALS THEY CALL 15-MINUTE SOUP WHICH I'M NOT VERY FOND OF BUT YOU MAY BE. TO MAKE THIS SPANISH SOUP, SAUTE A CLOVE OF GARLIC IN SOME OLIVE OIL, THEN POUR IT OVER A TRIMMED ROUND OF BROWN BREAD IN AN OVEN-PROOF BOWL. ADD A CUP OF HOT WATER, A LITTLE CHOPPED HAM, SOME SALT AND PEPPER, AND FINALLY, BREAK IN A RAW EGG. PUT THE DISH IN A MEDIUM OVEN UNTIL THE EGG WHITE SETS—ABOUT 10 MINUTES. NOURISHING, QUICK, INEXPENSIVE IT IS, BUT STILL NOT FOR ME.

SERVES 1

2 *slices French bread,*
   lightly toasted
4 *tablespoons grated Swiss*
   cheese
1 *cup milk (approximately),*
   heated
salt and freshly ground
   pepper
freshly grated nutmeg
1 *tablespoon butter*

Place a slice of bread in the bottom of a warm soup bowl, top with cheese, then put the other slice of bread over that. Season milk to taste with salt, pepper, and nutmeg, and pour enough in to nearly fill the bowl. Heat butter in a small saucepan until it turns golden (don't burn it, though) and pour over the soup. Serve immediately.

Cabbage Borscht

EVERYONE KNOWS THE WONDERFUL RUBY-RED BEET BORSCHT (WHICH ALSO TAKES A GOODLY AMOUNT OF EXPENSIVE BEEF FOR THE SOUNDEST VERSION), BUT BORSCHT AND BEETS ARE NOT SYNONYMOUS, AS THIS HUMBLE DISH SHOWS. IT MAY BE HUMBLE, BUT IT IS EASY TO PREPARE AND OF A LIVELY FLAVOR, IF NO GREAT JEWEL OF COLOR. WITH AN HONEST LOAF OF BREAD AND A SOUND FRUIT DESSERT SUCH AS OLD-FASHIONED APPLE DUMPLINGS (PAGE 343), THIS INDEED MAKES A FINE FAMILY SUPPER ON COLD NIGHTS.

SERVES 4

2 *slices bacon, cut in fine strips*
1 *medium onion, chopped*
1 *clove garlic, minced*
2 *carrots, pared and sliced*
1 *large potato, peeled and cut into ¼-inch dice*
½ *small cabbage, coarsely chopped*
4 *cups chicken stock*
salt
1 *tablespoon paprika*
1 *teaspoon dried dill*
1 *tablespoon red wine vinegar*
sour cream

Sauté bacon in a soup pot over medium heat. When nearly done (but not yet crisp), remove with a slotted spoon and drain on paper towels.

Cook onion and garlic in bacon fat until onion softens, then add carrots, potato, and cabbage to the pot. Add stock and season to taste with salt. (If the stock is well seasoned, you won't need any.) Add paprika, dill, vinegar, and the bacon. Cook, uncovered, 15–20 minutes over medium heat, or until potato and cabbage are done.

Ladle into soup bowls and add a dollop of sour cream to each.

Peasant's Potato Soup

A NORTHERN EUROPEAN SOUP OF AMAZING FLAVOR, CONSIDERING THE PLAIN INGREDIENTS. BUTTER CAN BE SUBSTITUTED FOR LARD, IF YOU WISH, THOUGH I BELIEVE LARD IS THE SECRET THAT GIVES THE SOUP ITS FIRM CHARACTER. IT IS, HOWEVER, QUITE AN ADAPTABLE SOUP. A LEEK COULD BE THROWN IN, OR A SPRINKLE OF FRESH HERBS OR CHEESE MIGHT GRACE THE TOP. PLOW IN.

SERVES 4
(for a first course,
2 for supper)

2 *cups peeled and diced
    potatoes*
1 *cup chopped onion*
4 *cloves garlic, 2 minced,
    2 slightly flattened and
    peeled*
4 *tablespoons lard (or
    butter)*
4 *cups light beef stock (or
    chicken stock or water)*
*salt and freshly ground
    pepper*
¼ *cup minced parsley*
4 *slices white bread,
    trimmed of crust and
    diced*

Place potatoes, onion, minced garlic, and 2 tablespoons of lard in a soup kettle and cook for about 10 minutes over medium-low heat, stirring now and again. Add stock or water and salt and pepper to taste. Simmer 15–20 minutes, or until potatoes are done. Put through a food mill or puree in a blender. Return to the kettle. Stir in parsley and heat through.

Prepare bread. Heat remaining 2 tablespoons of lard in a frying pan with flattened garlic cloves. When garlic is golden, remove from pan and sauté bread, tossing constantly, until golden and crisp. Drain on paper towels. Serve soup sprinkled with croutons.

WHAT MORE COULD ONE ASK FOR AT A LUNCH OR LATE SUPPER THAN THIS LIVELY, FORTIFYING SOUP? WELL, PERHAPS STEAMED TORTILLAS, A GLASS OF BEER, AND A FILLING DESSERT TO FOLLOW. IF

Yucatan Potato Egg-drop Soup

YOU DON'T HAVE FRESH JALAPEÑOS, ANY LITTLE CHILES WILL DO, OR YOU COULD USE A COUPLE OF PICKLED JALAPEÑOS INSTEAD.

SERVES 4

2 *tablespoons butter*
2 *medium onions, chopped*
1 *clove garlic, minced*
1½ *cups chopped canned tomatoes*
1 *jalapeño chile, seeded and minced*
2 *tablespoons minced fresh coriander (or parsley)*
2 *tablespoons flour*
5 *cups water*
4 *medium potatoes, peeled and diced*
salt and freshly ground pepper
2 *eggs*

Melt butter in a soup pot and sauté onions for a few minutes over medium heat. Add garlic, tomatoes, chile, and coriander. Cook gently 10 minutes, then stir in flour and cook a few more minutes. Add water and stir until it comes to a fine rolling boil. Add potatoes and simmer 30 minutes over low heat, or until potatoes are soft. Add salt and pepper to taste.

Finally, break eggs into the simmering soup. Cook 1 minute, then stir with a fork until eggs form strings. Serve hot.

Basque Bean Soup

THIS EXCELLENT SOUP IS ADAPTED FROM ELIZABETH DAVID'S *MEDITERRANEAN FOOD*. IT'S NOT VERY ECONOMICAL IF YOU HAVE TO BUY A WHOLE PUMPKIN, BUT I FIND THAT CANNED PUMPKIN WORKS JUST AS WELL SINCE IT COOKS TO MUSH ANYWAY. EITHER WAY IT SEEMS TO BE THE PUMPKIN THAT GIVES IT ITS SAVOR SINCE THERE IS VERY LITTLE ELSE TO IT. IT MAKES A PLEASANT LUNCH OR SUPPER WITH BREAD AND SALAD, OR IT CAN BE SERVED IN SMALL PORTIONS AS THE FIRST COURSE OF A MEAL.

SERVES 4–6

½ *pound dried small white beans*
1 *large onion, chopped*
2 *tablespoons butter (or lard)*
1 *small cabbage, cored and coarsely chopped*
1 *1-pound can pumpkin (or 2 cups diced fresh pumpkin)*
2 *cloves garlic, minced*
2 *quarts water (or stock)*
salt and freshly ground pepper

Place beans in plenty of water and bring to a boil. Simmer, covered, 5 minutes, then let sit 1 hour. Bring to a boil again and simmer 30 minutes, then drain the beans.

Sauté onion in butter in a soup kettle until the onion turns golden—about 15 minutes over medium-low heat. Stir now and again so it colors evenly. Add cabbage, pumpkin, garlic, beans, water, and salt and pepper to taste. Simmer, covered, 2½ hours, or until beans are quite tender.

Spanish Cocido

THOUGH NOT QUITE AS HEARTY AS A MINESTRONE, THIS EASY SOUP MAKES A PLEASANT WINTER SUPPER WITH CRUSTY BREAD AND A GLASS OF RED WINE. THIS IS THE SIMPLEST VERSION—AND THERE ARE MANY ACROSS SPAIN—BECAUSE IT HAS LESS MEAT. SOME USE COMBINATIONS OF HAM, BOTH SMOKED AND UNSMOKED, VEAL, BACON, SALT PORK, SAUSAGE, AND EVEN CHICKEN. THESE CAN MAKE A HEARTY TWO-COURSE MEAL, WITH THE SOUP SERVED FIRST AND THE MEATS IN ARRAY FOR THE SECOND COURSE. IF BENT ON ECONOMY, HOWEVER, THAT VEAL, SAUSAGE, AND CHICKEN MIGHT MAKE THREE OTHER MEALS.

SERVES 4–6

1 *cup dried small white beans*
6 *cups water*
1 *cup diced smoked ham*
¼ *pound slab bacon (or salt pork), in one piece*
1 *medium onion, chopped*
1 *clove garlic, minced*
½ *small head of cabbage, cored and coarsely chopped*
3 *turnips, peeled and diced*
1 *cup coarsely chopped turnip greens*
1 *cup peeled and chopped tomatoes (fresh or canned)*
salt and freshly ground pepper

Soak beans overnight in water. The next day, bring to a boil, turn down heat until pot just barely simmers, then add ham and bacon. Cover and cook 2–2½ hours over lowest heat, or until beans are tender.

Add remaining ingredients, with salt and pepper to taste, and simmer another 1½ hours. Remove bacon or salt pork, and cut into dice, then return to the pot. Serve hot in warmed bowls.

Split Pea and Barley Soup

I'M NOT MUCH A FAN OF SPLIT PEA SOUPS, USUALLY STODGY IN TASTE, COLOR, AND TEXTURE, BUT HERE THE BARLEY GIVES BOTH TASTE AND TEXTURE, AND THE CARROTS BRIGHTEN UP THE BOWL FOR A HEART-WARMING AND RIB-STICKING SOUP. VEGETARIANS MIGHT WANT TO LEAVE OUT THE BACON AND ADD SOME MORE BUTTER, OTHERS MIGHT WISH TO SUBSTITUTE A HAM HOCK OR BONE, OR THE BONE FROM A LEFTOVER LEG OF LAMB (THE BEST OF ALL!).

SERVES 4

2 *slices bacon, cut in small strips*
1 *tablespoon butter*
1 *onion, chopped*
1 *clove garlic, minced*
5 *cups hot water*
¾ *cup split peas*
⅓ *cup pearl barley*
¼ *teaspoon dried thyme*
1 *bay leaf*
salt and freshly ground pepper
2 *carrots, pared and thinly sliced*

Place bacon and butter in a soup kettle. Stir over medium heat until bacon is cooked but not yet crisp. Add onion and garlic, and cook until translucent. Add water, peas, barley, thyme, bay leaf, and salt and pepper to taste.

Bring to a boil, then lower heat and simmer, uncovered, 1 hour. Add carrots and cook another 30 minutes. Serve hot and steaming.

Esau's Potage, as lentil soup is often called, is a fortifying if usually dreary dish, but with a toss of peppery watercress and a squirt of lemon, it immediately becomes something quite special, fit for any occasion.

Lentil and Watercress Soup

SERVES 4

1 *cup lentils*
5 *cups light beef stock (or chicken stock)*
salt
1 *bunch (¼ pound) watercress*
2 *tablespoons butter*
1 *tablespoon lemon juice*
freshly ground pepper

Pick over lentils to make sure there are no stones among them, then wash well in a sieve. Put in a pot with stock and simmer until tender—the time depends on the lentils, but it shouldn't take more than 45 minutes. Add salt to taste toward the end of cooking.

Trim the watercress of the largest stems and wash well. Drain in a colander. Put butter in a large frying pan and toss watercress over medium heat until wilted. Add to the lentils and put in a blender. The soup can be thoroughly pureed, but I like to have it so there are bits and pieces of lentils and green watercress here and there. This is a matter of choice.

Return to the pot and add lemon juice and some pepper. Thin the soup with water as necessary, particularly when refrigerated, as it then needs more liquid.

Anchovy Soup

ADA BONI, WHOSE SOUND AND SIMPLE *TALISMAN ITALIAN COOK BOOK* HAS NOURISHED ME FOR SO MANY YEARS, CALLS THIS MOCK FISH SOUP. BUT SINCE IT HAS AN UNEXPECTEDLY COMPLEX TASTE FOR SUCH A SIMPLE DISH, I SEE NO REASON TO FUDGE. WHY NOT JUST CALL IT ANCHOVY SOUP, HONESTLY, UNLESS THERE IS SOMEONE IN THE FAMILY WHO DOESN'T THINK HE LIKES ANCHOVIES EITHER OFF OR ON PIZZA? IT CAN BE MADE BETTER BY USING A LIGHT FISH STOCK MADE FROM SCRAPS AND BONES, BUT DON'T USE BOTTLED CLAM JUICE BECAUSE THAT MAKES IT TOO TOO SALTY. THE GARLIC CAN BE TO YOUR TASTE—I LIKE IT WITH MORE GARLIC AND LESS TOMATO, BUT YOU MIGHT FEEL OTHERWISE. IT MAKES A FINE FIRST COURSE WITH AN ITALIAN MEAL, EVEN A SIMPLE PLATE OF PASTA (THOUGH A TRADITIONAL ITALIAN MEAL WOULD NOT INCLUDE SOUP AND PASTA). TRY IT, IT IS A SOUP FOR POETS, PEASANTS, AND JUST PLAIN PENNY PINCHERS.

SERVES 4

¼ *cup olive oil*
1–2 *cloves garlic, sliced*
1 *can flat anchovies*
2 *tablespoons minced parsley*
2–3 *tablespoons tomato paste*
5 *cups water*
4 *slices white bread, trimmed of crust, soaked in water, and squeezed dry*
freshly ground pepper
4 *slices white bread, toasted and cut in rounds*
Parmesan cheese (or Romano)

Place olive oil in a soup pot and add garlic and anchovies with the oil in the can. Cook 3–4 minutes over medium heat, stirring. Do not allow garlic to turn more than pale gold. Stir in parsley, tomato paste, and water. Bring to a boil over high heat, then lower heat and simmer 15 minutes.

Stir in bread and cook another few minutes. Put the soup through a food mill, or puree in a blender, and return to the pot. Add pepper to taste (with the salt of the anchovies to my taste it needs no salt). Simmer another 5 minutes. If allowed to set 1 hour or so, or even overnight in the refrigerator, this soup's flavor improves.

To serve, top toast rounds with cheese and set a few minutes in a medium oven to melt the cheese. Ladle hot soup into bowls and place the cheese crouton on top.

Nîmoise Fish Soup

THIS CLASSIC SOUP IS THE BASIS OF A *BOUILLABAISSE*, BUT IT IS SPLENDID EVEN WITHOUT ALL THE VARIOUS FISH SWIMMING IN AT THE END. IT CAN EVEN BE MADE WITHOUT SAFFRON, IF YOU CAN'T AFFORD A SPRINKLE, THOUGH SAFFRON AND GOOD OLIVE OIL ARE WHAT GIVE THE DISH ITS PIZZAZZ. IT CAN BE PUT TOGETHER IN A RATHER SLAPDASH WAY, SINCE NO TWO PERSONS MAKE THE SOUP EXACTLY THE SAME. HERE, I HAVE GIVEN THE MOST DOLLAR-STRETCHING WAY TO CONCOCT IT, THICKENED WITH POTATOES AND A BIT OF FLOUR RATHER THAN WHISKING IN BEATEN EGG YOLKS AT THE END. I'VE ALSO OMITTED THE GARLIC MAYONNAISE CALLED *AIOLI* THAT IS USUALLY ASSOCIATED WITH THE DISH, STIRRED IN JUST BEFORE SERVING, SINCE MORE AND MORE I DISLIKE THE AFTERTASTE OF RAW GARLIC IN QUANTITY. INSTEAD I MAKE A RATHER UNORTHODOX GARLIC PASTE BY BAKING A WHOLE HEAD OF GARLIC, WRAPPED IN FOIL, AT ABOUT 400° FOR AN HOUR. THE CLOVES CAN THEN BE DETACHED WHEN COOL AND SLIT WITH A KNIFE, AND ALL THE AMBER GOODNESS SQUEEZED OUT IN A BOWL. WHEN YOU HAVE COLLECTED IT ALL, ADD SOME OLIVE OIL AND SALT TO TASTE. THIS IS LOVELY SPREAD ON THE TOASTED CROUTONS, RATHER THAN CHEESE.

SERVES 4

1–2 *pounds fish scraps,
    heads, backbones, and
    so forth*
2 *onions, chopped*
1 *clove garlic, minced*
¼ *cup olive oil*
1 *tablespoon flour*
2 *medium potatoes,
    peeled and cubed*
⅔ *cup tomatoes (canned
    or fresh)*
*water (or half water, half
    white wine)*
2 *sprigs of parsley*
½ *teaspoon dried thyme*
1 *bay leaf*
2 *strips of orange rind*
*salt and freshly ground
    pepper*
½ *teaspoon saffron
    threads (optional)*
4 *slices white bread,
    trimmed, cut in
    rounds, and toasted*
*grated Parmesan cheese (or
    Swiss)*

Gather fish scraps—red snapper, bass, halibut, and cod are good for this. The heads are particularly fine because they give the soup some body and can be had for practically nothing.

Sauté onions and garlic in olive oil in a soup pot until soft. Stir in flour and cook 3–4 minutes. Add fish, potatoes, tomatoes, and water to cover. Bring to a boil, then lower to a simmer. Add herbs and orange rind tied in a cheesecloth bag, and salt and pepper to taste.

Simmer, uncovered, 30–40 minutes, then crumble in saffron and cook a few more minutes. Strain soup, remove fish bones and bag of herbs, and put vegetables through a food mill into the stock. Reheat the soup and serve with croutons sprinkled with a little cheese floating on top.

WITH SWEET SQUID AND EVEN SWEETER MUSSELS (BOTH SO INEX-PENSIVE), THIS MAKES A DISH AS DELECTABLE AS ONE WITH MANY VARIETIES OF RARE SEAFOOD. IT'S SO GOOD, IN FACT, THAT YOU CAN

Poor Man's Seafood Stew

SERVE IT AS A FIRST COURSE TO COMPANY—YOU DON'T *HAVE* TO TELL THEM ITS NAME.

SERVES 4

12 *fresh mussels (or clams)*
1½ *pounds squid*
3 *tablespoons olive oil (or vegetable oil)*
½ *cup chopped onion*
2 *cloves garlic, minced*
4 *tablespoons minced parsley*
1½ *cups chopped canned tomatoes*
1 *cup water (or dry white wine)*
¼ *teaspoon dried thyme*
1 *teaspoon dried basil*
1 *teaspoon fennel seeds*
salt and freshly ground pepper
½ *teaspoon red pepper flakes*
juice and grated rind of ½ lemon

Beard mussels and put in a bowl of salted water. Discard any that don't close up in 1 hour or so.

Clean squid (see page 69). Cut off the tentacles and reserve. Slit bodies up one side with a sharp knife and lay them out flat, then cut into 1½-inch squares.

Heat oil in a large pot over medium heat. Add onion and garlic, and cook until limp. Stir in parsley and tomatoes with their juice, then add water, herbs, and spices. (Go easy on the salt because the mussels will add some later.) Finally, add the squid squares and tentacles, and lemon juice, and rind.

Turn heat to low, cover pot, and cook gently 40 minutes. When squid is tender, put mussels in a pan with ½ cup of water, cover, and steam 10 minutes. Remove from pan and to remove any sand pour pan juices through a moistened paper towel set in a sieve. Add juices to the stew and taste for seasoning.

Serve the stew in warm soup plates with mussels in their shells on top as garnish. Accompany with plenty of fresh bread.

Any Minestrone

Like home-grown vegetable soup, minestrone hardly needs a recipe. Hearty American soup is usually based on a good beef bone, while most Italians use little if any meat—at the most a little dice of salt pork and a light stock. The soup is so chock-full of flavor, however, there is no need for either if you stick to your vegetarian guns. So throw the idea of authenticity to the winds and use whatever is inexpensive and available and colorful. Minestrone varies so much by district in Italy, and even from home to home, that there is no such thing as a definitive version anyway.

First you will need ¾ to 1 cup of dried beans cooked just to tenderness in a lot of water. These are usually white beans, but they can be kidney or (rare) cranberry or even something like our trusty pinto bean. Then put about 1 tablespoon of olive oil in a large pot with a bit of cut-up salt pork or bacon, if you wish, and begin sautéing gently about 1 cup of sliced onion and a couple of minced garlic cloves.

Start peeling and dicing vegetables and add to the pot when prepared: for example, some carrots, potatoes, perhaps celery or turnip, and certainly some zucchini. Stir in 1 cup of canned tomatoes and a little tomato paste, if you wish, but not too much for this is not a tomato soup!

Basil and parsley are usually added, though I've seen recipes that use sage and rosemary. Top well with water or stock, and cook about 45 minutes over low heat. The vegetables should not lose their shape. The last 15 minutes should include a few fistfuls of greenery coarsely chopped. Ordinarily this is cabbage, though I prefer Swiss chard leaves or spinach with their darker green color.

Taste as it cooks and add salt and pepper as needed. Some cooks add a tipple of wine at the last, and some use quite a bit more olive oil, which makes green-gold droplets on the top. Other vegetables to consider are green beans or peas in season, leeks, and a little yellow squash instead of some of the zucchini.

Finally, add about 1 cup of small pasta such as elbow macaroni or little seashells, or even the rice-shaped pasta, orzo. Simmer another 10–15 minutes. The soup should be as thick as stew, and if it gets too thick, add water little by little as the pasta cooks. Serve at the table with plenty of freshly grated Parmesan or Romano cheese to spoon on top. If you've used very little oil in the soup, you might like to serve a cruet of fine oil to sprinkle as well.

Minestrone is of the glorious family of dishes that are even better the next day, and the next, and will keep a week in the refrigerator. So make plenty. Most Italians consider it a course instead of pasta, but I respect either one as the center of a meal, with a loaf of bread, a glass of wine, a dessert such as Italian Glazed Oranges (page 346), with coffee.

With this thumbnail sketch in mind, here are two recipes of variations—one with no pasta at all, and one mostly all beans and pasta.

THE TUSCAN VERSION IS VERY SUAVE AND MELTING, WHILE PASTA E FAGIOLI IS A BARE BONES DISH MEANT TO USE UP THE LAST OF ANY BEANS AND BROKEN PASTA FROM THE BAREST CUPBOARD. HOWEVER, IT HAS A SIMPLE SOOTHING AIR ABOUT IT THAT IS HARD TO BEAT FOR A FILLING MEAL AT SO LITTLE COST. THE FLAVOR IS EXQUISITE IF YOU CAN FIND FRESH (OR EVEN DRIED) CRANBERRY BEANS, SO RICH AND TASTY, BUT THEY ARE AS SCARCE AS HEN'S TEETH IN THIS COUNTRY. WHITE BEANS WILL DO, OR A MIXTURE OF DIFFERENT COLORED BEANS MAKES FOR A MORE ATTRACTIVE DISH. WITH ANY MINESTRONE YOU MIGHT NOT DINE LIKE A KING, BUT YOU WILL HAVE SUPPED WELL AND SOUNDLY.

Tuscan Minestrone

SERVES 8

1 *pound dried Great Northern beans*
water
sprig of fresh sage (or ½ teaspoon dried)
1 *large clove garlic*
olive oil
1 *medium onion, chopped*
3 *carrots, pared and sliced*
2 *stalks celery, chopped with leaves*
¼ *cup minced parsley*
2 *tablespoons minced fresh basil (or 1 tablespoon dried)*
2 *medium zucchini, diced*
1 *small cabbage, chopped*
1 *bunch Swiss chard (or spinach), chopped*
4–5 *potatoes, peeled and diced*
light beef (or chicken) stock
salt and freshly ground pepper
freshly grated Parmesan cheese

Soak beans overnight in plenty of water. The next day drain them and cook in enough water to cover by 2 inches. Add sage, garlic, and 2 tablespoons of olive oil to the pot, and simmer several hours, or until quite soft. Pick out sage and garlic, and run the beans, juice and all, through a food mill. Reserve.

Prepare onion, carrots, celery, parsley, and basil, and stew them in ¼ cup of olive oil in a soup pot over medium heat. This will take about 15 minutes. Prepare the other vegetables beginning with those that may cook longest, and add them one by one. Stir the pot now and again to make sure they don't burn. The heat should be quite low after the onion softens. Finally, add enough stock to cover by 2 inches, cover, and let cook 20 minutes over low heat.

Add the puree of beans, taste for salt and pepper, cover the pot, and cook slowly another hour. If the soup gets too dense, add some more water; if it seems thin, uncover the pot and let cook down a little.

Serve in bowls with a cruet of olive oil and a dish of grated Parmesan cheese for guests to sprinkle over the soup.

Pasta e Fagioli

SERVES 8

1 *cup dried beans (Great Northern, cranberry, or a mixture of different beans)*

2 *slices bacon (or 2 thin slices salt pork)*

1 *small onion*

1 *celery stalk*

1 *carrot (optional)*

2 *tablespoons parsley*

2 *tablespoons olive oil*

1 *teaspoon dried basil (or 1 tablespoon fresh)*

1 *tablespoon tomato paste (or ½ cup canned tomatoes)*

6 *cups water*

salt and freshly ground pepper

1 *cup small pasta (or various broken pieces)*

grated Parmesan cheese (or Romano)

Soak beans overnight in plenty of water. Drain and place in a pot with fresh water to cover by 2 inches. Simmer until tender (the length of time will depend on the beans).

Chop bacon, onion, celery, carrot, and parsley until very fine, and sauté in olive oil in a soup pot. When starting to just turn golden, stir in basil and tomato paste, and add water and drained beans. Add salt and pepper to taste—this will take some adjusting because the beans have not been salted and will need some time to soak it in.

Simmer the soup 15 minutes. Smash some beans against the side of the pot and add pasta. Cook until pasta is done but not mushy. The soup should be very thick, almost a stew, but add a little water as necessary.

Serve hot with cheese sprinkled over.

How to
Surprise an Egg

*I*t is said there is no more perfect a food, more perfectly packaged, than the egg. This is not to say that a slapdash sizzle of them scraped on a plate, late at night when there's nothing else in the refrigerator, is perfect or even desirable. But cared for as something out of the ordinary, as done by any who slip one from under the hen, they may become the occasional herb omelet for supper, the billowy soufflé, the perfect scramble.

My only complaint about the egg is that it is always done in one of about four ways, each often badly. The British only feel comfortable frying them, and usually in meat drippings, while Americans scramble or flip an omelet as if the idea was to make what is naturally tender and delicate into something deliberately tough or coarse. This is balanced out, though, by the French, who know a good cheap thing when they see it. As Thomas Moore wrote: "Who can help loving a land that has taught us six hundred and eighty-five ways to dress eggs?"

41

Except for an omelet, with its fairly brisk heat, the one rule to remember with eggs is that they should just be gentled with flame. From there, they are infinitely various. With this in mind I've included instructions on how to go about a scramble and the best way to flip an omelet, but most of all my favorite methods to show them to advantage in meals other than breakfast: how to surprise (and be surprised by) the egg at hand.

Real Right Scrambled Eggs

VERY SIMPLE, YES, BUT ENTIRELY DIFFERENT FROM THE WAY MOST AMERICANS SCRAMBLE EGGS. PERHAPS IT IS A DIFFERENCE IN THE LANGUAGE, AS SCRAMBLE HAS A CONNOTATION OF MAD RUSH ABOUT IT WHILE THE FRENCH *BROUILLÉ* HAS MORE A SENSE OF JUMBLE AND CONFUSION.

THE RESULT IS A SMOOTH CREAMY MASS FIT FOR A KING. RATHER THAN SERVING TOAST ON THE SIDE, THE FRENCH USUALLY SERVE THESE ON THE TOAST OR ON A BUTTER-FRIED CROUTON, SO WITH EACH FORKFUL ONE GETS THE SENSATION OF CRISP AND CREAMINESS ALL AT ONCE.

SERVES 1

2–3 *eggs*
salt and freshly ground
pepper
1 *tablespoon butter*

Break eggs into a bowl and beat lightly with salt and pepper to taste. Put half the butter in the top of a double boiler set over barely simmering water. When it melts, add eggs and stir now and again until they begin to set but are yet creamy. This process should take at least 5 minutes. Stir in remaining butter and remove from heat.

THIS SOUNDS LIKE SICKBED FOOD, WHICH OF COURSE IT COULD BE, BUT THERE IS SOMETHING PARTICULARLY SATISFYING ABOUT THE LIGHT TEXTURE COTTAGE CHEESE GIVES THE EGGS I LIKE VERY MUCH, AND AT ANY TIME.

Boston Scrambled Eggs

SERVES 4

  3 *tablespoons butter*
  6 *eggs*
1½ *cups dry curd cottage cheese*
 ¼ *cup minced chives (or parsley)*
salt and freshly ground pepper
  4 *slices buttered toast*

Melt butter in a frying pan over low heat. Break eggs into a bowl and mix lightly with cottage cheese, chives or parsley, and salt and pepper to taste. Add to the pan and stir until the eggs are set but still creamy. Serve on toast.

BASQUE PIPERADE MAKES A DELICIOUS LIGHT MEAL THAT IS QUICKLY PUT TOGETHER, SLOWLY SAVORED. THE PROPORTION OF VEGETABLES CAN BE VARIED ACCORDING TO WHAT'S ON HAND——RED PEPPERS ARE PARTICULARLY FINE IF YOU HAVE THEM, FOR INSTANCE, AND YOU COULD USE A LITTLE MORE ONION, A LITTLE LESS GARLIC. I DON'T THINK THIS DISH SHOULD BE OVERLY TOMATOEY, HOWEVER. IN KENTUCKY THEY MAKE A SIMILAR DISH WITH BACON FAT RATHER THAN OLIVE OIL, FRESH CORN, A LITTLE GREEN PEPPER, AND CHOPPED PIMIENTO, SO DON'T WORRY ABOUT MERE AUTHENTICITY, USE WHAT YOU HAVE ON HAND.

Basque Piperade

SERVES 4

  4 *tablespoons olive oil*
  1 *large onion, chopped*
  3 *green peppers, cut in strips*
  2 *cloves garlic, minced*
1½ *cups chopped tomatoes (fresh or canned, well drained)*
  ¼ *teaspoon dried thyme*
Tabasco
salt and freshly ground pepper
  6 *eggs, lightly beaten*
minced parsley

Heat oil in a large frying pan and add onion and peppers. Cook 5 minutes over medium heat, then add garlic, tomatoes, thyme, a few drops of Tabasco, and salt and pepper to taste. Toss well and cook until peppers are soft. Pour in eggs and stir until they make soft curds. Serve on warm plates sprinkled generously with parsley.

A Maltese Curry

THIS AMAZING DISH IS FROM MARCEL BOULESTIN, THOUGH I'VE ADAPTED IT A BIT BECAUSE HE ADDS PEACHES AND APRICOTS, WHICH ARE SHIPPED SO GREEN THESE DAYS THEY HAVE LITTLE FLAVOR (THOUGH HE SUGGESTS GREEN OR RED PEPPERS, WHICH ARE FINE). IT AMAZES BECAUSE NO ONE WOULD EVER GUESS WHAT COMPOSES IT— CERTAINLY NOT THAT IT IS VEGETARIAN AND USES EGGS! BOULESTIN WAS AN AMATEUR WHO FELL INTO COOKING, CATERING, AND FINALLY THE RESTAURANT BUSINESS QUITE BY CHANCE (AND THE NEED FOR MONEY). BUT BY ALL ACCOUNTS HIS WAS THE FINEST RESTAURANT IN LONDON BETWEEN THE WARS. BEFORE THE DAYS OF ELIZABETH DAVID, HE ALMOST SINGLE-HANDEDLY CHANGED THE WAY THE BRITISH THOUGHT ABOUT FRENCH FOOD. HE ALSO WROTE COOKBOOKS THAT WERE SIMPLE, SENSIBLE ABOUT TIME AND METHODS, AND CHARMING THROUGHOUT. SOME OF HIS SAYINGS SHOULD BE AS WELL KNOWN AS THE APHORISMS OF BRILLAT-SAVARIN: "GOOD MEALS SHOULD BE THE RULE AND NOT THE EXCEPTION. ECONOMY IS A BASIC RULE IN FRENCH COOKING, WHICH IS RARELY EXTRAVAGANT. TRY TO STRIKE A BALANCE BETWEEN RICH AND SIMPLE FOOD. A GOOD COOKBOOK SHOULD ILLUSTRATE THE IDEA THAT *ON NE MANGE BIEN QUE CHEZ SOI.*" MOST OF HIS BOOKS ARE LONG OUT OF PRINT, BUT *BEST OF BOULESTIN* SEEMS TO BE STILL AVAILABLE. IT MAKES A FINE TROVE TO HAVE ON THE SHELF.

SERVES 4

2 *tablespoons bacon fat
(or butter)*
2 *large onions, chopped*
1½ *cups drained and
chopped canned
tomatoes*
2–3 *tablespoons curry
powder*
*salt and freshly ground
pepper*
1 *cup water*
1 *cucumber, peeled,
seeded, and grated*
1 *apple, peeled, seeded,
and grated*
1 *banana, peeled and
grated*
1 *teaspoon lemon juice*
pinch of sugar
4 *tablespoons heavy
cream (or sour cream
or yogurt)*
4 *eggs*
cooked rice
toasted slivered almonds

Put bacon fat or butter in a saucepan and let melt over medium heat. Sauté onions in it until they soften. Add tomatoes and cook 3–4 minutes, then add curry powder and salt and pepper to taste. Let cook another 3–4 minutes, then add water. Cover and cook 1½ hours over low heat. Check now and again to see if it has become too dry. When done the onions and tomatoes will have amalgamated into a suave mass with very little liquid. If the liquid cooks away before 1½ hours, add very little more because you will want it cooked away at the end.

Add cucumber, apple, banana, lemon juice, and sugar. Cook 10 minutes over medium-high heat. Beat cream into eggs and then stir eggs into curry quickly off the heat—they will cook being stirred into the hot curry. (If done over high heat, they will coagulate like scrambled eggs, and you want no visible trace of the eggs.)

Serve over hot fluffy rice and sprinkle with almonds.

The Omelet

The renown of the deft wrists of France's Mère Poularde persists as The Omelet's purest myth, though the famed Madame Bégué of New Orleans budges her a close second. Mère Poularde is within living, tasting memory. Farther, the nimbleness of Madame Bégué (born Elizabeth Kettenring), who "ruled the kitchen, her throne being the stove, her scepter a long-handled skillet"—the skillet she tossed her omelets with—was from the Civil War through the passing of the century. Their common secret was probably in the fearless quickness with which omelets should be turned out, only the slightest crinkle of gold on the outside, the inside just past flowing.

Of Mère Poularde much has been written, but I know only this clear recollection of Madame Bégué:

She was getting old—she was seventy-five or six when she died—so she sat throughout your breakfast, with her crutch at her side, and just before a shelf with specimens of her glassware. Above and behind her opened a room where cooking was in progress. Your eyes wandered thence, while you waited or took more white rock; for your companions were principally tourists, and conversation languished. Then came the second course, an omelette, with parsley, steaming hot and fine. . . . In the omelette you noticed odd bits of black spice, and detected a curious flavor. You questioned old Madame Bégué, as she ate hers at the side table, but she shrugged her shoulders and laughed.

This is from her obituary notice in the venerable *Boston Cooking School Magazine* by Felix J. Koch. "Madame Bégué is dead," he begins, "No more Epicurean breakfasts in the Quartier Latin for the bon-vivants of the nation."

It is a potent enough myth—the first serious pan I bought as a student was a cast-iron omelet pan. So trusty, it's traveled with me always, ready to flip out the world's most honored, simple meal. When you've done it a few times, it's more fun than a great fuss.

Much to-do has been made over just the perfect pan for an omelet and how to care for it so the eggs never, ever stick. Village wisdom has it that the pan, well chosen and seasoned, should never be washed or used for anything else. If anything should, after this precaution, stick, it must be scrubbed only with coarse salt. . . . Well, today there are fine light teflon pans made especially with sound bottoms, to which none of this very fine advice applies.

At any rate, if you buy one, it should be with sloping sides (so an omelet slips easily out) and with a fairly heavy botton (so eggs cook evenly), and the measurement of its bottom should be 6–7 inches (the perfect size for an individual omelet, the easiest to turn out). It should be called an "omelet pan," and it will tell you how to season it. If it doesn't, don't buy it, is my advice.

The following are what you want to turn out—three variations on a theme.

The Basic Omelet

THE FILLING FOR AN OMELET CAN BE PRACTICALLY ANYTHING, BUT REMEMBER THAT THIS IS PRIMARILY AN EGG DISH AND SHOULD NOT BE BURSTING WITH STUFFING. ONE OF MY FAVORITES IS A COUNTRY ONE WITH CUBES OF POTATO COOKED IN BACON FAT, WITH BITS OF BACON AND ONION, AND A SPRINKLE OF PAPRIKA TOWARD THE END. IF YOU HAVE GARDEN-RIPE TOMATOES, THESE CAN BE TOSSED QUICKLY IN A LITTLE BUTTER—THE SAME FOR MUSHROOMS SLIGHTLY SEASONED WITH TARRAGON. PRACTICALLY ANY GREEN VEGETABLE WILL DO, CHEESE OR SOUR CREAM, CUBES OF HAM. GRATED PARMESAN OR ROMANO CHEESE CAN BE STIRRED INTO EGGS BEFORE COOKING, AS CAN HERBS. THE FRENCH *FINES HERBES* OMELET CALLS FOR A TABLESPOON OF MIXED FRESH CHIVES, PARSLEY, AND TARRAGON OR CHERVIL. THAT IS PROBABLY THE BEST OF ALL.

SERVES 1

2 *large eggs*
salt and freshly ground
  pepper
2 *teaspoons water*
1 *tablespoon butter*

Break eggs into a bowl and stir lightly with a fork until just mixed. (Overbeating makes for a tough omelet.) Stir in salt and pepper to taste along with water—the water also ensures tenderness.

Heat pan over medium-high heat. It is the proper temperature when a small piece of butter on it sizzles immediately. Add butter, rotate the pan so it coats completely, and when the sizzling starts to die down, pour eggs in. They will start to set immediately, and as they do, tip the pan and lift the edges so that the uncooked egg can run beneath. The omelet is done when there is still a thin film of uncooked egg on top.

If you use a filling, quickly place it in the middle of the omelet, then flip over one flap and slide the omelet so it neatly folds over itself. If you wish, brush with a little more butter to make the top glisten.

The whole process should not take more than 30–45 seconds. To turn out a series of individual omelets, set them on warm plates in a very low oven. Be careful that the plates and oven aren't quite hot, for an omelet will go on cooking.

THE NEXT METHOD SEPARATES THE EGGS AND WHIPS THE WHITES SO YOU HAVE A KIND OF CROSS BETWEEN A SOUFFLÉ AND AN OMELET—CALLED, NOT SURPRISINGLY, AN OMELET SOUFFLÉ. IN FRANCE YOU SOMETIMES FIND THESE SLIGHTLY SWEETENED, FILLED WITH JAM OR PUREED FRUIT, AND THEN SPRINKLED WITH POWDERED SUGAR. THAT IS FINE IF YOU HAPPEN TO LIKE SUCH THINGS. I DON'T, THOUGH THERE ARE FEW THINGS MORE BLESSED THAN A REAL SOUFFLÉ FOR DESSERT.

Omelet Soufflé

SERVES 1

2 *eggs, separated*
salt and freshly ground
  pepper
1 *tablespoon minced chives*
  (*or parsley or Parmesan*
  cheese)
1 *tablespoon butter*
½ *cup light tomato sauce*
  (*optional*)

Beat whites until they make billowy peaks—be careful not to make them stiff or shiny. Beat in salt and pepper to taste. Lightly whisk yolks with chives and fold into the whites. Melt about ¾ of the butter in a 6–7-inch omelet pan over low heat.

Scoop eggs into the pan and smooth to the edge. As it cooks, run a fork around the edge to make sure it isn't sticking and constantly lift edges to see how the underpart is cooking. When the bottom is evenly golden, put pan under a broiler and cook just until it starts to take a little color. Don't broil too much or the omelet will be dry.

Fold over in half with a fork and slip out onto a warm plate. Rub top with remaining butter to make a shiny glaze. Serve in a pool of tomato sauce if you wish.

These take a little practice to make perfect, but they are worth it, for when the cupboard really *is* bare you have a dish that seems so much more than an ordinary omelet. They are less versatile, however, since anything mixed into the eggs should be fairly light and delicate. A hearty variation of my own is to mix the eggs with Parmesan cheese and chopped green chiles, then serve with a light red chile sauce in the southwestern manner.

Zucchini Frittata

THE THIRD OF THE OMELET FAMILY IS THE ITALIAN FRITTATA, FLAT AND ROUND RATHER THAN FOLDED, AND WITH VEGETABLES OR HAM COOKED INTO THE EGGS RATHER THAN STUFFED IN THE MIDDLE. THEY ARE DELIGHTFUL TO EAT AND PRETTY TO LOOK AT, AND ONE DOESN'T HAVE TO HAVE SUCH A DEFT HAND AT TURNING THEM OUT. THEY ARE ALSO A FAVORITE WITH THE THRIFTY COOK BECAUSE THEY ARE CHARMING WAYS TO USE UP LEFTOVERS—SAY HALF A TOMATO, A LITTLE ONION, A FEW STEAMED BROCCOLI FLORETS AND LEFTOVER SPAGHETTI. I GIVE A RECIPE FOR A SIMPLE ZUCCHINI FRITTATA BECAUSE IT'S ONE OF THE BEST WAYS I KNOW TO BRING OUT THE FLAVOR OF A RATHER BLAH VEGETABLE, BUT THE SAME RECIPE CAN BE USED FOR ARTICHOKES, ASPARAGUS, TOMATOES, GREEN BEANS OR PEAS, MUSHROOMS, HAM, OR WHAT HAVE YOU. THE ONLY THING TO REMEMBER IS THAT THEY SHOULD NOT BE MUSHY BUT RETAIN THEIR CUT SHAPE AND A GOOD DEAL OF THEIR TEXTURE.

SERVES 1

- 1 *small zucchini, thinly sliced (or ¾ cup mixed vegetables)*
- 1 *tablespoon olive oil*
- ½ *clove garlic, slightly flattened and peeled*
- 2 *large eggs*

salt and freshly ground pepper

- 1–2 *tablespoons grated Parmesan cheese*
- ½ *teaspoon fresh basil (or oregano, or ¼ teaspoon dry)*

Wash zucchini well before slicing. Put olive oil and garlic in a 6–7-inch omelet pan and cook over medium heat until the garlic starts to turn gold, then discard it. While garlic cooks, break eggs into a bowl and stir just until whites and yolks are mixed. Stir in salt and pepper to taste, Parmesan cheese, and the herb.

Fry zucchini just until it starts to have a little color, but don't wait for it to get limp. Lower heat and pour egg mixture over. Tip the pan this way and that so eggs cover the entire bottom of the pan. Lift up the edges to let uncooked eggs run under as the eggs begin to set. When the frittata is set well on the bottom and is lightly golden, put the pan briefly under a broiler to set the top. This should be only a few seconds—don't wait until it starts to color.

Slip onto a warm plate and sprinkle with a little more Parmesan cheese if you wish. Serve hot, at room temperature, or even cold.

Of course a frittata makes a delightful lunch or supper dish, with a good bread and a glass of wine. In Italy, larger ones are often made, sliced in strips and served cold as part of an antipasto.

The thrifty cook (a fine one, anyway) should always keep the versatility of omelets in mind for the easy, quick supper. They give a bit of elasticity to any budget and a lift to the palate.

Once, dining at Simpson's in London, stuffed to the gills on the almost obligatory ribs of beef and Yorkshire pudding, with all the trimmings right down to a scoop from the wheel of Stilton, I observed a couple at the table next, slip in to order an herb omelet and a split of champagne, after the theater, and thought it the most sensible yet romantic dinner possible.

LOVELY TO LOOK AT, SIMPLE TO PREPARE, AND VERY INEXPENSIVE. THE ZUCCHINI IS COOKED BUT STILL TOOTHSOME, AND THE CROUTONS GIVE AN UNEXPECTED CRUNCH TO THE MIDDLE. IT MAKES

Zucchini Omelet with Croutons

A FINE BREAKFAST OR LUNCH, BUT IT IS ALSO SUPERB AS A LATE SUPPER.

SERVES 1

1 *slice white bread, trimmed and cut into ¼-inch dice*
½ *clove garlic*
1 *tablespoon olive oil*
1 *small zucchini, coarsely grated*
1 *egg*
salt and freshly ground pepper
grated Parmesan cheese
1 *tablespoon butter*

Prepare bread. Place garlic and oil in a 6–7-inch omelet pan over medium heat. When garlic turns golden, remove it and sauté bread cubes in olive oil until crisp and golden. Remove and keep warm on paper towels in a warm oven.

In a small bowl, beat together zucchini, egg, salt and pepper to taste, and a little Parmesan cheese. Wipe out the omelet pan and place over medium heat again. When hot enough to make a bit of butter sizzle, add butter and then the zucchini mixture. Spread to the edges of the pan, lifting the edges as they set to let any liquid run under. When the bottom is set and the top seems done, fill with the croutons, slide the omelet out onto a warm plate, flipping over with the croutons inside. Serve at once sprinkled with a little more Parmesan cheese.

Reverse Potato Omelet

CRISP AND ATTRACTIVE, WHILE MANAGING TO BREAK ALL OMELET RULES, THIS IS AN IDEAL DISH TO MASTER. THE POTATOES ARE NOT ALL THAT TRICKY IN A SEASONED OMELET PAN, OR EVEN BETTER A NONSTICK TEFLON ONE. TO TURN OUT MORE THAN ONE OMELET, THE POTATO CAKES CAN BE COOKED IN RELAYS AND KEPT IN A WARM OVEN, THEN FILLED AT THE LAST MINUTE WITH THE EGGS.

SERVES 1

1 *large potato, peeled and
  coarsely grated*
3 *tablespoons butter*
*salt and freshly ground
  pepper*
2 *eggs, lightly beaten*
*herbs, sour cream, grated
  cheese, and so forth
  (optional)*

Wash potatoes through a colander or sieve and pat dry with paper towels. Melt 2 tablespoons of butter. Toss potato with melted butter and salt and pepper to taste, and spread into an omelet pan. Cook slowly until a crust forms underneath and you can shake the potato cake. If it sticks, run a knife around to loosen the edges. With a little practice you can achieve a good golden crust underneath, with the top potatoes anywhere from creamy to *al dente*.

When you judge the potatoes done, remove them from the heat and keep warm. Scramble eggs in remaining tablespoon of butter until just set. Toss them, if you like, with herbs or cheese, or fold them with a bit of sour cream. Place in the middle of potato cake and slide it out, folded like an omelet, onto a warm plate. Garnish with anything pretty and handy—parsley, watercress, or tomato, for example—and serve at once.

Omelet with French Fried Potatoes

A FRENCH OMELET—EVEN IF IT IS SERVED OPEN-FACED LIKE AN ITALIAN FRITTATA—AND A DELIGHTFUL ONE AS WELL. THEY ARE DIFFICULT TO SERVE TO MORE THAN TWO, HOWEVER, BECAUSE IF THEY SIT LONG, THE POTATOES WON'T STAY CRISP, BUT THEY ARE SO GOOD YOUR FAMILY WON'T MIND BEING SERVED IN ROUNDS, IF NEED BE. HOWEVER, WHAT COULD BE SIMPLER OR MORE SATISFYING FOR TWO—OR ONE? QUICKLY PUT TOGETHER OUT OF VERY LITTLE, WITH A TOSSED SALAD AND PERHAPS ONE OF THE SIMPLE FRUIT DESSERTS AT THE END OF THIS BOOK, ONE HAS FINELY DINED.

SERVES 1

1 *medium potato*
olive oil
1 *clove garlic, slightly*
  flattened and peeled
1 *bay leaf*
salt
2 *eggs, beaten lightly*
1 *tablespoon minced*
  parsley
freshly ground pepper
grated Parmesan (*or other*)
  cheese

Peel potato and cut in ¼-inch slices. Pour olive oil in a frying pan to a depth of ¼ inch and put over medium heat. Add garlic, and when it gets golden, remove it. Fry potatoes with the bay leaf until golden on both sides, then drain on paper towels. Sprinkle with a little salt and keep warm.

Grease an omelet pan with some olive oil. Set over medium heat again and place potato slices in a layer on the bottom. Stir eggs with parsley and salt and pepper to taste. When the potatoes begin to sizzle, pour eggs over. Tip the pan as they cook so any uncooked egg dribbles under the edges.

When the eggs have mostly set, put pan under a broiler for 1 minute or so, so they set on top. Remove and sprinkle with a little Parmesan cheese, then slide onto a warm plate.

Peruvian "Noodle" Eggs

THESE PENNY PINCHERS ARE ADAPTED FROM A JAMES BEARD RECIPE, AND THEY MAKE AN UNUSUAL KIND OF "PASTA," FUN FOR BRUNCHES OR A LATE SUPPER. THEY CAN, OF COURSE, BE FIDDLED WITH AS TO FLAVOR. PESTO IS EVEN NICER THAN TOMATO SAUCE, AND YOU COULD ADD CUMIN AND FRESH CORIANDER RATHER THAN THE BASIL, AND THEN SERVE ON A BED OF RED CHILE SAUCE.

SERVES 4

8 *eggs*
3 *tablespoons grated*
   Parmesan cheese
2 *tablespoons crushed*
   saltine crackers
3 *tablespoons milk*
½ *teaspoon dried basil (or*
   1 tablespoon fresh)
dash of Tabasco
salt and freshly ground
   pepper
butter
Home-Style Tomato Sauce
   (page 189)

Whisk eggs with Parmesan cheese, crackers, milk, basil, Tabasco, and salt and pepper to taste. Lightly butter an omelet pan and set over medium heat. Put in 2 tablespoons of the mixture, tip pan around to spread out the eggs, and cook like a crepe. Turn when it is set and starting to take color, and briefly cook the other side. Place each one on a plate as done and continue to make more until all the mixture is used. If necessary, butter the pan in between.

Roll the omelets up one by one and cut into noodles about ¼ inch wide. These may sit, covered, until you need them. To cook, toss in a frying pan with 2 tablespoons of butter and serve on a pool of sauce, sprinkled with a little more Parmesan cheese.

Celestial Eggs

THIS SPANISH DISH IS USUALLY SERVED AS A FIRST COURSE, BUT IT COULD MAKE A LIGHT MEAL ANY TIME OF DAY. IT MAKES AS FINE A SHOW AS ANY SOUFFLÉ, WITH A LOT LESS WORK AND CARE FOR TIMING. THE ONLY TRICKY PART IS TO MAKE SURE THE YOLKS STAY INTACT AS YOU SLIP THEM IN. INSTEAD OF OLIVES I RATHER LIKE FRESH HERBS OR CHIVES, AND THE WHOLE DISH IS OPEN TO EXPERIMENTATION ACCORDING TO WHAT YOUR IMAGINATION AND REFRIGERATOR SUPPLY. ALICE TOKLAS HAS A VERSION SHE CALLS "EGGS AS PREPARED IN THE CREUSE," WHICH OMITS THE TOAST AND OLIVES (THE WHITES BEING SPREAD IN A BUTTERED RAMEKIN); THE CHEESE IS SPRINKLED ON TOP AND CREAM RATHER THAN BUTTER IS DRIBBLED OVER THE YOLK—ALSO A LOVELY DISH.

SERVES 4

4 *eggs, separated*
¼ *cup finely grated Swiss cheese (or Parmesan)*
¼ *cup chopped pimiento-stuffed olives (or mixed herbs)*
4 *slices toast, buttered*
salt and freshly ground pepper
2 *tablespoons melted butter*

Preheat oven to 450°. Beat egg whites stiff but not dry. Fold in cheese, olives, and salt and pepper to taste. Spoon onto the toast, forming a nest in the middle of each with the bottom of a spoon. Slip an egg yolk into each nest and dribble a little butter over each yolk (you may want to sprinkle a little more cheese over as well).

Place the toasts on a baking sheet and bake 8 minutes. Serve immediately on warm plates.

I HAVE NOT DECIDED ABOUT THIS SAVAGE DISH FOR MYSELF, BUT I HAVE A COUPLE OF FRIENDS WHO DOTE ON IT AND INSISTED IT SHOULD BE HERE FOR OTHER FEARLESS PALATES.

Eggs à la Turque

SERVES 4

1 *cup plain yogurt*
1 *clove garlic, minced*
butter
¼ *teaspoon cayenne pepper*
8 *eggs*
vinegar

Mix yogurt and garlic together, and divide it among 4 plates—spreading it out with a spoon. Heat 3 tablespoons of butter with cayenne and keep warm.

Poach eggs in water with a little vinegar in it. When done to your taste, ladle them out with a slotted spoon onto yogurt-garlic mixture. Dribble a little butter over each and serve.

Refrigerator Eggs

A friend from Georgia once taught me these eggs while I sipped a glass of orange juice and champagne. He scoured the "ice box" (as it was called there) for "treasures." This turned up some fine green beans from the night before, a couple of new potatoes boiled in their skins, and some garden fresh tomatoes. These were cut into bite-size pieces. He then wilted some chopped onion in butter, threw in a strew of fresh rosemary, and tossed in the treasures for a minute. The mixture was placed in buttered ramekins. Over them he broke two eggs, dribbled a bit of butter over, and finally a sprinkle of salt and pepper. They were then placed in an oven heated to 350° and baked until the eggs were set—about ten minutes should do the trick. The essence of this kind of dish is that it is unrepeatable but whatever turns up in the way of treasure, infinitely delightful.

Eggs Bonne Femme

This classic French country supper dish, very close to what the French call "eggs tripe-style," is much better and a little richer. I've never understood why they liken the onions to tripe here because they are completely different in flavor and texture—perhaps it's the color. At any rate, this makes a very satisfying meal with bread and a tossed salad, particularly on cold winter nights when the pantry is bare.

SERVES 4

4 *medium onions, thinly sliced*
¼ *cup vegetable oil*
¼ *pound butter*
6 *hard-boiled eggs*
3 *tablespoons flour*
1 *cup milk, heated*
¼ *cup heavy cream*
salt and freshly ground pepper
2 *teaspoons dry mustard*
½ *cup grated Swiss cheese (or Cheddar)*

Preheat oven to 400°. Sauté onions in vegetable oil and half the butter over medium heat until transparent. This will take 8–10 minutes. Peel eggs and slice thinly. Make alternate layers of onions and eggs in a lightly greased 1½-quart casserole.

Heat the remaining butter in a saucepan over medium heat. Stir in flour and cook 3–4 minutes, then add the hot milk. Stir until thickened and smooth, then add cream, salt and pepper to taste, and dry mustard. Whisk to incorporate mustard, and simmer 5 minutes. Pour over eggs and onions, then top with cheese. Bake 12–15 minutes, or until heated through and starting to brown on top.

WITH ITS COMBINATION OF MILD EGGS AND CREAMY PIQUANT SAUCE, THIS MAKES A SATISFYING DISH FOR ANY TIME OF DAY. I LIKE TO SERVE IT WITH TOAST POINTS AND CHILLED DRY WHITE WINE.

Delicate Deviled Eggs

SERVES 4

 2 *cups milk*
½ *cup chopped onion*
 1 *bay leaf*
¼ *cup butter*
¼ *cup flour*
¼ *cup heavy cream*
 2 *egg yolks*
¼ *cup grated Parmesan cheese*
 1 *tablespoon dry mustard*
 2 *teaspoons water*
salt and cayenne pepper
 8 *hard-boiled eggs*

Preheat oven to 350°. Scald milk in a saucepan with onion and bay leaf. This should be done over low heat so the milk will have time to absorb the flavors.

In another saucepan, melt butter over medium heat, stir in flour and cook, stirring, 3–4 minutes. Strain the milk in and stir until you have a smooth thickened sauce. Beat cream and egg yolks together in a bowl, add a little of the hot sauce to incorporate, then stir them into remaining sauce.

Stir in Parmesan cheese. In a small bowl, mix mustard with water and then add to pan. Heat over low heat without letting the sauce come to a boil. Add salt and cayenne pepper to taste (it should be hot but not too hot) and cook a few minutes more.

Peel the hard-boiled eggs and slice thinly. Arrange in a shallow casserole or in individual heat-proof dishes. Pour sauce over them and bake about 5 minutes, or until starting to bubble.

Stuffed Curried Eggs

I FIRST HAD THESE IN A SMALL FRENCH INN, AS ONE COURSE OF A MEAL, BUT THEY MAKE A FINE SHOW ON THEIR OWN WHEN ONE IS FEELING THRIFTY BUT NEEDS TO NOURISH THE BONES. IF YOU HAVE IT ON HAND, IT'S ALSO NICE TO ADD A LITTLE CHUTNEY TO THE YOLKS WHEN YOU MIX THEM.

SERVES 4

4 *tablespoons butter*
6 *tablespoons flour*
4 *tablespoons curry powder*
3 *cups milk, heated*
salt and freshly ground pepper
8 *hard-boiled eggs*
½ *cup heavy cream*

Preheat oven to 425°. Put butter in a saucepan set over medium heat. When it starts to sizzle, add flour and stir smooth. Cook a few minutes, then stir in curry. Add milk and stir until it makes a smooth thickened sauce. Add salt and pepper to taste.

Cut eggs in half lengthwise. Remove the yolks and sieve them into a bowl. Stir in enough curry sauce to make a smooth thick mixture, then stuff back into the whites. Place in a shallow greased casserole. Stir cream into sauce and let it come almost to a boil, then pour over eggs. Bake 10 minutes, or until bubbly.

The Soufflé

Webster's dictionary tells us that this word translates poetically as "a breath of wind." It is also thought too fragile for mortal folk to cook. The poetry is correct, for a soufflé shows what magic the egg may hatch but what anyone can manufacture. There is only one secret: don't let them catch you afraid that they might not turn proudly up and out. To allow this is to release all their puff, and the result will be something resembling, but not as good as, a pancake.

Recipes tell you other secrets, such as not to open the oven door or jump up and down, and these are just plain common sense as any soufflé should be a wonder created for the moment—not to be sneezed at or cajoled, but snatched from the air for silent eating. It also should be obvious to any that this dish must be served immediately, if not sooner. For this reason I must admit that, though a soufflé shows a cook in all glory, I don't make them for guests. You can shout "NOW" to the family five minutes before one is to be whisked from the oven, but this is unseemly for visitors.

I've seen this problem handled with a great deal of tact and charm, however. During the Johnson administration, a family in Washington, D.C., there for the term since the father worked as an aide to L.B.J., served a lovely dinner and though there was no dessert, all felt well fed. About an hour later the kids clamored, "Hey, Mom, can we make a chocolate soufflé?" So the whole team bustled around the kitchen. Someone had the task of turning on the oven and assembling ingredients. Someone else handled the eggs, another the béchamel sauce, and so forth. And before you knew it, everyone had a plate of crusty, creamy, chocolaty stuff, with a dab of plain whipped cream melting over it. Thus, it seemed to me, families are made happy and complete. If I had such a team about, this would be ideal, but as it is I reserve my delectation for the restaurant table.

A seasoned cook can read the table of contents for a soufflé and know how to construct it, but for those who are novices, here are a few tips. Probably the most important is the treatment of the egg whites. They must be whipped using a bowl and a beater that are completely clean and free from fats. They should be at room temperature, preferably, and though it is said the lightest are made with a copper bowl and a balloon whisk, a pinch of cream of tartar can be added to imitate the acidity of the copper. And if beaten in an electric mixer, know the exact moment to stop.

When a recipe says to beat whites "until stiff but not dry," it means when the beater is lifted out, the mixture should stand up on it in a peak. So it is preferable to check along the way as you beat, after the whites become full of little bubbles. They should then be folded into the basic mixture as soon as they are ready, and the "folding" means tossing in and stirring about a third of the whites with a lifting motion. This gives you a lightened mixture to work with. Then the rest should be added to the bowl and quickly and deftly cut in (without a care, remember) and lifted up from center to side of the bowl, until the whole looks spongy and there are still perhaps little bits of white showing. If you fold and fold more, it only tends to deflate the soufflé. To respect the whites is to have the soufflé respect you.

So perhaps we can now get down to a basic recipe— Cheese Soufflé, perhaps the finest of all.

Cheese Soufflé

SERVES 4

3 *tablespoons butter*
3 *tablespoons flour*
1 *cup milk, heated*
1 *teaspoon salt*
pinch of freshly ground
   pepper
pinch of grated nutmeg
¾ *cup grated sharp*
   Cheddar cheese
4 *eggs, separated*
1 *extra egg white*
⅛ *teaspoon cream of tartar*
   (*optional*)

Preheat oven to 375°. Melt butter in a saucepan over medium-low heat. Stir in flour and cook several minutes. Add milk all at once and stir until it makes a smooth thick sauce. Let bubble a bit, then add seasonings. Remove from the heat and stir in Cheddar cheese and egg yolks. Allow to rest while you prepare the egg whites.

Beat whites until stiff but not dry (using cream of tartar unless you have a professional whisk and copper bowl). Scrape cheese sauce into a bowl with a rubber spatula. Quickly mix in about ⅓ of the whites, then gently but quickly fold in remaining whites. Only fold for about a minute, turning the bowl as you go. If there are specks of unincorporated whites, that's all right.

Pour mixture into a 1½-quart soufflé dish that has been lightly buttered. (A straight-sided round soufflé dish is not absolutely necessary, but it shows you have invested in a serious way.) Smooth the top with a spatula. Put dish in the center of the preheated oven. If there is a top shelf, it should be removed, for there is nothing more ghastly than to have a soufflé rise and reach through an oven shelf. Bake 30–35 minutes, or until it has risen about 2 inches above the rim of the dish, is golden and crusty on the outside, and still slightly creamy in the center. Always try to spoon out some of the dryer outside part as well as the softer center in each portion. Serve at once.

That's it. It only sounds like a lot of trouble to those who have never made a soufflé. Learn the knack and trust the soufflé to behave. Also learn how to vary ingredients and improvise. Practically any cheese can be used, for instance, or finely chopped meats, flaked fish, cooked and minced vegetables. All these in approximately ¾-cup measures. The fine thing about this is that you can taste the sauce and see if it might need some Dijon mustard, a flick of Tabasco, a sprinkle of herbs or onion—the test of a fine cook.

Seafood for a Song

Unless you hook them yourself, few known fish could any longer be called inexpensive, and shellfish of any stripe could break the back of even large budgets. But look closely, and on that chipped ice at the market may lie a few unlovelies, one or two beasties no one bothers to cook. These are the bargains.

Among them are what I call the three S's: squid, skate, and smelt. Strange stuff but for smelt, which is too tiny to think of. Mysterious among the shellfish nestle the mussels—cheap, sweet, delicate on both coasts, easy to prepare and to appreciate. I tried them recently on my parents, and though they'd once politely disliked some expensive oysters I laid out in honor of their landlocked Kansas, they ate every scrap of mussel and sopped up their oceanic juices with sourdough bread.

When I began this book I thought there was one slick monstrosity I could count on, the hideous monkfish. But overnight it has become trendy for its delicious, almost lobstery flesh, and markets chop off the dismaying huge head and strip its warty skin before it can be seen. And charge a fortune.

My only normal-seeming fish, also somehow snubbed, is the mackerel. All Mediterranean cuisines use it, and the French make it their most dependable cold hors d'oeuvre—why shouldn't we?

Squid and Their Cleaning

Fresh squid (also called calimari) are clean and sweet-smelling. If you detect any fishy odor, do not buy them. Also, West Coast squid can be very tiny, so if you wish to stuff them and have a choice as to size, try to get the larger ones—for any other purpose size does not matter. Squid freeze well because they have no blood, and even in the Midwest you will find 3- or 5-pound blocks for sale. They have a delicate flavor and cook tender in no time, and their little tentacles turn bright pinks and purples upon cooking—very pretty in a dish. They are one of the most versatile and delicious of all seafoods.

To clean, first cut off the tentacles just above the eyes and reserve them. Peel off the speckled skin—it should slip off easily by hand. If you wish, you may remove the back fins at this time, but it's not necessary because they are as good eating as the body. Pull out the head and beak from the body and discard, then squeeze out all the innards, starting from the tip and squeezing toward the head end. Reach in and find the transparent quill that resembles a plastic feather and pull it out. If necessary to get everything out of the body cavity, wash it out under the water faucet and squeeze dry.

Squid Sautéed with Parsley and Lemon

THIS NORTH ITALIAN RECIPE IS ONE OF THE SIMPLEST, QUICKEST, AND MOST DELICIOUS WAYS TO PREPARE SQUID. SQUID HAS AN ODD PROPERTY IN THAT IT SHOULD BE COOKED THIS LITTLE OR NEARLY A HALF HOUR. IN BETWEEN, IT TOUGHENS. IT WAS THIS DISH, MY FIRST SQUID, IN ITALY THAT MADE ME A CONVERT FOREVER. NOW IT IS A HOME FAVORITE, TIME AND AGAIN.

SERVES 4

3 *pounds small squid*
8 *slices white home-style bread, thinly sliced*
4–6 *tablespoons butter*
⅓ *cup olive oil*
2 *cloves garlic, slightly flattened and peeled*
salt and freshly ground pepper
¼ *cup minced parsley*
juice of 1 lemon
sprigs of parsley

Clean squid, reserving tentacles. Cut bodies into ¼-inch rings and keep them in a separate pile from the tentacles.

Trim bread of crusts so they are perfect squares, then stack them and cut diagonally so you have 16 triangles. Melt 4 tablespoons of butter in a frying pan and dip the triangles quickly so they are evenly coated on both sides— but not so they get soggy with too much butter. If you need more butter, use it. Fry bread over medium heat until both sides are golden brown. Place on plates and keep warm in the oven. It won't hurt them to stay awhile, they will only get crisper.

To cook squid, place garlic and olive oil in a frying pan and cook over medium-high heat until garlic turns golden. Discard garlic and add the tentacles. Cook 2–3 minutes over high heat, then stir in squid rings, parsley, and salt and pepper to taste. Cook another 2–3 minutes, lifting and tossing constantly. (They should only have time to stiffen slightly and turn opaque.) Remove from heat, squeeze lemon over squid, and lift out with a slotted spoon onto the bread croutons.

Boil pan liquid down until slightly reduced and pour over the squid. Serve immediately garnished with sprigs of parsley.

FRIED SQUID IS ONE OF THE MOST POPULAR SEAFOOD DISHES IN THE WORLD, THOUGH THE METHODS DIFFER FROM A SIMPLE FLOURING TO THE LACY TEMPURA BATTER OF JAPAN. THIS RECIPE HITS A GOOD MEDIUM IN BETWEEN AND IS VERY EASY TO MASTER. THE ONLY FINE POINT IS THAT YOUR OIL MUST BE KEPT AT 350° WHEN ADDING BATCHES OR THE SQUID WILL TAKE TOO LONG TO COOK AND SO WILL TOUGHEN. I SERVE IT WITH CRISP COLE SLAW AND BEER. SOME FOLKS LIKE TO DIP THEIR CRUSTY SQUID IN A BOWL OF THE GARLIC MAYONNAISE CALLED *AIOLI*, IN WHICH CASE YOU WOULD NOT WANT A CREAMY DRESSING FOR THE SLAW.

Deep-Fried Squid

SERVES 4

1 *cup flour*
vegetable oil
¼ *teaspoon salt*
¾ *cup warm water*
1 *egg white*
3 *pounds squid, cleaned*
lemon wedges

Sieve flour into a bowl and stir in 3 tablespoons of vegetable oil, salt, and water until it makes a smooth batter. Don't overbeat or the crust will be tough. Cover with plastic wrap and let sit at room temperature for at least 2 hours—3 or 4 is even better. Just before cooking squid, beat the egg white just until it holds peaks and fold into the batter.

Cut squid into ¼-inch rings and combine with tentacles. Heat oil in a deep-fat fryer or a cast-iron skillet to the depth of 1 inch or more. The oil should be at 350°.

Cook squid in batches of about ½ cup at a time. Put each batch in a small bowl, pour some batter over, and lift out with a fork into the hot fat. Cook only 1 minute or so, until they turn golden, then lift out with a slotted spoon (or the basket of a fryer) and drain on paper towels. Keep warm while you fry the rest.

Salt lightly and serve with lemon wedges.

"Ablonetti" with Cucumber Soubise

ABALONE IS A RARE AND EXTREMELY EXPENSIVE DELICACY EVEN ON ITS NATIVE CALIFORNIA SHORES. IT IS SO GOOD THAT CHEFS HAVE BEEN INVENTIVE WITH THE SQUID AND SO TITLE IT "ABLONETTI." WHEN PREPARED WELL IT CAN BE SO GOOD THAT ONLY ABALONE AFICIONADOS WOULD COMPLAIN. (INDEED, THE GENUINE, MAGNIFICENT UNIVALVE, WHEN SERVED IN RESTAURANTS, IS OFTEN STRAIGHT FROM A CAN SO THE CHEF DOESN'T HAVE TO GO THROUGH THE TROUBLE OF SLICING AND POUNDING THE RATHER TOUGH "FOOT" INTO GENTLE SUBMISSION.) THIS RECIPE IS MY RATHER TRENDY WAY OF SERVING SQUID, AND IT MAKES A FINE WAY TO START A COMPANY DINNER, NO MATTER WHOM YOU'VE INVITED. IF YOU DON'T WANT TO GO TO THE TROUBLE OF MAKING THE SAUCE, YOU COULD SERVE THE SQUID WITH A SQUEEZE OF LEMON AND SPRINKLE CAPERS ON TOP, A DISH CALLED EUPHONIOUSLY ABLONETTI SANTA BARBARA. FOR FURTHER INFORMATION ABOUT CALIFORNIA'S LOVE AFFAIR WITH THE ABALONE, SEE THE NEXT RECIPE.

SERVES 4

2½ pounds medium squid, cleaned
 1 cucumber
salt
 5 tablespoons butter
 3 cups chopped onion
flour
 1 cup bottled clam juice, heated
freshly ground pepper (or Tabasco)
freshly grated nutmeg
 2 teaspoons lemon juice (or to taste)
 ½ cup heavy cream (or more)
 1 tablespoon minced chives (or parsley)
 2 eggs, beaten
vegetable oil
cucumber slices
lemon slices

Prepare squid and reserve tentacles. Slit bodies up one side with a small knife and open them up flat. Place between waxed paper and pound gently but firmly with a rolling pin or kitchen mallet until they relax and soften. They should not be beaten to a pulpy mass.

Peel cucumber and slice in quarters lengthwise. Slice out all the seeds. Chop coarsely, sprinkle with salt, and let drain in a colander 30 minutes or so.

Put 4 tablespoons of the butter in a saucepan and cook onions in it over low heat until they start to soften. Cover pan and let them just sweat for about 15 minutes, or until quite soft but not browned in any way. Refresh the cucumber with water and squeeze gently with the hands. Add to the onions. Cook another 10 minutes. Add 4 tablespoons of flour and cook, stirring, 3–4 minutes, then add hot clam juice. Stir sauce until thick and smooth. Cook another few minutes, then puree through a sieve or in a blender.

Return puree to the saucepan and season to taste with salt (you may need none at all because of the clam juice). Add pepper, a hint of nutmeg, and lemon juice to taste. Thin sauce to desired consistency with cream—it should be about the consistency of sour cream. At the very last add chives or parsley for a speck of color.

To cook squid, dip each piece in flour lightly seasoned with salt and pepper, then into beaten egg, then again in the flour. Fry in a little hot vegetable oil for only 1 minute or so each side, or just until very lightly browned. If they tend to curl up, flatten with a pancake turner. Drain on paper towels and keep warm.

Put remaining 2 tablespoons of butter in a frying pan and toss tentacles over high heat just until they turn bright colors.

To serve, pour some of the sauce on one side of a warm plate, lay slices of squid down the center, and garnish the other side with a fan of alternate slices of thin lemon and cucumber. Sprinkle tentacles here and there over the plate.

YES, I HATE SUBTERFUGE, AND THIS SHOULD BE IN THE CHICKEN
SECTION, BUT THIS IS SO FRANKLY PHONY, WHY NOT? IT DOESN'T
QUITE RESEMBLE THE TEXTURE OF ABALONE, BUT IT DOES HAVE AN
IRRESISTIBLY DELICATE FISHINESS THAT IS NEAR
ENOUGH NOT TO FOOL BUT TO TEASE THE
PALATE.

Phony Abalone

SERVES 4

4 *half chicken breasts*
salt and freshly ground
  pepper
sugar
1 *bottle clam juice*
saltine cracker crumbs
4 *tablespoons butter*
lemon wedges

Skin chicken breasts and pull out white tendon on underside with the help of a small sharp knife. Place them
between sheets of waxed paper and pound each firmly but
gently with a rolling pin or kitchen mallet until they are
under ¼ inch thick. Peel off waxed paper carefully. Cut
each breast in half and rub with a little salt, pepper, and
sugar. Place in a shallow bowl and pour clam juice over.
Let marinate 6 hours in the refrigerator.

To cook, dip pieces in cracker crumbs to coat thoroughly. Heat butter, a tablespoon at a time, in a frying pan
large enough to hold 2 chicken pieces. Fry over medium-
high heat until golden crisp on each side and keep warm in
the oven. Serve with lemon wedges.

MOST ITALIAN SQUID RECIPES ARE REPLETE WITH LOTS OF TOMATOES, AND THOUGH THAT MAY BE VERY FINE, I RATHER LIKE SQUID UNSMOTHERED AND TOMATOLESS AS IN THIS RECIPE. IT'S GOOD, I THINK, TO SERVE IT WITH PASTA TOSSED SIMPLY WITH BUTTER AND PARMESAN CHEESE.

Italian Stuffed Squid

SERVES 4

2½ *pounds medium squid, cleaned*
1 *cup parsley*
1 *clove garlic, peeled*
½ *teaspoon dried basil (or oregano)*
4 *slices white bread, trimmed of crusts*
salt and freshly ground pepper
3 *tablespoons olive oil*
½ *cup dry white wine*

Preheat oven to 350°. Clean squid and reserve bodies and tentacles in different bowls. Chop parsley, garlic, and basil with tentacles until quite fine. Shred bread finely and mix in parsley mixture with salt and pepper to taste and 2 tablespoons of the olive oil. Stuff squid bodies with the mixture only until about half full (or the squid will burst in cooking). Skewer opening with a toothpick.

Place in a shallow casserole and pour wine around them, then sprinkle with the other tablespoon of olive oil. Cover with a lid (or foil) and bake 20 minutes. Place squid on warm plates, removing toothpicks as you do so, and pour cooking juices into a small saucepan. Boil down over high heat until thickened slightly, then pour over squid. Serve warm.

Squid Adobo

SERVES 4

2½ *pounds squid, cleaned*
  2 *medium ripe tomatoes*
  2 *medium onions*
  1 *cup rice*
  3 *tablespoons vegetable oil*
 10 *cloves garlic, peeled and thinly sliced*
  3 *tablespoons soy sauce*
 ½ *cup red (or white) wine vinegar*
  2 *cups water*
 ½ *teaspoon red pepper flakes (optional)*

A SIMPLE SPICY FILIPINO RECIPE FOR SQUID THAT CAN BE ADJUSTED LIKE A STIR-FRY DISH ACCORDING TO WHAT VEGETABLES ARE AT HAND. FOR INSTANCE, IF YOU DON'T HAVE GARDEN TOMATOES, YOU CAN ADD SOME DRAINED CANNED ITALIAN PLUM TOMATOES, AND A SPRINKLE OF BEAN SPROUTS IS WONDERFUL FOR THEIR TEXTURE. THE SOY SAUCE CAN BE ADJUSTED TO TASTE, SINCE SOME OF THEM ARE VERY STRONG AND SALTY, AND A PINCH OF SUGAR CAN BE ADDED AT THE END IF YOU FIND THE SAUCE TOO VINEGARY.

Cut squid bodies into ¼-inch rings and put in a bowl with tentacles. Slice tomatoes and onions in half vertically, then into thin vertical slices, and place in separate bowls. Put rice on to cook before cooking the squid, which takes only a few minutes.

Heat vegetable oil in a frying pan over medium heat. Add garlic and sauté until it just starts to turn color. Don't burn it. Immediately add onion slices and toss well. Add tomatoes, then squid, soy, wine vinegar, water, and pepper flakes if you use them. (I like this dish traditionally a little hot, but you might not.) Toss 2–3 minutes, or until squid just whitens. Remove vegetables and squid with a slotted spoon and place in a bowl. Keep warm in the oven.

Turn heat up high and boil pan liquid down until it starts to thicken. Serve squid over rice with sauce poured over it all.

Greek Stuffed Squid

MINT AND RAISINS IN A SEAFOOD DISH? YES, THE COMBINATION IS TYPICAL IN SOME GREEK DISHES AND MAKES MORE THAN A LITTLE SENSE HERE. THIS IS ONE HUMBLE, PLENTIFUL WAY TO PLEASE ANYONE WITH SQUID. THERE IS AN INHERENT SPIRIT OF GAIETY IN ALL GREEK RECIPES—AS IF WE ALL MIGHT GO OUT ON A PICNIC AT ANY MOMENT—THAT I ALWAYS RESPECT. THIS DISH CAN BE A FAMILY DINNER, A RESPECTABLE FIRST COURSE FOR COMPANY, OR A COLD GOURMET LUNCH THE NEXT DAY. ANY WAY YOU GO AT IT, THIS IS A DISH THAT SHINES.

SERVES 4
(for dinner,
6 as an appetizer)

2½ *pounds medium-sized squid*
4 *tablespoons olive oil*
½ *cup chopped onion*
⅓ *cup long-grain rice*
½ *cup minced parsley*
¼ *cup minced fresh mint (or 1 tablespoon dry)*
2 *tablespoons dry white wine*
¼ *cup raisins*
¼ *cup pine nuts*
salt
⅔ *cup water*
1 *cup chopped canned tomatoes, drained*
⅓ *cup dry white wine*
freshly ground pepper

Clean squid, reserving tentacles. Heat 2 tablespoons of olive oil in a saucepan, add onions, and sauté until limp. Stir in rice and coat with oil. When rice starts to turn opaque, add parsley, mint, wine, raisins, and pine nuts. Salt to taste. Add water, bring to a boil, cover pot, and simmer 18 minutes over low heat. The rice should still have a bit of bite to it.

Preheat oven to 350°.

Stuff squid bodies loosely with mixture (if you use too much they will split when the squid shrinks on cooking). Skewer the opening with a toothpick and lay in an oiled baking dish. Scatter any extra stuffing and tentacles among them.

Combine tomatoes, wine, and salt and pepper to taste in a saucepan, and simmer 6–8 minutes, then pour over squid. Dribble with remaining olive oil. Bake, uncovered, 20 minutes. Remove toothpicks and serve warm or at room temperature, as in the Greek style.

About Skate

The great skate looks rather like a gray-black kite, right down to the tail. Edible portions are the wings, and these are detached, skinned, and cut into portions before you see it in most markets. The flesh of these wings have a texture rather like crab, and unscrupulous restaurants used to use skate as a cheap adulterant for their crab dishes. Skate is very good and succulent on its own, however, and the only problem is that you probably have to live on the coast to find some because it is too unpopular to ship. If you have a source, there are all kinds of ways to go about preparing this creature—I've given only the tip of the iceberg here. Prepared in ways usually reserved for crab, as I've done here with Skate Creole and Skate Cakes, it can also stand in for other fish in stews and chowders—you name it.

THIS IS ONE OF THE BEST OF ALL FISH DISHES. IT IS A CLASSIC FRENCH BISTRO PRESENTATION, WHERE, AS ELIZABETH DAVID RECOUNTS, THE *PATRON* MAY RUN FROM STOVE TO TABLE WITHOUT A LOSS OF SIZZLE. IT IS USUALLY SERVED WITH LEMON WEDGES AND BOILED POTATOES SLOSHED WITH A LITTLE OF THE *BEURRE NOIR* AND PARSLEY. THIS METHOD MAY BE PUT TO USE WITH ANY SLICE OF POACHED FISH, ONCE ONE FINDS THE EASE OF PROPERLY BLACKENING BUTTER WITHOUT BURNING IT. EDOUARD DE POMIANE, IN HIS *COOKING WITH POMIANE,* POINTS OUT THAT IF BUTTER IS TOO EXPENSIVE, OIL CAN SUBSTITUTE. YOU THEN HAVE SKATE À LA VINAIGRETTE.

Skate with Black Butter

SERVES 4

2 *pounds skate wing, cut in serving portions*
1 *onion, peeled and quartered*
1 *bay leaf*
4 *tablespoons white wine vinegar*
salt
minced parsley
4 *tablespoons butter*
2 *tablespoons capers (optional)*

Poach skate in just enough water to cover, along with onion, bay leaf, and 2 tablespoons of wine vinegar. It should barely simmer for 10–12 minutes and will be done when the flesh flakes easily with a fork. Drain skate, place on plates, sprinkle with a little salt and minced parsley, and keep warm in the oven while you prepare the sauce.

Put butter in a small saucepan and heat over high heat. First it will foam up, then turn golden, then light brown. Very quickly it will turn a darker "hazelnut" color, and it is ready to snatch off the heat. Pour quickly over warm skate. Add remaining 2 tablespoons of wine vinegar to the pan and let it boil up, then pour it over the fish as well. Sprinkle with capers if you wish.

Skate Cakes

SERVES 4

2 *pounds skate wings*
salt
vinegar (or lemon juice)
  (optional)
½ *cup bread crumbs*
⅓ *cup melted butter*
¼ *cup minced onion*
¼ *minced celery (or green*
  pepper)
1 *egg, lightly beaten*
2 *tablespoons mayonnaise*
1 *teaspoon Worcestershire*
  sauce
¼ *teaspoon cayenne pepper*
2 *tablespoons butter*

THIS RECIPE IS BASED ON THE WONDERFUL CRAB CAKES COOKED DOWN SOUTH AND IS AN EXAMPLE OF HOW YOU GO ABOUT SUBSTITUTING SKATE FOR 1 POUND OF CRABMEAT IN A RECIPE. THEY MAY BE ACCOMPANIED BY LEMON WEDGES, OR TARTAR SAUCE AND A SPRIG OF PARSLEY, IF YOU WISH, BUT I DON'T THINK THEY REALLY NEED ANYTHING—EXCEPT PERHAPS FRENCH FRIES AND A CRISP SLAW.

Put skate in a large pot with about 2 inches of salted water and a little vinegar or lemon juice if you have it. Cover pot and cook 3–4 minutes, or just until skate turns white and can be flaked easily. The time will depend on the thickness of the wings. Remove from pot, let cool a little, then scrape flesh from the bones. You should have 1 pound of flesh, or about 2½ cups.

Mix skate with all ingredients except 2 tablespoons butter. Add salt to taste then shape mixture into 8 cakes about ½ inch thick. Chill in the refrigerator for 30 minutes or more.

Melt 2 tablespoons of butter in a large frying pan and sauté cakes about 5 minutes a side, or until a crusty golden. Serve hot.

A SUAVE YET LIVELY DISH, ALSO VERY EASY TO PREPARE, EASY ON THE POCKET. IT NEEDS ONLY A GLASS OF WHITE WINE.

Skate Creole Style

SERVES 4

1½ pounds skate wings
  2 tablespoons lemon juice
    (or wine vinegar)
 ½ cup dry Madeira (or
    sherry)
  2 tablespoons butter
 ⅓ cup minced green onion
    including part of tops
  1 clove garlic, minced
  1 tablespoon flour
 ⅛ teaspoon dried thyme
 ½ cup coarsely grated
    green pepper (discard
    skin)
 ¾ cup chopped tomatoes
salt and freshly ground
    pepper
cayenne
 ½ cup heavy cream
cooked rice

Poach skate in water to cover and lemon juice or vinegar. Lift them out after 3–4 minutes and let cool. Scrape flesh off both sides of the wings. The ribs of flesh should be cut in about 2-inch lengths. You should have 2 cups. Marinate in Madeira or sherry for 1 hour or more.

Heat butter in a large saucepan and sauté onion and garlic over medium heat until onion is limp. Stir in flour and cook several minutes. Add thyme, green pepper, tomatoes, salt, pepper, and cayenne to taste (it should be very slightly hot). Cook 5 minutes over low heat, then add skate with all its marinade along with cream. Simmer another 5–10 minutes. Serve over hot rice.

SKATE MAKES A PARTICULARLY DELICATE AND DELICIOUS CURRY. FOR LIKELY CONDIMENTS, SEE "ANYTHING EDIBLE . . . MAY BE CURRIED" (PAGE 317).

Skate Curry

SERVES 4

1½ *pounds skate wings*
  1 *onion, chopped*
  1 *clove garlic, minced*
  2 *tablespoons butter*
  1 *tablespoon curry
     powder (or to taste)*
  1 *tablespoon flour*
  1 *cucumber, peeled and
     coarsely grated*
  1 *apple, peeled, cored,
     and coarsely grated*
  ¼ *cup raisins*
salt
Tabasco
  ¼ *cup heavy cream*
  1 *teaspoon lemon juice
     (or to taste)*
pinch of sugar
cooked rice

Poach skate in water to cover, with whatever is handy: a slice of onion, a clove of garlic, parsley, a little lemon juice or white wine, a bay leaf, dried thyme, and so forth. These need cook only 3–4 minutes, or until the flesh flakes easily. Cool wings and scrape flesh off both sides. Return bones to the pot and cook another 20 minutes to make a stock. Strain it and reserve 2 cups.

In a large saucepan over medium heat, sauté onion and garlic in butter until onion softens. Stir in curry powder and cook 1 minute or so, then stir in flour and cook several minutes. Add fish stock and cook over high heat until the sauce is smooth and thickened.

Add cucumber, apple, raisins, and salt and Tabasco to taste. Stir and cook 30 minutes over low heat. Add skate, cream, and then lemon juice, and a bit of sugar to taste. Cook another 5 minutes and serve over rice with curry condiments.

Smelts and the Like

These tiny fish are no more than three inches long, and to call them smelt is purely generic, like the English term "whitebait." Actually, in New England they will be mostly herring, and other locales get alewives or pilchards. They can be used in any Mediterranean recipe calling for fresh sardines. The fine thing about them is that they can be eaten bones, heads, tail, and all, and need absolutely no fussing with beforehand.

I get them fresh year-round here in San Francisco, and my neighborhood supermarket (a Safeway) also sells them in pound bags frozen in Canada, so I suppose they are to be had for the asking all over the country. Any market will handle something easily obtained if there is a demand. The great thing about frozen smelt is that they don't even have to be defrosted; a little warm water run over them in a colander thaws them immediately. They are a wonderful resource to have waiting in your freezer.

Deep-Fried Smelts

I HAD NEVER TASTED OR SEEN THESE UNTIL I LIVED IN ENGLAND, WHERE THEY ARE A FAVORITE IN CHOP HOUSES EVERYWHERE, SERVED IN A HUGE CRISP MOUND AND GARNISHED WITH LEMON AND PARSLEY, SO MANY, YOU THINK IT IMPOSSIBLE TO EAT THEM ALL. AH, THEY DISAPPEAR, SO DELICIOUS ARE THEY, IN A MERE TWINKLING. THEY ARE INDEED SO GOOD THIS WAY YOU MAY NOT WANT ANY OTHER RECIPE, BUT I'VE FOUND SOME IN MY TRAVELS ALMOST AS EXQUISITE.

SERVES 2
(or 4 as a
first course)

1 *pound smelts*
1 *cup milk*
flour
salt and freshly ground
   pepper
vegetable oil for frying
1 *lemon, quartered*

Rinse smelts and dry on paper towels. Place in a bowl with milk, then shake in a bag of flour seasoned with salt and pepper. Heat at least 2 inches of vegetable oil to 370° in a roomy pan. Fry smelt in batches until crisp and golden— about 4 minutes. Drain on paper towels and salt lightly. Serve hot with lemon wedges.

I LIKE TO SERVE THESE CRUSTED BEAUTIES WITH PLAIN PASTA, TOSSED WITH PARMESAN CHEESE AND BUTTER. THEY ALSO MAKE A LOVELY FIRST COURSE, WITH A LOAF OF BREAD AND A GLASS OF WINE, OR THEY CAN BE PART OF A RANGE OF ANTIPASTI FOR ANY ITALIAN MEAL.

Italian Baked Smelts

SERVES 2
(or 4 for a
first course)

½ *cup bread crumbs*
2 *tablespoons minced*
  parsley
2 *cloves garlic, minced*
salt and freshly ground
  pepper
⅓ *cup olive oil*
1 *pound smelts*
1 *tablespoon lemon juice*
  (or *white wine vinegar*)

Preheat oven to 400°. Combine bread crumbs, parsley, garlic, and salt and pepper to taste. Stir in 1 tablespoon of olive oil until crumbs are moistened. Use a little more oil to grease an 8-inch casserole. Place a layer of fish in it, sprinkle half the crumbs over, place another layer of fish, then sprinkle with remaining crumbs. Dribble lemon or vinegar over and then remaining oil.

Bake 20 minutes, or until crusty and starting to turn golden. Serve hot or at room temperature.

THESE LITTLE TIDBITS ARE BEST PERHAPS AS PART OF AN HORS D'OEUVRE PLATTER, SAY WITH A TEPID RICE SALAD AND SLICED GARDEN TOMATOES DRIBBLED WITH A LITTLE OIL AND FRESH BASIL. A COUPLE OF SHALLOTS OUGHT NOT BREAK THE BUDGET, BUT THEY CAN BE SUBSTITUTED WITH NO GREAT LOSS BY A FEW GREEN ONIONS MINCED WITH PART OF THEIR TOPS. DON'T BE AFRAID TO TRY THEM, FOR THE ACTION OF THE LEMON JUICE "COOKS" THE FISH.

Marinated Smelts with Shallots

SERVES 2–4

1 *pound smelts*
3 *tablespoons minced shallots*
½ *cup lemon juice*

Cut heads and tails off smelts, then slit them open through their bellies and cut out backbones. Lay in a shallow casserole and sprinkle shallots over them, then pour lemon juice over. Refrigerate overnight, covered with plastic wrap.

A LOVELY, EASY MAIN DISH TO SERVE FOUR PEOPLE FROM ONLY A POUND OF SMELTS. IF YOU HAVE A LITTLE GRUYÈRE CHEESE LURKING IN THE REFRIGERATOR, IT CAN BE USED INSTEAD OF THE PARMESAN— OR BETTER YET, HALF AND HALF—BUT IT'S NOT NECESSARY. SERVE IT WITH A GREEN VEGETABLE AND A GLASS OF CHILLED WHITE WINE.

Smelts Mornay

SERVES 4

¾ *cup uncooked rice*
1½ *cups water*
salt
2 *tablespoons butter*
2 *tablespoons flour*
1 *cup milk, heated*
freshly ground pepper
freshly grated nutmeg
2 *tablespoons grated*
   Parmesan cheese
1 *pound smelts*
flour
¼ *cup vegetable oil*
lemon juice

Put rice into a saucepan of boiling salted water. Lower heat, cover pan, and cook 20 minutes. Let sit until it reaches room temperature. Melt butter in a saucepan over medium heat, stir in flour, and cook 3–4 minutes. Add hot milk and stir until you have a smooth thickened sauce, then season to taste with salt, pepper, and a whisper of nutmeg. Lower heat and simmer 5 minutes or more. Stir in Parmesan cheese.

Shake smelts in a bag of flour seasoned with salt and pepper. Put vegetable oil in a large frying pan over high heat. When the oil is hot, add smelts and cook 3–4 minutes, or until crisp and lightly golden. Sprinkle with a little lemon juice and remove with a slotted spoon to drain on paper towels.

To assemble the dish, butter 4 individual ramekins or scallop shells, or a pie plate for a family serving. Divide rice and spread it evenly, top with smelts, then pour sauce over the top. Put under a broiler until top starts to color and bubble.

To Prepare Mussels

Pull out the beard of seaweed and scrape the mussels together to clean them (or you can use a scouring pad). It's not necessary to remove small barnacles, however, because they add flavor to the cooking juices. Discard any that have broken shells and any that seem heavy—these are probably dead and filled with mud. Place the cleaned mussels in a bowl of salted water and leave for 30 minutes or so. This will help purge them of sand.

Mussels are the only inexpensive shellfish, and if you have an unpolluted beach nearby, they are free for the taking at low tide. They have a delicate sweet flavor, better really than most clams. They can be prepared in a host of ways, hot or cold, stuffed or not, all of them delectable. Many are grown specially for the market, these days, and need little preparation besides bearding for cooking.

The simplest, and maybe best, way to serve mussels. It is particularly fine with mussels that are so chock-full of seawater that they release the liquid into the cooking wine.

Mussels Marinière

SERVES 4
(as a first
course)

2 *pounds mussels*
1½ *cups dry white wine*
1 *medium onion,
chopped (or 6 green
onions or 2 cloves
garlic)*
½ *bay leaf*
4 *sprigs of parsley*
¼ *teaspoon dried thyme*
freshly ground pepper
4 *tablespoons butter*
¼ *cup minced parsley*

Prepare mussels according to method on page 88. Put wine and all other ingredients except minced parsley in a large kettle with a cover. Bring to a boil and cook several minutes, then add mussels. Cover kettle and let cook 5 minutes or so—just until they open their shells.

Lift out mussels into soup plates. Remove bay leaf and parsley sprigs and boil to reduce liquid 2–3 minutes. (Some people like to thicken the liquid with a little more butter worked with flour, others like to boil it down until it is a little syrupy. I like to really have something to sop up with bread rather than a sauce—this is up to you.) Add minced parsley at the last minute and serve mussels at once.

Italian Mussels in White Wine

THESE ARE AS EASY AS MUSSELS MARINIÈRE, BUT THEY ARE PREFERABLE FOR A SUMMER MEAL BECAUSE THEY ARE COLD. I LEARNED THEM FROM THE SAME ROBUST ITALIAN COOK WHO TAUGHT ME HOW TO MAKE *BACCALA* (SALT COD)—THE MOST MELTING AND TENDER DISH IMAGINABLE FROM SOMETHING RESEMBLING A BOARD.

SERVES 4
(as a first
course)

2 *pounds (or quarts)*
  mussels
2 *tablespoons olive oil*
½ *cup dry white wine*
2 *cloves garlic, minced*
¼ *cup minced parsley*

Prepare mussels according to method on page 88. Put olive oil in a wide-bottomed pan that has a lid and turn heat to medium. Add mussels. Cover while they steam 1 minute or so, then uncover and stir them. Remove any that have opened. Continue this until all the mussels have opened. Remove top shells and place mussels on a platter.

Strain liquid mussels have released in the pan through a piece of cloth or paper towel to remove any sand. Clean out the pan and return the liquid. Add wine, garlic, and parsley. Stir over high heat until the mixture starts to thicken slightly, then spoon over mussels. Chill thoroughly.

THIS MAKES A DELIGHTFUL LUNCH OR SUMMER SUPPER DISH, PERHAPS ON LETTUCE LEAVES AND GARNISHED WITH RADISH FLOWERS AND HARD-BOILED EGGS. IT CAN ALSO BE PART OF A COMPANY BUFFET.

Mussel and Potato Salad

SERVES 4

2 *pounds mussels*
2 *pounds new red potatoes*
4 *tablespoons dry white wine*
2 *tablespoons white wine vinegar*
1 *teaspoon Dijon-style mustard*
salt and freshly ground pepper
6 *tablespoons olive oil*
¼ *cup minced green onion, including part of tops*
2 *tablespoons minced parsley*

Prepare mussels according to method on page 88, then place in a large pot with about 1 cup of water. Cover pot and cook over high heat, shaking pan now and again, just until mussels open. Remove from pot, cool to room temperature, and remove from shells. It's not necessary, but the mussels will look better if you trim the black rim around them.

Scrub potatoes and boil in salted water to cover until they are just tender when pierced with a knife point. Drain and slice into a bowl when still warm. It's not necessary to peel them. Pour wine over them while they are warm and toss gently. Beat wine vinegar, mustard, and salt and pepper to taste in a small bowl. Beat in olive oil by drops, whisking as you go. Sprinkle potatoes with minced onion and parsley, add mussels, then toss with the dressing. Serve at room temperature or chilled.

Mussels Stuffed with Spinach and Mushrooms

A CLASSIC FRENCH PREPARATION WHICH GIVES A LITTLE SUBSTANCE TO THE MUSSEL, WITHOUT TAKING AWAY FROM ITS DELICACY. I RESOLVED TO LEARN HOW TO MAKE THEM AFTER HAVING THEM FOR LUNCH ON A TERRACE, IN A SUNNY SOUTHERN FRENCH VILLAGE, SOME FIFTEEN YEARS AGO. THEY REMAIN BRIGHT AND FRESH IN MY MIND, THOUGH I CAN'T REMEMBER THE VILLAGE OR THE NAME OF THE INN.

SERVES 4
(as a first
course)

2 *pounds mussels*
1 *cup water*
1 *pound fresh spinach*
2 *tablespoons butter*
½ *cup onion, minced*
6 *medium mushrooms,
   minced*
*salt and freshly ground
   pepper*
freshly grated nutmeg
bread crumbs
olive oil
lemon juice

Prepare mussels according to method on page 88, then place in a large pot with water. Bring to a boil, cover pot, and cook 5 minutes, or until they open. Remove cover and let cool.

Stem spinach and wash through several waters. Put in a large pot with only the water that clings to the leaves. Cover and cook over medium heat just until the spinach wilts. Run cold water over them, drain in a colander, and squeeze out all moisture with your hands. Mince finely.

Put butter in a saucepan over medium-high heat. Add onion and mushrooms. Cook, stirring now and again, until mushrooms have exuded their liquid and it evaporates, then start to brown lightly—about 15 minutes. Add spinach and salt, pepper, and nutmeg to taste. Stir and remove from heat.

Preheat oven to 375°. Discard top shells of mussels and take 24 of the largest and place in a shallow baking dish. Cut up smaller ones and divide among the 24. With your hands, smooth spinach mixture over mussels. Sprinkle lightly with bread crumbs, then dribble with olive oil.

Bake 15 minutes. Serve hot, sprinkled with lemon juice.

The Lowly Mackerel

Rich and oily mackerel is not to everyone's taste, but cut with some dry white wine, lemon juice, or acid tomato, it can be something you long for now and again, like persimmons as autumn turns, or the first spring lettuce. Your market will clean them for you and, if you wish, cut off the heads and tails. I usually like to leave them on, they give a bit more flavor to the cooked dish.

Mackerel in White Wine

MACKEREL WITH WHITE WINE IS ONE OF THE MOST COMMON AND PLEASING HORS D'OEUVRES SERVED THROUGHOUT FRANCE, FOR IT IS A FISH PARTICULARLY SUITED TO BE SERVED COLD. IT COULD BE SERVED AS ONE OF A SELECTION OF SMALL BOWLS, AS THE FRENCH DO, OR PERHAPS SIMPLY ON A LETTUCE LEAF WITH SOME TOMATO AND HARD-BOILED EGG WEDGES. IT IS ALSO A FINE MAIN DISH ON HOT SUMMER NIGHTS, SERVED WITH A RICE OR POTATO SALAD.

SERVES 4
(or 8 as a
first course)

  4 *1-pound mackerels,*
    cleaned
  1 *cup dry white wine*
  1 *cup water*
  1 *onion, sliced*
  ½ *teaspoon fennel seeds (or*
    a branch of fennel)
  2 *strips lemon peel*
10 *peppercorns*
  2 *bay leaves*
  1 *tablespoon Dijon-style*
    mustard
  ¼ *cup minced parsley*

Wash mackerel and pat dry with paper towels. Cut off heads and tails.

Put wine, water, onion, fennel seeds, lemon peel, peppercorns, and bay leaves in a saucepan. Simmer 10 minutes. Put fish in a frying pan large enough to hold them in a single layer. Strain the *court bouillon* from the saucepan over them and discard onion and seasonings. If the liquid does not just about cover the fish, add a little more wine or water.

Poach fish about 10 minutes over low heat. The liquid should just shimmer rather than come to a boil. The fish are done when no longer pink in the center and the flesh flakes easily. Remove from the heat and let them cool in their liquid.

Lift out the fish and gently remove the skin. Fillet them, removing all bones, and place in a dish. Boil down liquid to about half the volume and stir in mustard and parsley. Pour over fish and refrigerate. Allow to come almost to room temperature to serve.

THIS SIMPLE PROCESS IS USED FOR ALL KINDS OF FISH, BUT IT IS PARTICULARLY SUITED TO THE OILY MACKEREL. I SERVE THEM WITH PLAIN BOILED POTATOES, CUT INTO SLICES AND SPRINKLED WITH A LITTLE OF THE SAUCE.

Mackerel Maître d'Hôtel

SERVES 4

4 1-pound mackerels,
   cleaned
6 tablespoons butter
salt and freshly ground
   pepper
juice of 1 lemon
¼ cup minced parsley

Wash fish and pat dry with paper towels. Make 4 diagonal slashes through only the skin on each side. Sauté in butter in a frying pan large enough to hold them all. This will take about 15 minutes. If the butter starts to turn color, adjust heat so it won't burn.

Remove mackerel to warm plates. Season to taste with salt and pepper. Squeeze lemon into the butter and stir over high heat, then quickly stir in parsley and pour over the fish.

THE FIRST TWO RECIPES SHOW MACKEREL COOKED WITH WHITE WINE AND LEMON JUICE, AND THIS DEMONSTRATES HOW THE ACIDITY OF TOMATOES IS USED TO BALANCE THE OILINESS OF THE FISH. SERVE THEM WITH A HEAP OF PLAIN RICE TO EAT WITH THE SAUCE.

Portuguese Mackerel

SERVES 4

4 ¾-pound mackerels,
   cleaned
3 tablespoons olive oil
2 medium onions, thinly
   sliced
1½ cups chopped canned
   tomatoes
salt and freshly ground
   pepper
¼ cup minced parsley
1 cup dry white wine

Preheat oven to 375°. Wash mackerel and pat dry with paper towels. Cut off heads and tails if you wish. Put olive oil in a frying pan and toss onions over medium heat until they wilt and separate into rings. Add tomatoes and cook about 10 minutes over low heat. Add salt and pepper to taste and the parsley. Cook 1 minute or so, then add wine. Remove from heat.

Place mackerel in a lightly oiled shallow baking pan large enough to hold them in a single layer. Pour tomato mixture over and bake, uncovered, 40 minutes. Serve hot.

Meatballs and All

I read a food magazine quiz recently where they asked various glamorous chefs and stately cookbook writers what their favorite foods were. I was delighted when Craig Claiborne answered simply, "Any ground meat dish," for I don't remember ever having a meatball, meatloaf, or even a meatloaf sandwich I didn't relish. They may exist, but I've never met one. I dote on American chili and hamburgers, Greek moussaka, German klops, Italian bolognese sauce, French pâté, and sausages or stuffed cabbage dishes from anywhere—you name it. (Well, come to think, I don't admire British mince or bangers, but all rules must have a firm exception. I once asked the English artist Barbara Jones why their sausages were so awful, and she replied that everyone got used to sausages made mostly of bread during the war and now thought it a kind of sacred tradition!)

Here, we think first of ground beef, but there is ground pork to consider and ground lamb. Even ground veal is not too dear. I've even found some uses for the new ground turkey, though I think I would rebel if offered a turkeyburger.

HANDS-DOWN THESE ARE MY FAVORITE MEATBALLS. EVEN THE MANUSCRIPT PAGE FROM WHICH I TYPE IS SPATTERED WITH COOKING JUICES, THE SIGN OF EVERY SUCCESSFUL RECIPE. IN GERMANY VEAL IS ALWAYS USED, BUT I FIND THAT INEXPENSIVE GROUND TURKEY GIVES AN EVEN LIGHTER TEXTURE. (SOME RECIPES ALSO CALL FOR A SPLASH OF SODA WATER, WHICH THEY CLAIM MAKES THE BALLS LIGHTER, BUT I'VE TRIED THIS AND FIND IT UNDETECTABLE.) THE FINER THE STOCK YOU HAVE, THE BETTER THE SAUCE, SO IF YOU DON'T HAVE HOMEMADE STOCK ON HAND, TRY COOKING CANNED BEEF BOUILLON WITH SOME CHICKEN BACKS, A LITTLE ONION, A CARROT, A STALK OF CELERY, SOME PARSLEY, AND A BAY LEAF—WHATEVER YOU HAVE ON HAND. I ALSO KEEP A TUBE OF ANCHOVY PASTE AROUND BECAUSE THERE ARE FEW THINGS MORE USELESS THAN AN OPENED CAN OF ANCHOVIES IN THE REFRIGERATOR. EVEN IF YOU DON'T WANT TO COOK FOR FOUR, GO AHEAD AND MAKE THE WHOLE RECIPE AS THESE ARE PERHAPS EVEN BETTER THE NEXT DAY FOR A HOT MEATBALL SANDWICH.

German Meatballs with Caper Sauce

SERVES 4

½ *pound ground pork*
½ *pound ground veal (or turkey)*
¾ *cup fresh bread crumbs*
¼ *cup milk*
 1 *small onion, finely grated*
 2 *anchovies, finely minced (or 2 teaspoons anchovy paste)*
salt and freshly ground pepper
 1 *egg, slightly beaten*
¼ *teaspoon grated lemon rind*
 2 *tablespoons melted butter*
flour
 3 *cups stock (beef, veal, or chicken, or a mixture)*
 2 *tablespoons butter*
¼ *cup dry white wine*
 1 *tablespoon lemon juice*
 2 *tablespoons capers*
mashed potatoes

Put meats in a bowl. In another bowl, soften bread crumbs with milk, then mix in onion, anchovies, and a little salt and pepper (anchovies will make the mixture nearly salty enough). Mix in egg, lemon rind, and melted butter, then gently mix all this with the meats using your hands.

Shape meatballs into 1-inch balls and roll in flour. Poach these in stock, covered, 15 minutes. Remove with a slotted spoon, strain stock, and keep meatballs warm.

Melt butter in a saucepan over medium heat, stir in 2 tablespoons of flour, and cook several minutes. Pour in 2 cups of strained stock and cook until bubbling and smooth. Add wine, lemon juice, and capers. Cook 5 minutes or more over low heat. Pour sauce over meatballs and serve on a bed of creamy mashed potatoes.

Mildred Knopf's Buttermilk Meatballs

MILDRED KNOPF WAS A SELF-TAUGHT COOK WHO TURNED OUT THREE CHARMING AND INTELLIGENT COOKBOOKS IN THE '60S. THIS IS ADAPTED FROM HER *PERFECT HOSTESS COOK BOOK*. MANY OF THE RECIPES ARE A LITTLE RICH FOR OUR USE HERE. LARDED THROUGHOUT THE BOOK ARE RECIPES SHE LEARNED FROM HER MOTHER'S COOK, MARIE AGRESS, AN IMMIGRANT FROM AUSTRIA WHERE SHE HAD WORKED IN FRANZ JOSEF'S PALACE KITCHENS AT SCHOENBRUNN. MOST OF THESE ARE EASY TO SPOT FOR THEIR SENSE OF OLD-WORLD ECONOMY AND THEIR KNACK FOR USING AN INGREDIENT THAT MAKES ALL THE DIFFERENCE IN THE WORLD. THIS IS ONE SUCH, USING BUTTERMILK AND RYE CRUMBS TO GIVE THE MEATBALLS A CREAMY TEXTURE AND AN INSISTENT FLAVOR NOT POSSIBLE ANY OTHER WAY. MRS. KNOPF ADDS THAT THESE CAN BE COOKED WITHOUT FORMING INTO BALLS, IN THE COMBINED OIL AND BUTTER, RATHER IN THE MANNER OF A SLOPPY JOE, WHICH GUESTS AND FAMILY MIGHT ADMIRE, TOO.

SERVES 4

1 *pound lean ground beef*
1 *cup buttermilk*
½ *cup fresh rye bread crumbs*
salt and freshly ground pepper
flour
3 *tablespoons vegetable oil*
3 *tablespoons butter*
1 *cup sour cream*
4 *tablespoons dry sherry*
cooked noodles (or rice)
paprika

Place meat in a bowl with buttermilk and bread crumbs, and blend mixture thoroughly with your hands. Add salt and pepper to taste—not too much salt because the buttermilk tends to give the meat a lively enough flavor. Cover with plastic wrap and refrigerate 30 minutes.

Roll into 1-inch balls and roll lightly in flour. Put vegetable oil in a frying pan large enough to hold all the balls in a single layer. Cook over high heat until golden on all sides—about 5 minutes is enough, for they should not overcook. Scoop balls out into a bowl and discard the oil.

Put butter in the pan and heat over medium heat. Stir sour cream with sherry and then stir into the sizzling butter. Lower heat and stir the sauce smooth, adding a little salt as you wish. Do not let the sauce boil or it will curdle. When it is hot, stir in meatballs until they are coated. Serve over noodles or rice sprinkled with a blush of paprika.

I ADMIRE ANYTHING WITH THE GREEK EGG AND LEMON SAUCE, *AVGOLEMONO*, WITH ITS TART CREAMINESS, AND THESE MEATBALLS MADE LIGHT BY EGG WHITES AND RICE COOKED INSIDE ARE NO EXCEPTION. FOR A FIRST COURSE IT MAKES SENSE TO SERVE A SIMPLE GREEK SALAD OF SLICED RIPE TOMATOES SPRINKLED WITH A LITTLE VINEGAR AND OIL, TOPPED WITH CRUMBLED FETA CHEESE, AND WITH A LITTLE MOUND OF OIL-CURED OLIVES AT THE SIDE—THAT AND A LOAF OF BREAD AND GLASSES OF WINE FOR ALL.

Greek Meatballs with Egg and Lemon Sauce

SERVES 4

1½ *pounds ground lamb (or beef)*
1 *medium onion, grated (or minced)*
1 *clove garlic, minced*
⅓ *cup uncooked rice*
2 *tablespoons minced parsley*
1 *teaspoon dried basil (or mint)*
1 *teaspoon dried oregano*
salt and freshly ground pepper
3 *eggs*
2 *tablespoons vegetable oil*
chicken (or beef) stock
4 *tablespoons lemon juice (or to taste)*
cooked rice
minced parsley

Put meat in a bowl with onion, garlic, uncooked rice, herbs, and salt and pepper to taste. Beat 2 egg whites until they start to froth and add them as well (reserving yolks and the other egg for the sauce). Gently mix with a fork or your hands and form walnut-size balls.

Fry balls in vegetable oil over low heat. When lightly brown, remove with a slotted spoon to a saucepan. Add enough stock to cover meatballs and simmer, uncovered, 20 minutes. Pour off stock through a sieve and measure it. You will need 1½ cups for the sauce.

To make the sauce, beat egg yolks and the whole egg together until quite frothy. Whisk in lemon juice bit by bit, then whisk in hot stock bit by bit, beating steadily. Pour over meatballs and cook, stirring, over low heat until sauce thickens. Do not let it come to a boil, or it will separate.

Serve on a bed of rice, sprinkled with parsley.

Pork Balls Paprikash

I'D GO OUT OF MY WAY FOR ANY PAPRIKA DISH, AND THIS IS AMONG THE BEST. I WISH I COULD DUPLICATE THE PAPRIKA SAUCE AS I HAD IT ONCE AT THE HOME OF A YOUNG WRITER IN GERMANY, BUT WHEN I QUESTIONED HIS MOTHER, HE TRANSLATED THAT SHE HAD USED THREE KINDS OF PAPRIKA, ONE FRESHLY HARVESTED FROM THE GARDEN. AH, WELL, SOME THINGS DON'T AND WON'T TRAVEL. ALONG WITH THESE I SERVE A THINLY SLICED CUCUMBER SALAD, SLIGHTLY SWEETENED AND SPRINKLED WITH DILL.

SERVES 4

¾ *cup fresh bread crumbs*
½ *cup milk*
 1 *pound ground pork*
 2 *tablespoons finely grated onion*
 2 *tablespoons finely grated green pepper (flesh only)*
 1 *clove garlic, minced*
 1 *egg, lightly beaten*
salt and freshly ground pepper
flour
 4 *tablespoons lard (or bacon fat)*
 2 *onions, chopped*
 1 *tablespoon sweet Hungarian paprika*
 2 *cups chicken stock, heated*
 1 *cup sour cream*
cooked egg noodles

Soak bread crumbs in milk until soft. Place pork in a bowl. Add grated onion, green pepper, garlic, and bread crumbs. Add egg, and salt and pepper to taste, then mix with a fork or your hands as gently as possible. Shape into golf-size balls, roll in flour, place on a plate, and refrigerate for 1 hour or so before cooking.

To cook, heat fat in a large frying pan and sauté pork balls over medium-high heat until they start to brown. Add chopped onion and cook until it softens. Careful of the meatballs, stir in paprika, then 2 tablespoons of flour, and cook for several minutes. Add stock all at once and stir until sauce thickens and is smooth.

Cover the pan, turn heat down low, and cook 30 minutes. Finally, add sour cream and heat, stirring, just until the mixture is warmed through. The sour cream will curdle if the mixture boils. Serve over cooked noodles.

These meatballs are particularly mild and light textured from the whipped egg white (a good trick to remember!). Rather than an anemic American beer, splurge a little and

Belgian Meatballs Cooked in Beer

get something with a little body to it, and the sauce will be more interesting. I serve these as the Belgians do, with plain boiled potatoes, quartered and cooked right in with the meatballs. But if you don't have a pan big enough for all this to fit in and snuggle down, you can steam them on the side. The meatballs are also good with mashed potatoes. Serve beer with them, certainly, and some may be pleased with a little pot of mustard or horseradish alongside.

SERVES 4

1 *pound ground pork*
¾ *cup fresh bread crumbs*
¼ *cup milk*
¼ *cup minced green onion*
  including part of tops
1 *tablespoon butter*
½ *cup minced mushrooms*
salt and freshly ground
  pepper
freshly grated nutmeg
1 *egg, separated*
vegetable oil
1 *12-ounce bottle of beer*
1 *bay leaf*
¼ *teaspoon dried thyme*
minced parsley

Place pork in a bowl. Soften bread crumbs in milk and add them to the bowl. Sauté onion in butter until soft and add along with mushrooms, salt, pepper, and nutmeg to taste. Add the egg yolk and lightly mix all together with a fork or your hands. Finally, beat the egg white stiff and gently fold into mixture.

Shape into oval patties approximately 2½ inches by 1½ inches (there will be 12 patties). Always be gentle with the mixture as you shape the patties. Fry them in a film of vegetable oil in a frying pan large enough to hold them all. When golden on both sides, tip out most of the accumulated fat.

Add beer, bay leaf, and thyme, cover the pan, and simmer 30 minutes. Lift out patties onto warm plates and cook sauce down over high heat until slightly thickened. Stir in some parsley and pour over the meatballs.

Chinese Lion's Head

LION'S HEAD, ALMOST AN IMPERIAL CONCEIT WITH ITS MEATBALL LION IN A RUFF OF CRINKLY CABBAGE, SEEMS TO BE A HOME DISH ONLY. AND IT IS THE KIND WE DREAM OF ON THE UNTRANSLATED SIDE OF A CHINESE MENU, THOUGH I DOUBT IT EVEN EXISTS THERE, SO REDOLENT IT IS OF LONG, SLOW HOME COOKING, NOT TO BE TURNED OUT IN A FLASH. BUT IT IS EASY FOR ANY KITCHEN IN REACH OF FRESH GINGER, AND CERTAINLY IT IS AN HONORABLE STAPLE OF MINE. WHEN THE BUTCHER HAS GROUND PORK, IT MIGHT BE SAID I HANKER FOR LION'S HEAD. (A THRIFT NOTE: SINCE WE DON'T USUALLY HAVE FRESH WATER CHESTNUTS ON HAND, A CAN WILL HOLD MORE THAN IS NEEDED AND DOES NOT FREEZE WELL. TOSS THE LEFTOVERS, SLICED, WITH A SPRINKLE OF WHITE WINE VINEGAR AND A LITTLE SUGAR—OR BETTER YET, RICE WINE VINEGAR—AND SERVE THEM IN SALAD THE NEXT DAY.)

SERVES 4

- 1 *pound ground pork*
- 3 *tablespoons soy sauce*
- 1 *tablespoon sherry*
- 3 *green onions, minced with part of tops*
- ¼ *cup chopped water chestnuts*
- 1 *teaspoon grated fresh ginger root*
- 1 *egg, lightly whipped*
- 1 *clove garlic, minced (optional)*
- 2 *tablespoons minced fresh coriander (optional)*

cornstarch

- 1 *head Napa cabbage (approximately 1 pound)*
- 2 *tablespoons vegetable oil*
- ½ *cup chicken stock*
- ½ *teaspoon sugar*
- 1 *teaspoon soy sauce*
- ¼ *cup water*

cooked rice

Lightly mix pork in a bowl with all seasoning ingredients, egg, garlic, and coriander if you use them. Place plastic wrap over the bowl and refrigerate 1 hour or so—the mixture is a very moist one, and this gives it time to firm up a bit.

Form pork into 8 equal balls and place on waxed paper. Shake a measure of cornstarch out on a plate, roll balls in it, and place them back on the paper. Reserve the rest of the cornstarch for later.

Cut bottom off cabbage and separate the leaves. Split stem up the middle of each leaf, then slice off top half so each leaf is in 3 pieces. Place them in the bottom of a casserole.

Heat vegetable oil in a frying pan over high heat. Toss balls into the pan, lifting with a slotted spoon as they cook and brown, to keep them as plump and round as possible. Place balls on top of the cabbage. Add chicken stock, sugar, and soy sauce to the pan, stir well, then pour over the casserole.

Cover and simmer 30 minutes. Mix 1 tablespoon of cornstarch with ¼ cup of water and stir in. Let simmer about 10 minutes to thicken slightly. Serve cabbage with meatballs and sauce on top, with a mound of rice on the side.

I DON'T KNOW WHY MORE MARKETS DON'T CARRY GROUND LAMB, FOR IT'S AN IDEAL WAY TO USE UP THE SCRAPS. I HAVE A SOURCE THAT ALWAYS CARRIES IT, BUT YOU MAY HAVE TO LOOK AROUND

Deviled Lamb Patties

AND ASK. IT'S THE IDEAL WAY TO SATISFY YOUR TASTE FOR LAMB ON A BUDGET. OUTSIDE ON A SUMMER EVENING THEIR PERFECT PARTNER IS TABBOULEH (PAGE 286), THE BULGUR WHEAT SALAD, BUT INSIDE ON WINTER NIGHTS I PREPARE EGGPLANT CUT AS FOR FRENCH FRIES, MARINATED IN MILK TO COVER, AND THEN SHAKEN IN A BAG OF FLOUR FLAVORED WITH SALT, PEPPER, AND NUTMEG. THESE ARE THEN DEEP-FRIED UNTIL THEY PUFF AND TURN GOLDEN.

SERVES 4

1½ *pounds ground lamb*
  1 *clove garlic, finely minced (or 2 tablespoons grated onion pulp)*
Dijon-style mustard
  1 *tablespoon Worcestershire sauce*
freshly ground pepper
  ¼ *teaspoon Tabasco (optional)*
salt (optional)
  ⅓ *cup bread crumbs*
  1 *tablespoon butter*
  1 *teaspoon dried basil (or oregano)*

Put lamb in a bowl and add garlic, 2 tablespoons of mustard, Worcestershire, and rather a lot of freshly ground pepper. If you like hotness, add a shake or two of Tabasco, but I don't think they need any salt—maybe later on the outside but not in the meat. Mix gently and shape into 4 oval patties about 1 inch thick, then set aside to gather flavor.

To cook, either ready a charcoal grill or get out the frying pan. Prepare bread crumb topping by sautéing crumbs in butter with some basil crumbled in. When golden, have the crumbs and mustard pot handy.

Ideally, these should be pink inside and quite brown out. On a charcoal grill this is easy, but inside remember ground lamb is usually so greasy you will need no fat to cook it, and you will actually have to keep tipping fat out as they cook so they brown well. Over high heat they will take about 5 minutes a side to cook—poke a fork in one to test for pinkness. If too pink, lower heat and cook a few minutes more.

At this point slather mustard on the tops of the birds, and be generous. Sprinkle bread crumbs evenly over the tops, let cook a few minutes more, then lift out onto warm plates.

A GLORIOUS OLD-FASHIONED FAMILY DISH TAKES A LITTLE TIME AND CARE BUT IS WELL WORTH IT. IF YOU DON'T HAVE A LARGE FAMILY, DON'T WORRY, FOR THIS IS GREAT COLD THE NEXT DAY.

American Stuffed Meatloaf

SERVES 4–6

3 *tablespoons butter*
1 *large onion, chopped*
1 *teaspoon dried crumbled sage*
½ *teaspoon dried thyme*
2½ *cups home-style white bread, cut in dice*
½ *cup chicken stock (approximately)*
salt and freshly ground pepper
¼ *cup minced parsley*
1 *pound ground beef*
½ *pound ground pork*
1 *egg, beaten*
1 *clove garlic, minced*
4 *tablespoons catsup*
1 *teaspoon Worcestershire sauce (plus)*

Put butter in a frying pan and sauté onion about 10 minutes over medium-low heat, or until starting just to turn golden. Stir in sage and thyme. Put bread cubes in a bowl and toss with onion. Add enough stock to make the dressing moist. This will depend on the bread, and remember, you want it lightly moist and not a paste. Add salt and pepper to taste, and finally stir in parsley.

Preheat oven to 350°. Mix beef and pork lightly with egg, garlic, 2 tablespoons of catsup, and the Worcestershire sauce. This "mixing lightly" is the secret of all meatloaves and meatballs.

Reserve about ½ cup of meat mixture and spread out the rest on waxed paper in a 9-inch by 14-inch rectangle. Pat it as you go and smooth as much as possible. Pat the dressing over meat, lightly pressing it in. Leave about a 1-inch margin all around the edges so it will be easier to seal and keep the stuffing inside.

Using the edge of the waxed paper to help, roll up meat, patting and smoothing as you go, so you end up with a 9-inch roll. Lay this, seam side down, in a regular loaf pan. Use reserved meat to smooth over the top like an icing. Make this as even and smooth as possible. This process is to keep the loaf from splitting its seams as it cooks. Then smooth over the top the remaining 2 tablespoons of catsup, mixed with a little extra Worcestershire sauce.

Bake 30 minutes. Pour out juices that have accumulated and let loaf rest 5 minutes or more for easier cutting. Cut in slices and serve.

THIS HAS BEEN A STAPLE OF MY HOUSEHOLD FOR YEARS, GATHERING A FEW INGREDIENTS ALONG THE WAY—THE SPINACH, FOR INSTANCE, WHICH IS NICE BUT NOT NECESSARY (ALSO, YOU MAY USE FROZEN). FOR COMPANY I SOMETIMES MAKE IT IN A ROUND FORM SO IT LOOKS LIKE A GIGANTIC MEATBALL. THIS IS PUT ON A PLATTER SURROUNDED BY PASTA THAT HAS BEEN LIGHTLY TOSSED WITH A GOOD TOMATO SAUCE, AND THEN CUT AT THE TABLE IN PIE-SHAPED WEDGES. THIS IS A LITTLE TRICKY TO FORM, BUT YOU CAN USE AN 8-INCH BOWL AND TURN IT OUT ONTO A BAKING PAN. BE SURE TO SEAL IT AS WELL AS YOU CAN, AND PINCH, PAT, AND SMOOTH AFTER IT HAS BEEN TURNED OUT.

Ricotta-stuffed Italian Meatloaf

SERVES 4–6

1 *pound ground beef (or half veal, half beef)*
1 *cup bread crumbs*
½ *cup water*
3 *eggs*
¼ *cup minced parsley*
¼ *cup minced green onion*
1 *clove garlic, minced*
salt and freshly ground pepper
1 *pound spinach*
¾ *pound ricotta cheese*
¾ *cup grated Parmesan cheese*
2 *teaspoons dried basil*
freshly grated nutmeg
2 *tablespoons vegetable oil*

Place beef in a bowl. Reserve 2 tablespoons of bread crumbs and soak the rest in water. Add this, along with 2 eggs, 1 tablespoon of parsley, green onion, garlic, and salt and pepper to taste. Mix lightly with a fork. Using ⅔ of the mixture, line a loaf pan, sides and bottom. Reserve the rest. Preheat oven to 375°.

Stem spinach and wash in several waters. Place in a large pan with only the water that clings to the leaves. Cover pan and let spinach just wilt over medium heat. Run cold water over, drain in a colander, squeeze out moisture with your hands, and mince finely. Place in a bowl with ricotta cheese, the remaining egg, the rest of the parsley, Parmesan cheese, basil, and a good amount of nutmeg. Add salt and pepper to taste—not too much salt because the Parmesan is salty.

Place ricotta in meat-lined pan and carefully pat the rest of the meat over the top. Be careful to seal all edges well. Sprinkle loaf with reserved crumbs, then dribble with vegetable oil. Bake 40–45 minutes, or until top is crusty brown and inside is set. Let stand 10–15 minutes before slicing.

EVER SINCE SUPERMARKETS STARTED MARKETING GROUND TURKEY I'VE WONDERED WHAT IN THE WORLD TO DO WITH IT. THIS WAS THE FIRST AND MOST OBVIOUS ANSWER, AND IT IS A FAVORITE, USING A

Turkey and Stuffing Loaf

GOOD-TEXTURED BREAD AND SPLURGING ON A TURKEY WING TO MAKE THE STOCK. FOR THOSE WHO LIKE CRANBERRY SAUCE, WHEN CRANBERRIES ARE OUT OF SEASON YOU CAN ZIP UP CANNED WHOLE BERRY SAUCE BY HEATING IT GENTLY WITH SOME GRATED ORANGE RIND AND PERHAPS A SPLASH OF DRY SHERRY.

SERVES 4

1 *pound ground turkey*
8 *slices home-style white bread, trimmed of crusts*
¼ *cup milk*
1 *egg, lightly beaten*
1 *tablespoon grated onion pulp*
salt and freshly ground pepper
1 *onion, chopped*
2 *stalks celery, chopped with leaves*
2 *tablespoons minced parsley*
4 *tablespoons butter*
¼ *teaspoon dried thyme*
¼ *teaspoon crumbled sage*
chicken (or turkey) stock
3 *slices bacon*
paprika

Preheat oven to 350°. Put turkey in a bowl. Soak 2 slices of bread in milk, then crumble into the turkey, adding egg, onion pulp, and salt and pepper to taste. Mix gently but thoroughly and let sit while you make the stuffing.

Sauté onion, celery, and parsley in butter in a large saucepan over medium heat. When onion is quite soft, add herbs and cook a few more minutes. Remove from heat. Cut remaining bread into dice and toss with onion mixture. Add enough stock to moisten dressing but not enough to make it soggy. This amount will depend on the kind of bread used.

Press half the turkey into the bottom of a greased loaf pan, top with dressing, then smooth a layer of remaining turkey over. Make sure no stuffing shows through. Place bacon strips on top and sprinkle with a little paprika. Bake 45 minutes to 1 hour—when done the loaf should be firm and the bacon crisp on top.

Let sit 10 minutes. Serve in slices.

Lamb Stuffed with Mushrooms and Fontina

A SUPERB DISH FIT FOR COMPANY ANYTIME, AND NOT TOO HARD ON THE POCKET EVEN WITH VELVETY FONTINA AND A FEW MUSHROOMS. SERVE IT PERHAPS WITH ZUCCHINI JOSEPHINE (PAGE 315) OR ZUCCHINI FANS (PAGE 316), A GOOD LOAF OF BREAD, A BOTTLE OF RED WINE. . . .

SERVES 4–6

2 *pounds ground lamb*
1 *cup fresh bread crumbs*
¼ *cup milk*
2 *eggs, lightly beaten*
2 *tablespoons grated Parmesan cheese*
2 *tablespoons minced parsley*
½ *teaspoon dried crumbled sage*
salt and freshly ground pepper
½ *pound Fontina cheese, coarsely grated*
½ *pound mushrooms, finely chopped*
3 *green onions, finely chopped*
2 *tablespoons butter*
2 *cloves garlic*

Preheat oven to 350°. Put lamb in a bowl. Soak crumbs in milk and squeeze dry with your hands. Add this to the bowl with eggs, Parmesan cheese, parsley, sage, and salt and pepper to taste. On a sheet of waxed paper, pat lamb out in a rectangle about ¼ inch thick—its size doesn't matter because you're not cooking it in a loaf pan.

Sprinkle with Fontina cheese. Sauté mushrooms and onions in butter until lightly browned, then sprinkle over the cheese. Use the waxed paper to help roll up carefully, then make sure the roll is sealed on the seam and at the ends. The best way to do this is with wet fingers, pinching and patting.

Place in a lightly greased baking pan, with 2 peeled garlic cloves on either side. Bake 1 hour. Baste occasionally as it cooks with the juices that accumulate. Remove from oven and let rest about 10 minutes, then slice and serve on warm plates.

Veal Loaf with Prunes, or How Not to Write a Recipe

How to write a recipe is the recipe itself, how not to is another, unsung story. Consider this dish abandoned after trial, involving perhaps wrong choices all down the road. I dug it out of my files, unspotted (which in my case means never made) but of a color to make me believe it to be at least twenty years old, probably from my stay in England. Thinking to put a crown on my loaves here, I step by step deciphered my file shorthand:

2 lbs ground veal, 1 egg, 1 egg yolk, s & p & nutmeg, flour & butter. Sauce: ¼ lb prunes, 1 c red wine, 1 t cornstarch, ½ c stock, s & p. Mix meat with eggs & season to taste. Form a roll, sprinkle with flour & fry in butter. Soak prunes, remove pits & mash with wine. Pour over the meat in the pan. Dilute cornstarch in stock or water & add. Season with s & p & simmer until meat is done, adding a little more water if necessary. Serves 8.

Now this sounds interesting, I thought, maybe with more prunes lining the center it would look proud sliced on a plate. And then that prune sauce would glaze it on the outside, and maybe form a little sauce for after. I considered how bland and dry veal is, and decided to add a minced shallot, with perhaps bacon wrapping the inner prunes. The shallot won, but I was out of bacon. So I measured out prunes, dividing for half a recipe—ah, how to divide an egg and a yolk: try one? The stock was to be chicken because I had some frozen, and I firmly believed the loaf should be cooked in the oven rather than on top. Was this my great mistake?

So butter slathered it, the oven heated to 425° to brown it, and the roll was popped in to wait for sizzle. The prune sauce had been pureed and simmered to perfection. Two teaspoons of lemon juice, it took. This was spread over the roll after twenty minutes, and the oven turned down to 350°. A mistake? Another fifteen minutes, and popping the oven door open I find a savory loaf leaking butter, obviously meant to be spooned over. Why not pour the rest of the sauce around, to absorb those juices? None of this looks like a mistake, so why ever not?

It cooks in all an hour, when it first perfumes the kitchen. After sitting fifteen minutes to firm and draw in juices, it is sliced and placed on a warm plate with creamy mashed potatoes. The sauce looks black, so forget the subtle sauce. The veal presents a pretty slice, the mounds of potato drip butter. But, but, but—at the first forkful the cook knows this is not a dish for friends or strangers, the family will never ask for it, it won't even make a good sandwich the next day. Some dishes you can work and work with, because you know they will go just right, but there are some like this, wherever you might have shied wrong, you know you'll never make come right.

I don't know how you know this, but I trust it, and how not to write a recipe.

My Stuffed Cabbage

I COULD PRAISE STUFFED CABBAGE ALL DAY, FOR SURELY IT IS ONE OF THE BEST PEASANT DISHES EVER DEVISED. AND HOW ELSE COULD YOU SERVE SO MANY PEOPLE, SO WELL, ON A POUND OF MEAT? ANY COUNTRY THAT GROWS CABBAGE ALSO STUFFS IT. THE FRENCH LIKE TO STUFF THE WHOLE HEAD BETWEEN LEAVES AND THEN TIE IT UP IN A HUGE BALL TO COOK. AND THOUGH I PREFER RICE TO THEIR BREAD STUFFING, PRACTICALLY ANY MEAT CAN BE USED—HAM, LEFTOVER TURKEY, CHICKEN OR GAME, ROAST BEEF, BRAISED PORK. IF YOU HAVE A SMALL FAMILY, IT FREEZES FAIRLY WELL, THOUGH I MUST CONFESS WHEN I MAKE A POT I USE IT FOR LUNCH AND DINNER UNTIL IT VANISHES, FOR IT IS ONE OF THOSE KINDLY DISHES THAT GET BETTER ON REHEATING. UNLESS YOU FEED IT TO COMPANY (AN IDEA I HEARTILY APPROVE), YOU TRULY NEED ONLY BREAD AND BUTTER AND A GLASS OF WINE OR BEER FOR A SATISFACTORY MEAL.

I USE EXACTLY THE SAME STUFFING WITH TOMATO SAUCE MIXED IN FOR STUFFED PEPPERS. I CHAR THE PEPPERS AND STEAM IN A BAG BEFORE PEELING, THEN HALVE THEM, AND PLACE IN AN OILED BAKING DISH. I SALT THEM LIGHTLY, DRIBBLE A LITTLE OLIVE OIL IN, THEN STUFF THEM. THEY ARE THEN BAKED WITH A SLICE OF CHEDDAR CHEESE ON TOP, UNTIL THEY ARE WARMED THROUGH AND THE CHEESE IS MELTED.

SERVES 6–8

1 *large head cabbage (2–3 pounds)*
1½ *tablespoons butter*
1½ *tablespoons vegetable oil*
1 *large onion, chopped*
2 *cloves garlic, minced*
1 *pound ground beef (or pork, or half and half)*
2 *cups cooked rice*
¼ *cup minced parsley*
½ *teaspoon dried thyme*
salt and freshly ground pepper
1 *cup beef stock*
1 *cup tomato sauce (canned)*
1 *bay leaf*
minced parsley

Peel off any wilted outer leaves of cabbage and cut out core with a small knife. Place, core down, in a large pot with 2 inches of boiling water. Cover and cook 5 minutes, or until the leaves can be separated easily. Peel until you come to unwilted leaves, then put cabbage back in for a few minutes. Repeat this as necessary. Lay the leaves out on paper towels to drain as you go.

Place butter and vegetable oil in a frying pan over medium-low heat, and sauté onion and garlic until onion softens. Remove to a bowl and sauté ground meat in the pan until it starts to brown. If too much fat accumulates, drain meat, then add to the bowl of onion and garlic. Stir in rice, parsley, thyme, and salt and pepper to taste.

Put about 3 tablespoons of stuffing in each big leaf, and round the cabbage with your fists lightly to make a ball. Place balls in layers in a casserole. As the leaves get smaller use 2 at a time and then even 3 if you must, to use all the stuffing. Pour stock and tomato sauce over the rolls and add the bay leaf. Cover the casserole. This dish can simmer 1 hour on top of the stove or in oven at 350°.

Serve sprinkled with parsley.

Classic Moussaka

MOUSSAKA HAS BECOME SYNONYMOUS WITH EGGPLANT, BUT THE GREEKS ALSO USE OTHER VEGETABLES—ZUCCHINI IS A PARTICULAR FAVORITE. AS IT IS USUALLY COOKED, EGGPLANT GETS SO GREASY THAT MOUSSAKA SOMETIMES IS NOT A WISE CHOICE IN A RESTAURANT, BUT AS I DO IT HERE THE EGGPLANT DOES NOT SPONGE UP OIL AND IS ONE OF THE WORLD'S GREAT INEXPENSIVE DISHES SUITABLE TO SERVE ANYONE. JUST TWO BLOCKS AWAY FROM MY HOUSE IS A GREEK ORTHODOX CHURCH THAT HAS A FOOD FESTIVAL EVERY YEAR. THE MOUSSAKA THERE IS SO DELICATE AND MELTING I'VE TRIED TO BUDGE THE SECRET OUT OF A FEW MEMBERS, BUT THEIR RECIPE SEEMS NO DIFFERENT FROM THIS. PERHAPS IT'S JUST THEIR FINGERS. . . .

SERVES 8–12

olive oil
  1 *cup chopped onion*
1½ *pounds ground lamb*
    (or beef)
½ *cup dry white wine*
1½ *cups chopped canned*
    tomatoes, drained
  4 *tablespoons minced*
    parsley
¼ *teaspoon dried oregano*
salt and freshly ground
    pepper
  2 *eggs, separated*
½ *cup bread crumbs*
    (approximately)
2½ *pounds eggplant (about*
    2 large)
  3 *cups milk, heated*
  6 *tablespoons butter*
  6 *tablespoons flour*
freshly grated nutmeg
  1 *cup grated Parmesan*
    cheese

Heat 2 tablespoons of olive oil in a frying pan, then add onion and cook until limp. Add ground meat, chopping at it with a spoon or fork until it separates, then cover the pan and simmer 5 minutes. Add wine, tomatoes, and herbs, and season to taste with salt and pepper. Cover and simmer 30 minutes. Remove from heat and let sit until cool. Stir egg whites to a froth and add to mixture with 2 tablespoons of bread crumbs.

Peel eggplant and cut crosswise into ⅓-inch slices. Drop slices in batches of boiling salted water and cook only 2 minutes. Remove and drain on paper towels. Fry lightly in 3 or more tablespoons of the oil just until lightly golden. Remove to a plate.

Begin to warm milk in a small saucepan. Melt butter in a larger saucepan and stir in flour. Let it cook over medium heat, stirring, 3–4 minutes. Add hot milk and stir until you have a smooth thick sauce. Season to taste with salt, pepper, and nutmeg. Allow to cook 5 minutes or so. Remove from heat and stir in egg yolks and half of the grated Parmesan cheese.

Preheat oven to 350°. Oil a 9-inch by 12-inch by 2-inch baking pan and sprinkle lightly with remaining bread crumbs. Line the bottom of the pan with half of eggplant slices, cover with meat mixture, and spread evenly. Layer remaining eggplant slices over meat, cutting slices if necessary to fit them in. Spread cheese sauce over and sprinkle with remaining cheese and bread crumbs.

Bake 35–40 minutes, or until golden brown on top. Remove from oven and let sit at least 10 minutes before slicing into squares. Moussaka can also be served at room temperature, as it is in Greece.

I DON'T KNOW WHAT CAVALRY CLUB THIS ORIGINATED IN, BUT THE RECIPE TAKES HAMBURGER TO ANOTHER REALM, ONE SO SAVORY, WHO NEEDS A MORE EXPENSIVE LEG OF LAMB? TRUE, IT'S NOT VERY

Dry Curry Cavalry Club

PRETTY TO LOOK AT, SO I MAKE A RING OF RICE ON THE PLATE, DOLLOP CURRY IN THE CENTER, PUT ¼-INCH-THICK HALF-SLICES OF LEMON AROUND, FILL THEIR SPACES WITH YOGURT, PLOP CHUTNEY IN THE CENTER, THEN GIVE THE WHOLE A GRAND CAST OF SLIVERED, TOASTED ALMONDS. IF YOU DON'T HAVE TIME TO STICK WITH IT FOR 2 HOURS, COOK IT IN A PRESSURE COOKER FOR 30 MINUTES ANYTIME DURING THE DAY, THEN COOL IT AND COOK IN AN OPEN FRYING PAN WHILE YOU PREPARE THE GARNISH.

SERVES 4

1 *pound lean ground beef*
1 *apple*
2 *bananas (preferably not too ripe)*
1 *cucumber*
1 *large onion*
1 *clove garlic*
2 *tablespoons curry powder*
3 *tablespoons butter*
1 *cup beef stock*
salt
Tabasco
½ *cup heavy cream*
1 *tablespoon lemon juice*
cooked rice
garnish: lemon slices, yogurt, chutney, toasted almonds

Put meat in a large bowl. Then prepare the fruits and vegetables. They should be peeled, seeded, and chopped very fine. If you have a food processor, it goes like a breeze using pulsing movements with the metal blade, but if not, you just have to knuckle down with a large sharp knife and get them as fine as possible.

Mix these into the meat along with the curry powder. Heat butter in a large frying pan and sauté the mixture over high heat. It won't really brown, but the meat should be cooked beyond pink. When it looks well mixed and sizzly, add stock, bring to a boil, lower heat, cover, and let simmer 2 hours over very low heat. Peek now and again, and stir. Taste for salt and hotness after the first hour, and add a sprinkle of salt and a few drops of Tabasco.

When ready, all liquid should have cooked away and the whole mixture should be brown. Uncover it for the last 15 minutes of cooking to evaporate liquid if need be. Near the end, when it is a nice brown mass, stir in cream and lemon juice. Serve over hot rice, and garnish with lemon slices, yogurt, chutney, and almonds.

How to Partner Sausages

There are hundreds of types of sausages—long and thin, fat and stubby, fresh and smoked, bland and spicy. They are usually made from pork, but sausages can be of beef or veal or game birds, and combinations thereof. Any way you look at it, though, they are all ground meat. The dry types are usually sliced thin and used as cold cuts, but depending on where you live, your market will have quite a selection of sausages available for a quick, inexpensive, tasty hot meal.

Here, I'd like to present three cabbage partners, perfect with any boiled, fried, or grilled sausage, along with simple boiled or mashed potatoes. Oh yes, and a pot of grainy mustard! The first is more or less the way the late James Beard prepared one of his favorites, the humble sauerkraut. Once you've tried this method you'll understand why he was an addict. The next is the German method of cooking red cabbage with red wine, and then an unusual cabbage stuffed with apples.

Sauerkraut with Juniper Berries

SERVES 4

2 pounds sauerkraut
　　(fresh or canned)
4 slices bacon
freshly ground black pepper
1 bay leaf
¼ teaspoon dried thyme
2 sprigs of parsley
2 cloves garlic
8–10 juniper berries,
　　crushed
chicken stock (or beer)

Place sauerkraut in a bowl of water, then drain in a colander. Krauts differ, and fresh is very salty, so test by biting a strand or two. Wash through water until it has lost some of its acidity—not all, but enough to make a mellow dish.

Line the bottom of a large pot with bacon slices. Make layers of kraut with a good sprinkle of pepper between them. Put bay leaf, thyme, and parsley in a cheesecloth bag (or simply tuck in and remove later) and add it with garlic and juniper berries. Add enough chicken stock or beer to come to the top of the kraut.

Bring to a boil, reduce to a simmer, and cook, covered, 2–4 hours. Four hours is preferable because the longer it cooks, the better it becomes.

Red Cabbage Braised with Wine

SERVES 4

1 *small head red cabbage*
3 *tablespoons bacon fat (or*
   goose fat, or butter)
salt and freshly ground
   pepper
1 *cup red wine*
2 *apples, peeled, seeded,*
   and diced
2 *tablespoons brown sugar*
1 *tablespoon red wine*
   vinegar

Remove any limp leaves from outside of the cabbage. Cut in quarters and slice out the core, then shred finely with a knife. Put in a bowl of cold water 15–20 minutes. Drain well in a colander.

Put bacon fat in a large saucepan over medium heat. Add cabbage and stir several minutes to coat with fat. Add salt and pepper to taste, then wine. Simmer several more minutes, then add apples, brown sugar, and wine vinegar. Simmer, covered, about 15 minutes, or until cooked but still with a bit of bite.

My Cabbage Stuffed with Apples

SERVES 4

1 *head cabbage*
2 *tablespoons butter*
1 *large onion, chopped*
4 *tart apples, peeled, seeded, and thinly sliced*
pinch of dried thyme
salt
½ *cup chicken stock (or dry white wine, or a mixture)*
paprika

Cut out part of the cabbage core so the leaves will loosen easily. Place in a pot, core down, with about 2 inches of boiling water. Cover with a lid and steam 4–5 minutes. Remove and carefully peel off 8 large leaves—if the inner leaves are not wilted enough, place cabbage back in the pot 1 minute or so to soften. Reserve remaining cabbage for other uses.

Melt butter in a frying pan and cook onion several minutes over medium heat. Add apples and toss well. Cover pan and cook over low heat until apples soften.

Divide apple mixture among the cabbage leaves and fold leaves around to make a bundle. Place, seam side down, in a pan that can hold all the bundles in a single layer, pour stock or wine around, and sprinkle with a blush of paprika. Cover pan and simmer 30 minutes over low heat. (If need be, these can also be cooked 30 minutes in a 350° oven.)

Remove with a slotted spoon to warm plates and serve.

Another favorite is the lightly curried Shaker Cabbage in Caraway Cream in my book, *The American Table*. This cabbage is particularly fine with bland sausages such as bockwurst. With these excellent partners, and the next three recipes—my favorite dishes using three common sausages—you'll never be without ways to offer this useful tribe.

Italian Sausage and Green Peppers

THIS IS ONE OF MY FAVORITE MEALS WHEN DINING ALONE AND NOBODY TO PLEASE BUT MYSELF (AND MY WALLET). I'VE TINKERED WITH IT THROUGH THE YEARS BY ADDING SOME GARLIC OR SOME WHITE WINE AND TOMATOES OR TOMATO PASTE, BUT IT'S BEST JUST THIS WAY.

SERVES 1

1 *tablespoon olive oil (or vegetable oil)*
2 *fresh Italian sausages, sweet or hot*
1 *small onion*
1 *small green pepper*
salt
pinch of crumbled red pepper flakes (optional)
pinch of fennel seeds (optional)
pinch of dried oregano (or basil)

Put olive oil in a frying pan and sauté sausages over high heat until browned on both sides. Cut onion vertically in 8 pieces. Cut pepper in quarters, remove seeds, and cut quarters in ½-inch strips. Add them to the sausages, turn heat down to medium-low, toss several minutes, and add salt to taste along with other seasonings. (Use what you have on hand, but if the sausage doesn't have pepper or fennel, it's nice to add a little.)

Cover pan and cook 30 minutes over low heat, or until both onion and pepper are quite tender. Uncover, turn up heat, and stir 4–5 minutes. Serve with either plain pasta tossed with butter and Parmesan cheese, or best of all with Polenta (page 214).

Bockwurst or Bratwurst with Onion Sauce

SOMEHOW THIS IS ONE OF THOSE COMFORTING MEALS ONE COMES BACK AND BACK TO FOR MORE THAN SIMPLE SUSTENANCE. THE ONLY TROUBLE WITH IT IS THAT YOU END WITH EVERYTHING PALE, BUT THIS CAN BE REMEDIED BY A BLUSH OF PAPRIKA AND A DAB OF YELLOW MUSTARD.

SERVES 4

3 *tablespoons butter*
2 *large onions, thinly sliced*
3 *tablespoons flour*
½ *teaspoon dry mustard*
¾ *cup milk, heated*
¾ *cup chicken stock, heated*
salt and freshly ground pepper
pinch of sugar
2 *tablespoons prepared horseradish* (optional)
8 *bockwurst* (or *bratwurst*)

Melt butter in a saucepan over medium heat. Add onions and sauté until they soften. Don't let them take color, and lower heat if necessary. Cover pan and stew gently 10 minutes. Gradually sprinkle in flour and dry mustard and stir several minutes, then add milk and chicken stock, and stir until you have a smooth thickened sauce. Season to taste with salt, pepper, and a hint of sugar. If you like, add a little horseradish to perk things up. Let the onion sauce cook 15–20 minutes while you boil the sausages in a little water.

To serve, ladle onion sauce onto warm plates and place sausages on top. Serve with steamed parsleyed potatoes.

THERE'S NO ACCOUNTING FOR QUITE HOW GOOD THIS IS, BUT IT CERTAINLY BRINGS A LITTLE POLISH SAUSAGE A LONG WAY TOWARD BEING A FAMILY FAVORITE, FOR KEEPS. (OR ALMOST KEEPS—I GOT SO I SERVED THIS SO OFTEN THERE WAS A

Hungarian Sausage and Potatoes

KITCHEN REBELLION, AND I AM NOW ONLY ALLOWED IT ONCE A MONTH.) WHEN RED PEPPERS ARE IN SEASON, IT'S GREAT TO PREPARE THIS WITH ONE GREEN AND ONE RED, FOR RED PEPPERS SEEM TO MAKE THE PAPRIKA SING.

SERVES 4

6 *medium potatoes, peeled and sliced ¼-inch thick*
¾ *to 1-pound kielbasa (or other smoked, precooked sausage), sliced in rings*
6 *slices bacon, cut in small strips*
1 *tablespoon butter (or lard)*
1 *large onion, chopped*
2 *medium green peppers, seeded and sliced in thin strips*
1 *tablespoon sweet Hungarian paprika*
½ *cup canned tomato sauce (or 2 tablespoons tomato paste stirred in ½ cup water)*
½ *cup beef stock (or water)*
salt and freshly ground pepper

This should be cooked in any wide skillet or oven-top casserole that has a lid. First prepare the potatoes and drop them into a bowl of water. Then cut up sausage. Put pan over medium heat, add bacon and butter, and cook until the bacon begins to curl and brown. Add onion and peppers, and cook until onion is limp. Stir in paprika, then drain potatoes and add them along with sausage. Stir to coat.

Finally add tomato sauce and stock, and turn heat up until the pot bubbles. Stir and add salt and pepper to taste. Cover and cook 35–40 minutes, or until the whole looks and smells savory. Peek now and again to make sure there is enough liquid, and give the sausages a gentle turn into the sauce at the same time.

Cheap Cuts

Good meat markets will show forth a range of innards—hearts and tongues and lungs and brains and tripe—all fine if you like such, and most under a dollar a pound. I happen to admire some of these, particularly hearts and brains, but most folks write off the lot. Fortunately, there are other cuts, usually down at the end of the counter, that nobody knows much to do with. They could become secret favorites of your family, recipes your friends ask for.

The most unlikely would seem to be the breasts of lamb and veal, the first a treasure of day-to-day cooking and the other, fit party fare for economical epicures when well stuffed and slowly braised. Succulent lamb shanks go for little, as do both kidneys of veal and lamb. As far as I'm concerned, only people who have been force-fed overcooked gray liver as children don't like liver. Prepared well, it is a joy not a duty.

No matter the state of my bank account, I use these all frequently. Any market that sells lamb has a couple or more kidneys a day, at least. These I pick up on sight, and tuck them in the freezer until I've enough for a meal. Good veal generally must be discovered in a specialty market, but lamb breast and shanks can be *picked up nearly everywhere. My love affair with both has been of long standing because for pennies you have all the flavor but none of the stiff price of leg or chops.*

Of Lamb Shanks

These ought to be fresh, dark pink, and showing a good deal of flesh at the cut. Some recipes call for peeling off the "fell" membrane, as you do with most lamb cuts, but I see no good reason with a piece of meat that must be braised several hours, for this is one time lamb must be so well done as to be falling almost apart. Any red meat is more delicious near the bone, and this is no exception. When your budget is also near the bone and you want something warm and soothing on a particularly lean night, remember the shank of lamb. Whole, they are difficult to deal with at the table; but if you don't care to saw and gnaw, I've included only one recipe for them this way. The others pare a recipe down to just half a shank per person, to be heaped on a plate and eaten in proper forkfuls.

LAMB SHANKS NEED SLOW, LONG BRAISING, AND THIS IS ONE OF THE SIMPLEST AND BEST WAYS TO DO SO. THEY ARE PARTICULARLY FINE WITH A PILAF OF BULGAR WHEAT, BUT PROBABLY EQUALLY GOOD IS PASTA TOSSED SIMPLY WITH BUTTER AND PARMESAN CHEESE.

Rosemary Lamb Shanks

SERVES 4

4 *lamb shanks*
4 *cloves garlic, peeled*
1 *teaspoon dried rosemary*
⅔ *cup dry white wine*
*salt and freshly ground
　　pepper*

Preheat oven to 300°. Put shanks in a casserole large enough to hold them in a single layer. Add garlic cloves, rosemary, wine, and salt and pepper to taste. Cover casserole with foil and a lid, and bake 2½ hours.

Remove shanks to warm plates. The liquid should have cooked down to a good sauce already, but if not, bring to a high boil and cook down until it thickens slightly. (The garlic cloves can either be discarded or crushed into the sauce, as you like.) Pour sauce over the shanks and serve.

Lamb Shanks with Orzo and Feta

A GREEK DISH THAT MAKES LAMB SHANKS STRETCH A LONG, DELECTABLE WAY, THIS IS ONE OF MY VERY FAVORITES—EVEN FOR COMPANY. IT NEEDS ONLY A LOAF OF FRENCH BREAD AND A TOSSED SALAD TO MAKE A GREAT MEAL. ORZO IS A RICE-SHAPED PASTA AND CAN BE FOUND IN GREEK OR ITALIAN MARKETS (WHERE IT IS SOMETIMES CALLED "PUNTINE"). ORZO IS A FINE PRODUCT TO KEEP ON THE SHELF, FOR IT MAKES A GOOD ADDITION TO SIMPLE SOUPS AND CAN BE COOKED IN CHICKEN STOCK AND SERVED WHERE YOU MIGHT ORDINARILY FIND RICE OR A RISOTTO. FETA IS A FRESH CHEESE PICKLED IN BRINE, AND IT IS EASILY FOUND THESE DAYS IN LARGE SUPERMARKETS.

SERVES 4

2 *lamb shanks*
2 *tablespoons olive oil*
1 *medium onion, chopped*
2 *cloves garlic, minced*
1½ *cups coarsely chopped canned tomatoes*
½ *teaspoon dried oregano*
freshly ground pepper
water
1 *cup orzo (rice-shaped pasta)*
1 *cup slightly crumbled Feta cheese*
¼ *cup minced parsley*
½ *cup dry white wine*

Pat shanks dry with paper towels. Put olive oil in a frying pan and sauté shanks over medium-high heat until golden. Place them in a casserole and sauté onion and garlic over low heat, in the same fat, until onion softens. Pour over shanks and add tomatoes with their juice, oregano and pepper to taste. Salt is unnecessary because the cheese will add enough later. Add ½ cup of water (unless you cook the shanks in a pressure cooker, for they will need none then). Simmer, covered, 3 hours (or 1 hour in a pressure cooker). Check now and again to make sure they still have some liquid around them—if not, add a little more water.

When very tender, remove shanks and strip meat from the bones. Skim as much fat off the vegetables as possible, and if there is too much liquid, boil down quickly so it mostly evaporates. Add meat to the pan and discard bones. At this point the dish may be held until you are ready to serve.

Cook orzo in lightly salted water 10–15 minutes, or until almost tender. Drain in a colander and add to the pot, along with Feta cheese, parsley, and wine. Simmer 5 minutes, stirring, to make sure it doesn't stick to the bottom of the pot. Serve on warm plates.

Lamb Shanks with Eggplant and Macaroni

THE RICH FLAVORS OF EGGPLANT AND LAMB ARE NATURAL PARTNERS, AND HERE THEY COME INTO THEIR OWN IN A SATISFYING, COMFORTABLE DISH—A FAMILY AFFAIR, NO DOUBT, BUT WHO'S TO SNEER AT THOSE? IT CAN BE FIDDLED WITH AND FUDGED ON AS YOU GO ALONG—LESS TOMATOES OR TOMATO SAUCE, OREGANO OR MARJORAM THE PRINCIPAL HERB, ANOTHER CHEESE. I FIRST HAD SOMETHING LIKE IT IN A GREEK HOUSEHOLD WHERE IT WAS BRASSY WITH OREGANO, DRIPPING WITH OIL, AND ABSOLUTELY DELICIOUS, THOUGH THIS IS MORE THE WAY I COOK IT NOW.

SERVES 4

2 *lamb shanks*
2 *tablespoons olive oil*
1 *large onion, chopped*
2 *cloves garlic, minced*
1½ *cups coarsely chopped canned tomatoes*
salt and freshly ground pepper
1 *bay leaf*
¼ *teaspoon dried thyme*
water
1 *medium eggplant, peeled and cut in dice*
2 *tablespoons minced parsley*
½ *teaspoon dried basil (or 1 tablespoon fresh)*
2 *cups macaroni*
Parmesan cheese

Rinse shanks and pat dry with paper towels. Place olive oil in a large saucepan or frying pan with a lid. Sauté shanks over medium-high heat until golden. Add onion and garlic, and cook over low heat until onion wilts, then add tomatoes with their juice, salt and pepper to taste, bay leaf, thyme, and ½ cup of water (unless you cook them in a pressure cooker).

Simmer, covered, 3 hours, or until lamb is very tender (this takes only 1 hour in a pressure cooker). Peek now and again to make sure pot is not too dry and add more water if necessary.

While the meat cooks, prepare eggplant and place in a colander. Toss well with salt and place over a bowl to catch the juices. When lamb is done, run cold water over eggplant and dry with paper towels.

Remove shanks from pan and let cool a bit, then strip off meat and discard the bones. Return to the pan with the eggplant, parsley, and basil, and cook, covered, 15–20 minutes.

Meanwhile, cook macaroni in plenty of salted water, according to package directions. When done, but still a bit *al dente,* drain and stir into the lamb. Cook another few minutes, then serve sprinkled with Parmesan cheese.

The Breast of Lamb

According to the tone of your market, these might be found trimmed down to lamb riblets, cut in double ribs for barbecue, or in a whole slab (sometimes doubled around for packaging). These untrimmed whole breasts are the ones to watch for. You have to trim off any fell—that membrane outside all lamb—and any top fat right down to where the breast appears almost all red meat. Don't cut too deep, though, this is but a thin meat layer covering a lot of fat. All good recipes explain the ways this layering fat through the breast may be tamed or put to good use. It is easy to cut between the ribs of the whole breasts, cracking the bones a bit if need be on the larger pieces.

THE MOST POPULAR WAY TO PREPARE BREAST OF LAMB IN FRANCE, THIS IS PROBABLY ALSO THE BEST WAY TO BEGIN TO USE AND TASTE AND SERVE THIS CUT. IT IS ALSO A KIND OF TEST METHOD OF WHAT YOU SHOULD SEEK IN A RECIPE: POACHING REMOVES MOST OF THE FATTY LAYERS, A SOUND BROWNING REMOVES EVEN MORE, AND A SUCCULENT MEAT IN A FRAGRANT CRISP TOPPING REMAINS FOR THOSE WHO, LIKE ME, ENJOY GNAWING A BONE NOW AND AGAIN.

Breast of Lamb Provençal

SERVES 4

2 *breasts of lamb (about 4–5 pounds)*
salt and freshly ground pepper
1 *cup bread crumbs*
½ *cup minced parsley*
2 *cloves garlic, minced*
2 *tablespoons olive oil (or vegetable oil)*

Trim fell and fat off breasts, put in a large pot, add water to cover, bring to a boil, and skim off any scum that rises to the top. Cover the pot and simmer 1 hour. Remove meat and let cool slightly. (The stock can be saved for soup.)

Preheat oven to 375°. Salt and pepper breasts and bake in a large roasting pan 30 minutes. If necessary to fit the pan, cut the breasts in two.

Mix bread crumbs, parsley, garlic, and olive oil together. Pat mixture gently over the breasts, then bake another 30 minutes. To serve, cut between the ribs and fan them out on warm plates.

Hungarian Breast of Lamb

I HAVE A THEORY THAT ANY DISH WITH THIS MANY ONIONS MUST BE WONDERFUL, AND I DON'T THINK I'VE EVER BEEN PROVEN WRONG. CERTAINLY THIS IS A CASE IN POINT. SERVE WITH BEER RATHER THAN WINE, PLUS A SALAD OF THINLY SLICED CUCUMBERS MARINATED IN A LITTLE VINEGAR, A PINCH OF SUGAR, AND DILL. AND TUCK IN.

SERVES 4

2 breasts of lamb (about 4–5 pounds)
2 tablespoons vegetable oil
salt and freshly ground pepper
2 tablespoons butter
6 medium onions, peeled and sliced
1 tablespoon flour
1 tablespoon sweet Hungarian paprika
1 clove garlic, minced
⅛ teaspoon grated lemon rind
1 cup beef (or chicken) stock

Trim fell and fat off breasts and cut into 2-rib sections. Add vegetable oil to a large frying pan and brown ribs in batches, sprinkling with salt and pepper. Place in a casserole. Rinse and dry pan. Add butter and sauté onions over medium-low heat until they start to turn golden. This will take stirring now and again, and some patience, for it will take 20–30 minutes, but it will be worth it.

When onions are done, stir in flour, paprika, garlic, and lemon rind. Cook 3–4 minutes, then add stock and stir until you have a smooth thickened mixture. Taste for salt, then pour over the lamb. Cover and simmer very gently 1¼ hours.

Serve with plain boiled potatoes rolled in minced parsley.

Lamb Ribs with Sauerkraut and Barley

I found this little gem in a spiral-bound Armenian church social cookbook, almost falling apart and marked fifty cents on the flyleaf. (Always look at these amateur efforts, especially by church ladies, for there is likely to be something you can use time and time again.) In this dish, where only a little meat goes a long and tasty way, you'll be surprised at how well barley and sauerkraut combine to make a hearty winter meal, for pennies, too. Serve with beer.

SERVES 4

1 *breast of lamb (about 2–2½ pounds)*
2 *tablespoons vegetable oil*
1 *cup pearl barley*
1½ *cups sauerkraut (fresh or canned)*
½ *cup tomato sauce (fresh or canned)*
salt and freshly ground pepper

Trim breast of fell and fat and cut into rib sections. Heat vegetable oil in a large frying pan and sauté ribs until golden all over. Lift ribs into a casserole with a slotted spoon and add barley and water to cover.

Simmer, uncovered, 45 minutes. Add sauerkraut, tomato sauce, and salt and pepper to taste. Cover and simmer another 30 minutes.

Lamb Breast with Turnips

SERVES 4

2 *breasts of lamb (about 4–5 pounds)*
salt and freshly ground pepper
½ *teaspoon dried rosemary*
4 *cloves garlic, unpeeled*
6 *medium turnips, peeled and quartered*
4 *carrots, scraped and cut in 2-inch lengths*
2 *tablespoons butter (optional)*

Preheat oven to 375°. Trim breasts of fell and fat, and cut into 2-inch sections. Place in a roasting pan, sprinkle with salt, pepper, and rosemary, and scatter garlic among them. Bake 30 minutes.

Meanwhile, parboil turnips and carrots in boiling salted water 15 minutes, then drain and reserve. Turn the pieces of lamb and add turnips and carrots, tossing so they are coated in the fat. (If the lamb has not released enough fat, add butter.) Bake another 45 minutes, basting and turning vegetables every 15 minutes or so.

To serve, discard garlic and lift out glazed vegetables and meat with a slotted spoon onto warm plates.

Breast of Veal

This cut is usually stuffed to give a little savor to the meat and the dish a bit more substance, though there are various other and simpler ways to cook it. Don't worry about preparing it for stuffing, however, because anywhere you find a veal breast there will also be a butcher to cut a pocket in it for you. There's not a great deal of meat on the breast, but since what's there is near the bone, it is unusually tasty, and it is also the only part of the veal that sells for a reasonable price these days.

Stuffed Breast of Veal

TO COOK THIS EXCELLENT DISH CONSIDER THE SIZE OF YOUR PAN—I FIND IT EASIER TO HAVE THE BUTCHER CUT THE VEAL IN TWO PIECES, AND CUT POCKETS IN EACH RATHER THAN HAVE SO LONG A CUT OF MEAT. LOOK AT ANY COOKBOOK—THE KINDS OF STUFFING DEVISED FOR BREAST OF VEAL ARE AS DIVERSE AS THOSE FOR THE CAVITY OF TURKEY. SOMETIMES A VEAL OR PORK (OR BOTH) FORCEMEAT IS USED TO ROUND OUT THE SERVED PORTION, OR A PILLOW OF SPINACH, MUSHROOMS, AND RICE. THESE ARE PARTICULARLY NICE IF YOU STUFF A BONED BREAST OF VEAL AND MAKE STOCK—THUS SAUCE—FROM THE BONES, AS IN BREAST OF VEAL MARENGO (SEE BELOW).

SERVES 4

1 *3-pound breast of veal, cut with a pocket*
salt and freshly ground pepper
7 *tablespoons butter*
½ *cup chopped onion*
1 *clove garlic, minced*
2½ *cups soft bread crumbs (or bread cut into dice)*
3 *tablespoons minced parsley*
½ *teaspoon dried rosemary*
½ *teaspoon dried thyme*
flour
½ *cup water (or stock)*
white wine (or heavy cream) (optional)

Sprinkle veal inside and out with a little salt and pepper. Put 4 tablespoons of butter in a saucepan over medium heat, then sauté onion and garlic until onion softens. Scoop into a bowl and mix with bread crumbs, parsley, and herbs. Stuff the pocket with this and skewer it or close with toothpicks.

Flour veal lightly. Put remaining 3 tablespoons of butter in a large frying pan over medium heat and sauté meat until light golden on both sides. Add water or a light beef or chicken stock, cover, and simmer 2 hours over low heat, or until quite tender.

Remove meat and cut into serving portions along the line of the bones. If you wish, a sauce can be made from the pan drippings with a little dry white wine or cream.

Breast of Veal Marengo

I SUPPOSE THIS IS A KIND OF MOCK RECIPE, FOR WHICH THERE CAN BE NO EXCUSE, BUT I MAINTAIN IT IS ONE OF THE MOST EXCELLENT WAYS TO SERVE UP A VEAL BREAST THERE IS. THE "MARENGO" STYLE OF COOKING, SAID TO BE SERVED ON THE BATTLEGROUND FOR NAPOLEON IN HASTE WITH INGREDIENTS AT HAND, REMAINS WITH US AS CHICKEN MARENGO, AND FOR ALL I KNOW TURKEY MARENGO, SIMPLY BECAUSE IT MAKES A SAUCE THAT ANY MOUND OF MASHED POTATOES LONGS FOR. ON THE BATTLEGROUND, I BELIEVE, IT INCLUDED A FEW RARE FRIED EGGS FILCHED FROM THE COUNTRYSIDE, A GARNISH BEST FORGOTTEN.

SERVES 4

1 *3-pound breast of veal*
salt and freshly ground pepper
¼ *cup vegetable oil*
3 *tablespoons butter*
1 *large onion, chopped*
3 *carrots, scraped and chopped*
3 *cloves garlic, minced*
2 *tablespoons flour*
1 *cup dry white wine*
2½–3 *cups veal stock*
1 *bay leaf*
¼ *teaspoon dried thyme*
2 *tablespoons minced parsley*
1 *cup chopped and drained canned tomatoes*

Cut the flap of meat off rib bones, remove the membrane that covers it, then cut meat into 2-inch pieces. Because the breast is made up of layers that slide over each other, it is difficult to cut even with a sharp knife. The best way is to use a serrated bread knife in a sawing motion.

Cut rib bones into manageable pieces and make a veal stock with them. The easiest way is in a pressure cooker because it will make a fine stock in only about 1 hour, but you can boil the bones with water to cover for 3–4 hours, skimming any surface foam, with a little onion, carrot, celery, parsley, and a seasoning of peppercorns, bay leaf, thyme, and so forth. This can be strained and boiled down to 3 cups, then seasoned to taste with salt.

To cook the meat, salt and pepper it lightly and fry quickly in vegetable oil until golden on both sides. Remove from pan and reserve. It's best to do this in batches so the meat browns well.

Melt butter in a casserole and cook onion, carrots, and garlic 8–10 minutes over medium-low heat. When onion is quite soft, stir in flour and cook another 5 minutes. Add wine and let bubble up, cook another few minutes, then add stock, meat, and remaining ingredients.

Cover casserole and simmer 1½ hours, or until veal is cooked and sauce is rich and tasty. Serve with mashed potatoes, noodles, or rice.

Cooking with Kidneys

I'm not much a fan of strong-tasting beef kidneys—the ones with which the British construct their old standby, beef and kidney pie—but I love sweet and tasty veal or lamb kidneys. The veal are hard come by, except from specialty markets, but any store that sells lamb will also have their kidneys, at a remarkably low price, too. They can be used interchangeably in these recipes, substituting one veal for every three lamb kidneys. Some recipes tell you to soak kidneys in milk to cover for an hour before cooking, but if they are very fresh (and why buy them otherwise?), they don't need anything but peeling off any membrane and cutting out the nubbin of fat from the middle. One of the admirable things about kidneys is that they are quickly prepared, for those always in a rush.

IF I HAD SOMEONE TO COOK FOR ME, AND COULD ORDER IT UP FOR A SOLITARY MEAL, THIS IS ONE DISH I'D PUT ON FILE, WITH A FOOTNOTE: "STIR IN A LITTLE DIJON MUSTARD SINCE IT ALWAYS SUITS KIDNEYS."

Kidneys with Garlic and Parsley

SERVES 4

8 *slices white home-style bread, thinly sliced*
butter
10–12 *lamb kidneys (or 3–4 veal)*
2 *tablespoons butter*
2 *cloves garlic, minced*
¼ *cup minced parsley*
salt and freshly ground pepper
2 *tablespoons lemon juice*

Trim crusts from bread to make perfect squares, then stack them and cut diagonally so you have 16 triangles. Melt 4 tablespoons of butter in a frying pan and dip triangles quickly so they are evenly coated on both sides—but not soggy with too much butter. Use more butter if you need it. Fry bread over medium heat until both sides are golden. Place on plates and keep warm in the oven. It won't hurt them to stay awhile as they only get crisper.

Cut kidneys in ⅓-inch slices and cut out knobs of white fat. Melt 2 tablespoons of butter in a frying pan over medium-high heat. Toss in garlic, then after a minute the kidneys. Cook until they just lose their pinkness. Add parsley, salt and pepper to taste, and then the lemon juice. Toss well and serve over the hot croutons.

AN UNUSUAL BUT NEAR PERFECT WAY TO COOK KIDNEYS. I LIKE
THEM BEST SERVED ON CROUTONS (AS IN THE PRECEDING RECIPE),
BUT THEY ALSO PAIR NICELY WITH MY OVEN-ROASTED POTATOES.

Kidneys Liègeoise

SERVES 4

12 *juniper berries*
2 *tablespoons lemon juice*
10–12 *lamb kidneys (or 3–4 veal)*
4 *tablespoons butter*
salt and freshly ground pepper
¼ *cup white wine*

Flatten berries with the side of a large knife, then chop them very finely. Soak them in lemon juice. Remove any membrane from the kidneys and cut them in ⅓-inch slices. Cut out knobs of white fat in the slices.

Put 3 tablespoons of butter in a large frying pan over high heat. As soon as it sizzles, add kidney slices and toss quickly until they lose their pinkness a bit—about 1 minute. Add lemon juice with berries and the white wine. Cook 3 minutes, tossing kidneys at the same time. Scoop out kidneys to warm plates and cook pan juices down 1 minute or so. When they start to thicken slightly, add remaining tablespoon of butter, stirring to bind the sauce. Pour over kidneys and serve.

Kidneys are most often cooked with white wine, but this French preparation with red wine, tarragon, and gracing mushrooms makes a delicious change. They also always need

Tarragon Kidneys in Red Wine

some bland foil for their sauce—creamy mashed potatoes or a buttered crouton, but I like to serve these with an easy rice pilaf made with a little onion and chicken stock and a simply dressed green vegetable.

SERVES 4

½ teaspoon dried tarragon
1 tablespoon red wine vinegar
8 lamb kidneys (or 3 veal)
2 tablespoons flour
salt and freshly ground pepper
2 tablespoons butter
¼ pound mushrooms, thinly sliced
⅓ cup chicken stock
⅓ cup red wine

Stir tarragon into wine vinegar and let soak 15 minutes or more to gather flavor. Remove any membrane from kidneys and cut into ⅓-inch slices. Cut out knobs of white fat in the slices, and shake in a bag with flour seasoned with salt and pepper to taste.

Heat butter in a frying pan and add kidney slices, tossing over high heat 1 or 2 minutes. Add tarragon-vinegar mixture, mushrooms, and any flour left over. Toss a bit more and add chicken stock and wine. Lower heat and cook, stirring, a few more minutes. The kidneys should lose their pinkness but should not cook longer or they will toughen.

If the sauce seems the right consistency, serve as is, but if too thin, lift out kidneys and mushrooms onto plates and cook sauce down over high heat until it thickens slightly, then pour over kidneys and serve.

REDOLENT OF THE BRITISH BREAKFAST SIDEBOARD IN ITS GREAT HEYDAY, TO BE FORKED UP ALONG WITH A KIPPER, PERHAPS, AND EGGS IN SEVERAL VERSIONS, CRISP TOAST, THESE STILL MAKE A FINE QUICK SUPPER WITH, SAY, BEER AND SLAW AND BREAD TO SOP UP THE SAUCE. ANYONE TRAVELING IN ENGLAND, IRELAND, WALES, OR SCOTLAND SHOULD REMEMBER THAT IT IS POSSIBLE, AND EVEN SOMETIMES SPLENDID, TO LIVE OFF BREAKFAST AND TEA THERE. THE ORDINARY BREAKFAST OF "BED AND BREAKFAST" IS FILLING AND ALWAYS THE SAME, BUT AT GRANDER ESTABLISHMENTS THE TABLE GROANS WITH THINGS WE'VE NEVER HEARD OF—MOST ALL DELICIOUS. AFTERNOON TEA CAN INCLUDE NOT ONLY ALL SORTS OF SWEET CAKES AND JAMS AND MUFFINS DRIPPING COUNTRY BUTTER, BUT ALSO SANDWICHES AND OTHER SAVORY SNIPPETS, ALL WORTH A GOOD STUFFING. THERE ARE NOW MUCH BETTER RESTAURANTS THAN WHEN I FIRST WALKED ALL OVER THE COUNTRY, BUT ONE CAN STILL BE CAUGHT IN STRANGE CORNERS WHERE RESTAURANTS SERVE SUCH WARTIME DELICACIES AS CANNED BAKED BEANS ON TOAST. . . .

English Deviled Kidneys

SERVES 4

10–12 *lamb kidneys (or*
      3–4 veal)
flour
salt
cayenne pepper
  4 *tablespoons butter*
  2 *tablespoons*
     Dijon-style mustard
  2 *teaspoons*
     Worcestershire sauce
 ½ *cup chicken stock*

Peel any membrane off kidneys and cut into ⅓-inch slices. Cut out knobs of white fat and shake in a bag with flour seasoned with salt and cayenne pepper to taste. This is to be a hot dish so be generous with the cayenne.

Melt butter in a frying pan over medium-high heat. Add kidneys, turning them quickly in the sizzling butter—they should not cook more than 2 minutes or so. Add mustard, Worcestershire, and chicken stock, and stir until the sauce thickens. Toss another minute, or until kidneys have lost any trace of pinkness. Serve immediately.

Beef Liver

I know people who order liver and onions in restaurants but never cook it at home. Why is this? I wonder—sweetbreads, with all their picky preparation I can see, but liver takes no time at all to get ready for cooking, and that goes like a breeze in summer. We generally get it in convenient slices, and at the best stores it will already have been peeled of its outer membrane. If not, simply make a cut at the edge, start peeling it back with a small knife, and the whole thing strips off easily once you get a pull. Cut out any tough veins, and it's ready to cook. Calves liver is, of course, the finest, but there's nothing wrong with regular beef, and the new "baby beef liver" is not nearly as expensive and nearly as delicate as calves liver. I like not only liver and onions but also these favorites, and in many other ways, for I believe liver is not only good for you but good period.

THE SIMPLEST AND PERHAPS BEST OF ALL LIVER DISHES. THE TUSCANS USE ONLY CALVES LIVER, SLICED THINNER THAN WE GET IT, BUT USE WHATEVER IS AVAILABLE, AND IT STILL WILL BE DELIGHTFUL.

Liver with Sage, Tuscan Style

IF YOU HAVE FRESH SAGE GROWING, IT IS EVEN BETTER TO OMIT RUBBING SAGE INTO THE LIVER AND SIMPLY ADD SOME FRESH SAGE LEAVES TO THE OIL WITH THE GARLIC.

SERVES 4

1½ pounds liver (preferably baby beef), sliced
½ teaspoon dried crumbled sage (*not powdered*)
flour
⅓ cup olive oil (or vegetable oil)
1 clove garlic, slightly flattened and peeled
salt and freshly ground pepper
1 lemon

Pat liver dry with paper towels and rub with sage. Dredge in flour. Heat olive oil with garlic in a frying pan over medium-high heat. When garlic turns golden, remove it and sauté liver slices until golden brown on the outside but still pink in the middle. Remove from pan and place on warm plates. Sprinkle with salt and pepper to taste.

Add juice of one lemon half to the pan juices, let it bubble up, stir to get any brown pieces unstuck, and pour over liver. Cut the other lemon half in 4 wedges and place beside the liver.

WHO KNOWS WHERE MY FILES PICKED UP THIS RECIPE? I DO KNOW WHY I STARRED IT TO COOK AGAIN, AND HOW WELL IT PAIRS WITH BUTTERED EGG NOODLES.

Liver with Onions and Apples

SERVES 4

1½ *pounds liver (preferably baby beef), sliced*
juice of ½ lemon
  ¼ *teaspoon dried crumbled sage (not powdered)*
  5 *tablespoons butter*
  2 *medium onions, chopped*
  2 *large apples, peeled, seeded, and chopped*
salt
  ¼ *teaspoon caraway seeds*
freshly ground pepper

Trim liver, if necessary, and place on a plate. Sprinkle with lemon juice and sage. Turn to coat lightly.

Melt 3 tablespoons of butter in a saucepan and add onions and apples. Stir and cook until onions wilt, then sprinkle lightly with salt, and add caraway seeds. Cover and cook 15–20 minutes over low heat. Uncover and cook another 4–5 minutes, or until the mixture starts to turn golden. Keep warm.

Put remaining 2 tablespoons of butter in a frying pan large enough to hold all the slices (otherwise do them in batches). When the butter begins to sputter over medium-high heat, sauté slices quickly, 3–4 minutes per side, depending on thickness. They should brown but still be a bit pink inside. Salt and pepper to taste and place on warm plates. Nestle onion and apple mixture beside and serve at once.

OKAY, MAYBE THIS IS THE BEST WAY TO COOK LIVER?

Liver with Mustard Tarragon Sauce

SERVES 4

1½ *pounds liver (preferably baby beef), sliced*
flour
salt and freshly ground pepper
3 *tablespoons butter*
⅓ *cup chopped onion*
½ *cup beef stock*
2 *tablespoons red wine vinegar*
½ *cup chopped canned tomatoes, drained*
¼ *teaspoon dried tarragon*
⅓ *cup heavy cream*
5 *teaspoons Dijon-style mustard*

Pat liver dry with paper towels and dredge in flour seasoned with salt and pepper. Melt butter in a large frying pan over medium-high heat and sauté liver until brown on both sides but still a bit pink in the middle. Remove to plates and keep warm in the oven.

Add onion to the pan and cook, stirring, until limp. Add beef stock, wine vinegar, tomatoes, and tarragon. Stir to pick up any brown bits from pan, then cook several minutes over high heat. Add cream and boil until you have a slightly reduced sauce. Stir in mustard well and pour over liver. Serve immediately.

Liver au Poivre

I'M ALWAYS EAGER TO SNIFF OUT NEW DISHES WHEN I TRAVEL IN FRANCE, SO I STEER CLEAR OF THE USUAL STEAK AU POIVRE. THAT, I KNOW ABOUT. INSTEAD I COOK, AT HOME, THIS DISH WITH A FRENCH NAME THAT I ACQUIRED IN ENGLAND FROM A JEWISH COOK. SUCH ARE THE TRAVELS OF RECIPES. USE A STACK OF FRENCH FRIES TO GO WITH IT.

SERVES 4

1½ *pounds liver, sliced*
½ *cup Dijon-style mustard*
peppercorns, coarsely ground or cracked
2 *tablespoons butter*
2 *tablespoons vegetable oil*
minced parsley

Pat liver dry with paper towels, coat with mustard, and sprinkle with quite a lot of pepper. (The traditional way to crack pepper is with a mortar and pestle, but it's simple to roll a wine bottle over them to get a good rough consistency.) Place on waxed paper and chill in refrigerator 30 minutes to set the coating.

Heat butter and vegetable oil in a large frying pan over medium-high heat and cook liver until crusty brown on the outside but still a bit pink in the middle, about 3 minutes a side. Serve sprinkled with minced parsley.

Liver with Agliata Sauce

AGLIATA IS A KIND OF CROSS BETWEEN PESTO SAUCE AND THE GREEK SKORDALIA, THOUGH THERE ARE BREEDS LIKE IT ALL OVER THE MEDITERRANEAN. IT HAS A LITTLE LESS OF A RAW GARLIC PUNCH THAN MOST OF THESE, WITH THE EXTRA FRAGRANCE OF BASIL, AND IT IS PLEASING IN WAYS THE ITALIANS NEVER IMAGINED: INDEED, I MAKE A DOUBLE BATCH AND KEEP IT IN THE REFRIGERATOR TO MAKE UP NEW DISHES. TO BEGIN WITH, IT MAKES A SUPERIOR GARLIC BREAD OR OMELET FILLING, AND A LITTLE STIRRED INTO A VINAIGRETTE CAN MAKE IT SING. . . . THE ITALIANS RESERVE IT, AS FAR AS I KNOW, FOR FRIED LIVER OR SALT COD—BOTH WONDERFUL—BUT IT CERTAINLY TAKES LIVER TO HEIGHTS YOU MAY NEVER HAVE DREAMED OF.

SERVES 4

1 *cup soft white bread crumbs (or cubes)*
2 *tablespoons water*
1 *teaspoon wine vinegar (red or white)*
1 *tablespoon minced fresh basil (or 1½ teaspoons dried)*
1 *tablespoon minced parsley*
1–2 *cloves garlic*
¼ *cup olive oil*
salt and freshly ground pepper
1½ *pounds liver, sliced*
flour
vegetable oil (or olive oil)

Sprinkle bread with water, let soak a few minutes, then squeeze out any extra moisture with your hands. Place in a blender with wine vinegar, basil, parsley, and garlic. Blend over low, then medium speed until the mixture has only little specks of green. (The Italians do this with a mortar and pestle, which is fine, but not necessary.) Pour in olive oil bit by bit until you have a smooth thick sauce. Add salt and pepper to taste. This can be made at any time and will keep for several days in the refrigerator.

To cook the liver, trim slices, pat dry with paper towels, and dust lightly with flour. Heat vegetable oil in a frying pan over medium heat and cook slices about 3 minutes a side—they should be crusty brown outside and light pink within. Serve with the sauce slathered over.

Remember the Chop

If steaks and lamb chops and such are well out of bounds here, though not the cheapest of the cheap, a meaty pork chop can save you with the family when you've dodged the budget once too often. A fine thick one can even be stuffed for a company splurge—and who would sniff at that? Not I. One of the best things about them is that they *are* one of the delights of home cooking, for they need long, slow, moist methods after their first browning, and restaurants prefer meats that can be quickly seared on a grill, then served up with a fancy sauce and garnish.

If you bought wisely, only one is needed per person, so look for loin chops with a good ratio of meat to fat, and if necessary, trim a little of the fat around the edges, lest they be too greasy in the end. When no company is on the way I eat them simply fried, sprinkled with salt and pepper, then set to braise awhile with a little liquid (or even barbecue sauce) since I love all the things Southerners surround them with: crisp corn sticks, stewed greens, baked yams, pickled crabapples, and so forth. I never tire of them this way, but when aunts and uncles or even friendly gourmets are at hand, I remember recipes like those following, fit to grace any company table.

ABSOLUTELY DELICIOUS—NOT TOO MUCH TOMATO, THE SECRET OF MANY ITALIAN DISHES. IT IS ALSO A DISH TO BE IN THE KITCHEN WITH, TO HEAR HUM AND PURR. I COOK THE PORK CHOPS WHILE STIRRING A POT OF POLENTA TO POUR OUT AND SLICE BESIDE, OR MASHED POTATOES, SOAKING THE JUICES.

Pork Chops Modena

SERVES 4

4 *large pork loin chops*
1 *teaspoon dried rosemary*
1 *teaspoon dried crumbled sage (not powdered)*
1 *clove garlic*
salt and freshly ground pepper
3 *tablespoons butter*
¾ *cup chopped canned tomatoes*

If the pork chops are very fat around the edges, trim a bit, then pat dry with paper towels. Chop rosemary, sage, and garlic together until almost a paste. Rub chops with this on both sides and sprinkle with salt and pepper to taste.

Take a frying pan large enough to hold the chops in a single layer and sauté them in butter over medium heat. This should be done rather gently because you don't want either the garlic or butter to burn—don't worry about making them absolutely golden on each side for they will brown later.

Pour in tomatoes with about ¼ cup of their juices (reserve any other juice, as you might need it later). Cover pan, turn heat low, and cook 1 hour, turning the chops once.

Check now and again to see whether juices have boiled away. If so, add a little more tomato juice (or water). When done, remove chops to warm plates. If the pan juices are ample, turn heat up and boil sauce down to a rather thick consistency. If they look dry, add some more juice or water and stir over high heat to make a sauce.

Pork Chops with a Currant Glaze

THERE ARE A LOT OF RECIPES THAT SAY TO COOK PORK CHOPS WITH ALL KINDS OF FRUIT NONSENSE AND THE PURE MEAT FLAVOR GETS LOST, BUT THESE SLIGHTLY SWEET-TART ONES ARE JUST RIGHT. SERVE THEM WITH SWEET POTATO CAKES (PAGE 303).

SERVES 4

    4 *large loin pork chops*
salt and freshly ground
      pepper
    3 *tablespoons vegetable
      oil*
 ¼ *cup chicken stock*
 ¼ *cup currant jelly*
 1½ *tablespoons Dijon-style
      mustard*
    2 *tablespoons red wine
      vinegar*

If the chops are fatty, trim them a little. Pat dry with paper towels, and salt and pepper to taste. Put vegetable oil in a frying pan large enough to hold chops in a single layer. Set over medium-high heat and fry chops until golden on both sides.

Pour out all but 1 tablespoon of fat, add chicken stock, cover the pan, and cook 30 minutes over low heat. Check now and again to make sure liquid does not boil away—if it tends to, lower heat and add a little more stock.

After 30 minutes, melt jelly and mustard together in a small pan, stirring until smooth. Pour over chops and cook another 15 minutes, turning chops once in order to glaze both sides. Finally, remove them to warm plates. Add wine vinegar to pan and stir over high heat until a rich sauce is achieved. Pour over chops and serve.

A VERY SUAVE DISH BECAUSE THE RATHER SWEET PICKLES AND SHARP MUSTARD ARE TAMED IN A CREAMY SAUCE. THIS IS EVERY INCH A COMPANY DISH, NEEDING ONLY A COMPLEMENTARY MOUND OF MASHED POTATOES.

Pork Chops Dijon

SERVES 4

4 *large loin pork chops*
salt and freshly ground
  pepper
2 *tablespoons vegetable oil*
1 *tablespoon butter*
¼ *cup chopped onion*
1 *clove garlic, minced*
¼ *cup thinly sliced rounds*
  sweet gherkin pickles
⅓ *cup dry white wine*
⅓ *cup heavy cream*
2 *tablespoons Dijon-style*
  mustard
minced parsley

Preheat oven to 350°. Pat chops dry with paper towels and sprinkle both sides with salt and pepper. Heat vegetable oil in a frying pan large enough to hold chops in a single layer, and sauté on both sides until golden—about 5 minutes a side over medium-high heat. Wrap each in foil and place in the oven. Bake 30 minutes, or until quite tender.

Discard any fat from the frying pan and add butter. Cook onion and garlic over medium heat until onion softens, then add pickles and wine. Cook down over high heat until wine has become almost a glaze, then add cream and mustard. Whisk until you have a smooth, slightly thickened sauce.

Remove chops from oven, unwrap, and place on warm plates, then pour sauce over. Sprinkle with parsley and serve.

Pork Chops with Rye Bread Stuffing and Sour Cream Gravy

SERVES 4

YOU MIGHT MAKE A PASSABLE BREAD PUDDING FROM THE LAST OF A RYE LOAF, SAY WITH APPLES, RAISINS, CINNAMON, EGGS, MILK, AND SUGAR, BUT YOU SHOULD ALSO REMEMBER THIS GLORY TO AMPLIFY THE LOAF. SIT DOWN TO THESE WITH APPLE SLICES FRIED IN BUTTER, SPRINKLED WITH A LITTLE BROWN SUGAR, OR SIMPLY WITH A MOUND OF APPLESAUCE.

4 *large loin pork chops,
    about ¾ inch thick*
*salt and freshly ground
    pepper*
½ *cup chopped onion*
1 *clove garlic, minced*
3 *tablespoons butter*
1 *cup soft rye bread
    crumbs*
¼ *teaspoon caraway seeds*
3 *tablespoons minced
    parsley*
1 *tablespoon vegetable oil*
water
2 *tablespoons flour*
½ *cup sour cream*

Cut pockets in chops, and salt and pepper lightly. Sauté onion and garlic in 2 tablespoons of butter until onion softens, then combine with bread crumbs, caraway seeds, and parsley. Stuff chops with this mixture and close openings with toothpicks.

Heat remaining tablespoon of butter and vegetable oil in a frying pan large enough to hold chops in a single layer, then sauté lightly on both sides. Add ½ cup of water, cover pan, and cook 40 minutes over low heat, or until chops are tender and succulent. Turn after 20 minutes to make sure that both sides brown, and check for liquid. If they tend to get dry, add a little more water—not too much because all liquid should be boiled away by the end.

Remove from pan, slip out toothpicks, and keep warm. Pour fat from pan and return 2 tablespoons to pan. Add flour and stir over low heat until it begins to turn light brown, then stir in 1 cup of water. Let cook several minutes, stirring to smooth the sauce. Finally, add the sour cream and salt and pepper to taste, and heat gently. (Don't let it boil.) Serve chops with gravy.

IF I'M BREAKING OUR BUDGET ON SMOKED PORK CHOPS, SO WHAT?
NOW AND AGAIN IT'S WORTHWHILE MAKING THIS RARE DISH FOR
FAMILY OR GUESTS. HAUL OUT YOUR BEST NOODLES AND DUMPLINGS,
YOUR SWEET POTATO CASSE-
ROLE, YOUR MASHED OR FRIED
OR PUREED MASSES. . . .

Braised Smoked Pork Chops with Juniper Berries

SERVES 4

4 *large smoked pork chops*
2 *tablespoons bacon fat*
   (or butter)
2 *large onions, chopped*
3 *carrots, scraped and*
   sliced into rounds
½ *cup white wine*
1 *cup beef stock*
freshly ground pepper
6 *juniper berries, crushed*
cornstarch
water
minced parsley

Trim extra fat off chops if necessary. Melt bacon fat or butter in a casserole large enough to hold chops in a single layer, and add onions and carrots. Cook over medium heat until onions wilt, then add wine, stock, pepper to taste, and juniper berries. (You probably won't need any salt, as the chops are salty and the stock is well seasoned.) Let this bubble up and place the chops on top, nestling them down slightly into the vegetables and juices.

Cover and simmer 1 hour. Remove chops to warm plates and thicken juices with a little cornstarch mixed with water. Add this bit by bit and stir—you don't want the sauce to be too thick, only a little body. Taste for seasoning and add salt if necessary.

Cover chops with sauce and serve sprinkled with parsley.

The Feathered Trove

Here is surely where any near pennyless cook may shine for family and guest alike. Any good cook knows that a blue-ribbon all-get-out recipe for chicken is a pot of home gold—with three or four in hand you've got an audience. Not only is today's market chicken (and recently, parts of turkey) economical, whether baked or fried or fricasseed, grilled over coals, or sautéed on the front burner, but it seems to take to any personal trick, turn of culture, shift of seasonings. There is practically no way not to cook a chicken if it is honest and the result is succulent.

A whole book could be written about such recipes, a good many of which would include brandy and cream, shallots and mushrooms, chestnut stuffings, sleek sauce, and stately garnish, but here are simpler ones my neighbors and I serve up near the end of the month, with relish and a call for more.

Market Chicken

Anyone with an eye to thrift will learn to cut one up. Look at it: you have one meal of dark meat for two, and another of elegant white, and also the prospect of a fine stock from the backs, wing tips, and giblets, and parcels of liver and wings to freeze toward other meals. Our ancestors knew that everything about this bird can be used, every ounce of rendered fat saved, feathers fit to stuff a mattress, combs sauced with truffles under glass bells, even feet to make delicate gelatins. We needn't go this far into the past, but we can make the bigger bits count.

To cut, first slice off the wings. Slice from the back, where the joint wiggles—just slip the knife in and trust it. It's easy to cut off the tips of the wings to save for stock. Then cut from the front for the thigh joint, cutting through the skin carefully so as not to rob a covering for the breast—just where it wiggles. I usually leave the thigh and leg in one piece, but if you push back the skin at the joint, you'll see a line of fat you should aim for, to divide them. Next, just whack down between the back and breast, halfway, then crack off the first back section. Cutting the next part of the back is a little tricky, and you'll have to slip your hands around the wishbone to pull it out, but just slice down through the ribs. Put the breast skin side up and flatten it with your fist, then turn over and cut up the middle bone— preferably with a good heavy knife. It's elementary, if not child's play, once you do one.

Mock Pheasant

THIS RECIPE IS BASED ON A POLISH CONCEIT, AND IT REALLY DOES GIVE A SLIGHTLY GAMEY TASTE TO OUR MODERN CHICKENS. IF NOT EXACTLY LIKE PHEASANT, IT IS ASTONISHINGLY SUCCULENT ON ITS OWN. I LIKE TO CARRY ON THE GAME CONCEIT BY SERVING IT WITH DEEP-FRIED POTATO SLICES (CALLED SARATOGA CHIPS), BUT FRENCH FRIES OR WHOLE PAN-FRIED LITTLE POTATOES AS THE FRENCH DO THEM ARE EXCELLENT, TOO. YOU DON'T HAVE TO USE THE MOST EXPENSIVE MADEIRA FOR THIS DISH, EITHER, SEVERAL BRANDS ON THE MARKET ARE EXCELLENT FOR COOKING WITHOUT BEING COSTLY. I KEEP SOME HIDDEN IN THE CUPBOARD, FOR IT IS WONDERFUL IN MANY SAUTÉS AND STEWS.

SERVES 4

1 *3-pound chicken*
12 *juniper berries, finely crushed*
2 *tablespoons butter*
salt and freshly ground pepper
1 *medium onion, sliced*
3 *sprigs of parsley*
2 *bay leaves*
2 *slices bacon*
¾ *cup dry Madeira*
1 *cup stock (if nothing better, half chicken, half canned beef)*
1 *tablespoon currant jelly*
a few drops of lemon juice
watercress (or parsley)

At least a day before, rub chicken inside and out with juniper berries. Place chicken in a plastic bag and refrigerate—24 hours is the minimum, and another day is even better.

To cook, preheat oven to 325°. Rub chicken with part of the butter, and salt and pepper. Sprinkle cavity with salt and pepper, add remaining butter, and stuff with onion slices and parsley. Cross bacon over breast and either truss or put in a deep casserole about the size of the bird. (If so, cross his wings behind his back as if he were feeling proud of himself, but tuck his legs in as much as possible.)

Pour Madeira around and bake 2 hours, basting every 15 minutes or so. When done remove bacon slices and discard, and keep chicken warm in the oven with the door open.

Pour pan juices into a jar or measuring cup so you can skim off fat that rises. Spoon out as much of it as possible, then pour juices into a saucepan. Add stock to baking pan or casserole and stir over high heat to loosen little pieces at the bottom. Strain this into the saucepan and stir over high heat until smooth. Whisk in jelly until it melts. Reduce a few more minutes, and if you'd like a more thickened sauce, whisk in some butter kneaded with flour—only little pieces at a time—until silky.

The final sauce should be neither sweet nor sour, so taste it and add lemon juice a drop or so at a time. If it gets too sour, simply whisk in a little more jelly.

While sauce cooks, carve chicken and place on warm plates. Spoon sauce over each portion and garnish with watercress or parsley.

My Roast Chicken with Rosemary and Garlic

AN EASY DISH THAT MAKES AN EXCEPTIONALLY TENDER CHICKEN WITH LOVELY CRISP SKIN. IT CAN BE DONE WITH A WHOLE CUT-UP CHICKEN, BUT THE BREASTS CAN EASILY GET DRY SO I PREFER TO USE DARK MEAT ONLY FOR THIS DISH. OTHER HERBS SUCH AS SAGE OR TARRAGON CAN BE USED, AND YOU CAN ADD MORE GARLIC OR NONE AT ALL. IT'S NICE TO SERVE WITH RICE TOSSED WITH THE BAKING JUICES.

SERVES 4

4 *chicken legs and thighs*
3 *tablespoons butter*
1 *sprig of fresh rosemary*
  (or 1 teaspoon dried)
2 *cloves garlic, peeled*
salt and freshly ground
  pepper
⅔ *cup dry white wine*

Preheat oven to 325°. Place chicken in a baking pan large enough to hold them in a single layer. Dot with pieces of butter, sprinkle rosemary around, tuck in garlic, and add salt and pepper to taste. Pour wine around and bake 1 hour, basting every 15 minutes. When done the skin ought to be quite crisp and brown.

THE SIMPLEST, AND PERHAPS BEST, VERSION OF CHICKEN CACCIATORE—SO-CALLED BECAUSE HUNTERS USED A SAUCE OF VINEGAR, WINE, GARLIC, AND ROSEMARY TO SPARK THEIR VENISON. IN ITALY IT WOULD BE SERVED AS A COURSE ON ITS OWN, WITH BREAD TO SOP UP THE JUICES, BUT I LIKE TO SERVE IT WITH PASTA DRESSED SIMPLY WITH BUTTER AND PARMESAN CHEESE.

Hunter's Chicken

SERVES 4

1 *chicken, cut up*
3 *tablespoons olive oil
    (or vegetable oil)*
2 *cloves garlic, flattened
    slightly and peeled*
1½ *teaspoons dried
    rosemary*
*salt and freshly ground
    pepper*
¼ *cup white wine vinegar*
½ *cup dry white wine*

Pat chicken dry with paper towels. Put olive oil and garlic in a frying pan large enough to hold all the pieces. Heat over medium heat until garlic cloves are golden, then discard garlic.

Fry chicken until golden on both sides, adding rosemary and salt and pepper to taste as it cooks. When chicken is golden, add wine vinegar (it will bubble furiously). When it stops, add wine and let it bubble up and die down.

Cover pan, lower heat, and cook 20–30 minutes, or until chicken is tender. Remove to warm plates and cook pan juices down until they make a golden sauce. If the juices have cooked down too much, add some water and stir over high heat until the same effect occurs.

A savory French country dish, just the thing for a hearty autumn or winter meal when you want something with gusto that sticks to the ribs. It doesn't need anything but a tossed green salad and perhaps French bread.

Chicken with Turnips and Garlic

SERVES 4

1 *chicken, cut up*
1½ *tablespoons olive oil
   (or vegetable oil)*
1 *tablespoon butter*
*salt and freshly ground
   pepper*
4 *turnips, peeled and
   quartered*
2 *medium onions, peeled
   and quartered*
6 *cloves garlic, unpeeled*

Pat chicken dry with paper towels. Heat olive oil and butter in a frying pan over medium heat. When sizzling, add chicken (in batches, if necessary) and cook until golden on both sides. Remove and set aside. Salt and pepper to taste. To the pan add turnips, onions, and garlic. Sauté 15 minutes, turning from time to time so the turnips brown lightly and evenly.

Return chicken to the pan, cover, and cook 20 minutes over low heat, or until turnips are cooked. To serve, remove garlic and arrange chicken on plates with vegetables at the side. If you like, the garlic pulp can be squeezed from the cooked cloves and spread over the chicken.

YOU DON'T HAVE TO GROW TOMATOES TO PREPARE THIS FINE DISH, FOR IF YOU LOOK CLOSELY AT ALL THOSE TOMATOES IN THE MARKET THAT WERE PICKED TOO EARLY, YOU WILL FIND SOME THAT HAVE ESCAPED WHATEVER GAS THEY USE TO TURN TOMATOES PINKISH. THE TARTNESS OF GREEN TOMATOES IS A WELCOME ADDITION TO MANY DISHES. FOR BOTH COLOR AND FLAVOR I SERVE THESE WITH TURMERIC RICE (PAGE 307).

Chicken with Green Tomato Sauce

SERVES 4

3 *large green tomatoes*
¼ *cup raisins*
1 *chicken, cut up*
2 *tablespoons butter*
1 *tablespoon vegetable oil*
1 *medium onion, chopped*
salt and freshly ground
    pepper
1 *teaspoon curry powder*
¼ *teaspoon freshly grated*
    ginger root (optional)

Place tomatoes in a pot of boiling water about 2 minutes, or until skins start to split, then drain and peel them. Cut in half, gently squeeze out seeds, then cut into dice. Put raisins in a small saucepan, cover with boiling water, let sit to plump up, then drain.

Dry chicken parts with paper towels. Put butter and vegetable oil in a large frying pan over medium-high heat. When sizzling, add chicken and sauté until golden on both sides. Remove chicken to a plate and add onion to the pan. Cook several minutes, then stir in tomatoes, raisins, salt and pepper to taste, curry powder, and also ginger if you use it. Let bubble a few minutes, then nestle the chicken down into the sauce.

Cover pan and simmer 30 minutes, or until the chicken is done. Place on warm plates. Turn up heat under the pan and stir until tomatoes make a fine sauce. Pour over chicken and serve.

Chicken Paprika

ONE OF MY FAVORITE OF FAVORITES, THIS RECIPE IS THE FIRST TIME I REALIZED THAT A SUBTLE DIFFERENCE IN SOME DISHES IS THE USE OF MORE ONIONS THAN ONE WOULD SUSPECT. IT IS MOST DELICIOUS IF YOU USE HUNGARIAN "ROSE" PAPRIKA, AND I KEEP A TIN OF IT ON THE SHELF—ONE OF THE TIMES PENNY-PINCHING DOESN'T PAY. TO SAVE TIME, THIS IS A PERFECT DISH FOR A PRESSURE COOKER, WHERE IT WILL TAKE ONLY 15 MINUTES. FOR THE BEST OF ALL WORLDS I SERVE IT WITH SPAETZLE, SPRINKLED WITH CRISP CROUTONS OF WHITE BREAD CUBES COOKED IN BUTTER UNTIL GOLDEN. TO MAKE SPAETZLE, SIMPLY STIR TOGETHER 1½ CUPS OF FLOUR WITH ½ CUP OF WATER, ½ TEASPOON OF SALT, AND ¼ TEASPOON OF BAKING POWDER. ADD A LITTLE FRESHLY GRATED NUTMEG AS WELL. DROP FROM A SMALL SPOON INTO A POT OF BOILING SALTED WATER—JUST DIP THE SPOON INTO THE WATER AND THE DOUGH WILL SLIP OFF. THEY NEED TO COOK ONLY A FEW MOMENTS BEFORE DRAINING IN A COLANDER AND SPRINKLING WITH CROUTONS.

SERVES 4

1 *chicken, cut up*
4 *medium onions, thinly sliced*
4 *tablespoons butter*
2 *tablespoons paprika*
salt
1 *tablespoon flour*
1 *cup sour cream*

Place chicken in a bowl of water. Sauté onions in butter over medium-low heat until soft and starting to turn golden—this will take about 15 minutes. Stir in paprika well, nestle chicken parts among the onions (without drying them), and salt to taste. Cover pan and cook 30 minutes over low heat.

Uncover pan and turn chicken pieces. Check liquid: there should be enough from the water on the chicken and the onion juices, but if not add a little water. Cover pan again and cook another 45 minutes.

Remove chicken and place on warm plates. Mix flour and sour cream together well and stir into the onions. Cook 3–4 minutes over low heat, then pour over chicken and serve.

An easy, filling, colorful one-dish meal I picked up from chef and writer Jack Sharpless, who wheedled it from a hole-in-the-wall restaurant. For even more color you might cook the rice with some green or red pepper, or sprinkle the finished dish with chopped pimiento and parsley, but you don't need do anything to improve the flavor. Though inexpensive, it's at the same time such a crowd pleaser I see no reason not to make it a favored company dish—with a large tossed salad and a jug of white wine, why not?

Syrian Chicken with Turmeric Rice and Chick-Peas

SERVES 4

2 *tablespoons butter*
1 *medium onion,*
  chopped
2 *cloves garlic, minced*
1 *cup long-grain rice*
1 *teaspoon ground*
  turmeric
¼ *teaspoon dried*
  marjoram (or oregano)
salt and freshly ground
  pepper
2¼ *cups chicken stock*
1 *1-pound can*
  chick-peas, drained
1 *chicken, cut up*
2 *tablespoons melted*
  butter
1 *teaspoon lemon juice*

Preheat oven to 350°. Heat butter in a saucepan over medium heat. Sauté onion and garlic several minutes, then stir in rice. Stir until rice turns opaque. Add turmeric, marjoram, salt and pepper to taste—not too much salt if the chicken stock is well seasoned. Add 2 cups of stock to the rice and bring to a boil. Turn heat down low, cover pan, and cook 12–15 minutes, or until most of the liquid is absorbed. Stir in drained chick-peas, then place mixture in a casserole large enough to hold chicken in a single layer.

Place chicken over stuffing. Stir together remaining ¼ cup of stock with melted butter and lemon juice. Salt and pepper chicken lightly and brush with some of the mixture. Bake 45–50 minutes, brushing with mixture twice as it cooks. When done, the chicken should be lightly browned and tender.

Serve on a platter with stuffing in a ring around the chicken.

A SUMPTUOUS COMPANY DISH, ITS SECRET BEING THE EGG YOLKS, WHICH TURN THE SAUCE INTO A SLIGHTLY PUFFED AND DELICATE COATING. (USE THE WHITES FOR MERINGUES.)

Chicken Breasts in Parmesan Cream

SERVES 4

4 *half chicken breasts*
salt and freshly ground
   pepper
2 *tablespoons butter*
2 *tablespoons flour*
¾ *cup heavy cream, heated*
½ *cup grated Parmesan*
   cheese
3 *egg yolks*
½ *cup bread crumbs*

Preheat oven to 350°. Bone and skin chicken breasts and sprinkle with salt and pepper. Heat butter in a frying pan and when it starts to foam add the breasts. Roll them in the butter and cook about 3 minutes on each side over medium heat (the butter shouldn't burn). Remove from pan and place in a greased baking pan.

Add flour to frying pan and cook several minutes, then add cream and stir until you have a smooth thickened sauce. Stir in 1 tablespoon of Parmesan cheese, beat egg yolks with a little of the hot sauce, then stir them in as well. Coat breasts with this sauce, sprinkle with remaining Parmesan cheese mixed with bread crumbs, and place in the oven.

Bake 10 minutes, or until chicken is done, and sauce is set and slightly puffed. If you wish, these can be placed under the broiler for 1 minute or so to brown lightly.

Filipino-Style Chicken

A DELICIOUS STIR-FRY DISH THAT CAN BE COOKED IN A SAUTE PAN IN LESS TIME THAN IT TAKES TO COOK A POT OF RICE. IT HAS THE SLIGHTLY UNUSUAL ADDITION OF VINEGAR TO GIVE CHARACTER, AND I LIKE THE OCCASIONAL SNAP OF A PEPPERCORN, BUT IF YOU DON'T, SIMPLY ADD A LOT OF CRACKED PEPPER.

SERVES 4

 4 *half chicken breasts*
¼ *cup vegetable oil*
¼ *cup wine vinegar (white or red)*
 2 *bay leaves*
 2 *cloves garlic, minced*
16 *peppercorns*
½ *cup soy sauce*
cooked rice

Cut each breast into 4 pieces, leaving them on the bone. Brown pieces in hot vegetable oil, stirring quickly—this will take only 3 minutes or so.

Add wine vinegar, bay leaves, garlic, and peppercorns. Cook, stirring to coat the pieces 3 more minutes. Then add soy sauce, cover pan, and cook about 4 more minutes. Uncover pan and stir to coat pieces well with the sauce. Remove bay leaves and garlic, and serve over rice.

A SUAVE DISH IN WHICH ALL THE FLAVORS SEEM TO BALANCE FINELY ON THE TASTE BUDS. IT TAKES SO WELL TO A MOUND OF MASHED POTATOES (IF THEY ARE VERY CREAMY AND FLUFFY) THAT I CAN'T IMAGINE ANY OTHER ACCOMPANIMENT—WELL, YES, A CHILLED GLASS OF WHITE CALIFORNIA WINE.

Chicken with Tarragon and Tomato Sauce

SERVES 4

4 *half chicken breasts (or 4 thighs and legs)*
2 *tablespoons butter*
½ *cup chopped onion*
1 *cup chopped canned tomatoes*
½ *cup dry white wine*
½ *teaspoon dried tarragon (or 1 teaspoon fresh)*
⅛ *teaspoon dried thyme*
salt and freshly ground pepper
½ *cup heavy cream*

Pat chicken dry with paper towels. Melt butter in a frying pan large enough to hold all the pieces in a single layer. Sauté over medium-high heat until lightly brown on both sides. Be careful the butter doesn't burn. Remove pieces to a warm plate.

Add onion to the pan and sauté several minutes until it softens. Add tomatoes with their juices. Stir well and return chicken to pan. Pour in wine, then sprinkle with herbs and salt and pepper to taste. Spoon tomato-onion mixture over chicken, cover pan, and cook 15–20 minutes over low heat. White meat will take 20 minutes of cooking time, and dark meat about 25.

To test for doneness: poke with a fork, and the juices that flow should no longer show pink. Remove chicken pieces to warm plates. Add cream to pan, turn heat high, and stir 2–3 minutes, or until sauce is smooth and starts to thicken. Pour over chicken and serve.

Teriyaki Chicken Wings

THESE WERE ORIGINALLY APPETIZERS, BUT AFTER I REALIZED HOW MUCH EVERYONE LOVED THEM, I TURNED THEM INTO A DINNER DISH. NO ONE HAS EVER COMPLAINED THAT I'M ONLY SERVING CHICKEN WINGS. I SERVE THEM OVER PLAIN WHITE RICE, WITH MAYBE A LITTLE SOY SAUCE FOR THOSE WHO WISH IT, AND WITH A SIDE DISH OF SNOW PEAS AND WATER CHESTNUTS. SESAME SEEDS ARE EXPENSIVE IF YOU BUY THEM IN LITTLE PACKETS, BUT IN HEALTH FOOD STORES YOU OFTEN FIND LARGER BAGS AT REASONABLE PRICES. THEY CAN BE KEPT IN THE REFRIGERATOR SO THEY DON'T GO STALE. THEY ARE NUTRITIOUS AND DELICIOUS STIRRED INTO PLAIN RICE, THEY CAN TOP HOMEMADE ROLLS OR BROAD LOAVES, BE MADE INTO THE SPICY LITTLE WAFERS THE CHARLESTONIANS CALL BENNE WAFERS, AND CAN ADD A BIT OF ELEGANCE TO ANY TOSSED SALAD.

SERVES 4

12 *chicken wings*
 1 *cup soy sauce*
¾ *cup sugar*
¼ *cup white wine*
 2 *cloves garlic, slightly flattened and peeled*
 4 *slices fresh ginger root (or ½ teaspoon dried ginger)*
½ *cup sesame seeds*

Cut off wing tips and reserve to make stock. Cut wings at the joint to make 2 pieces of each. Put in a bowl. Heat soy sauce with sugar, wine, garlic, and ginger root. When sugar is dissolved, pour mixture over wings. Marinate in refrigerator for several hours, turning now and again.

Preheat oven to 300°. Place wings in a baking dish large enough to hold them in a single layer and pour a ladle of marinade over them. Bake 30 minutes, turn, and bake another 30 minutes. If the marinade dries out, add some more.

Put sesame seeds in a dry frying pan and toast them several minutes over low heat, stirring, until they turn golden. Roll chicken wings in the seeds and serve.

Spezzatino of Chicken Wings

IN ITALY, SPEZZATINI ARE USUALLY MADE WITH YOUNG CHICKENS, AND THE DARK MEAT IS COOKED LONGER THAN THE WHITE TO ENSURE THAT BOTH KINDS ARE MOIST AND SUCCULENT. BUT THIS PUNGENT SAUCE IS INTERESTING ENOUGH TO MAKE EVEN THE HUMBLE CHICKEN WING TAKE FLIGHT. THEY CAN BE SERVED WITH A MOUND OF BUTTERED PASTA OR PERHAPS RICE DUSTED WITH GRATED PARMESAN CHEESE.

SERVES 4

12–16 *chicken wings*
flour
salt and freshly ground
      pepper
  ½ *cup vegetable oil*
   1 *sprig of fresh*
     rosemary (or ½
     teaspoon dried)
   4 *anchovy fillets (or 1*
     heaping teaspoon
     anchovy paste)
   2 *cloves garlic, peeled*
  ½ *cup wine vinegar*
     (red or white)

Cut tips off chicken wings and reserve to make stock. Shake wings in a bag of flour seasoned with salt and pepper. Heat vegetable oil and rosemary in a frying pan large enough to hold all the wings. If you let the rosemary get too dark, remove it; otherwise, cook with the wings.

Fry wings over high heat until golden on both sides. While they cook mash anchovies and garlic with wine vinegar—either in a mortar and pestle or in a blender.

When chicken is cooked, remove to a platter and drain all but 1 tablespoon of oil from the pan. Add vinegar mixture and reduce over high heat to about half its volume. Return wings to the pan, cover, and cook 5 minutes over low heat.

Serve chicken on warm plates with sauce poured over.

A VERY PLEASANT HEARTY DISH WITH A FINE SWEET-SOUR TANG, THIS IS BEST WITH HOMEMADE TOMATO SAUCE, IF NONE IS ON HAND, CANNED WILL DO NICELY. SINCE IT IS A ONE-DISH MEAL, I USUALLY SKIP ANY SALAD OR BREAD, AND GO ON TO SOME RESOUNDING DESSERT.

Chicken Podgorny

SERVES 4

1 *slice bread, trimmed*
2 *tablespoons milk*
½ *pound ground beef*
1 *teaspoon dried dill*
¼ *teaspoon allspice*
salt and freshly ground
 pepper
8 *chicken wings*
2 *tablespoons vegetable oil*
1 *cup tomato sauce*
juice of 1 lemon
1 *tablespoon brown sugar*
1 *small cabbage, coarsely*
 chopped

Soak bread in milk in a mixing bowl until it crumbles easily and add beef and spices. Combine lightly with your hands and shape into balls the size of walnuts. You should have approximately 20 meatballs.

Cut tips off chicken wings and reserve to make stock. Pat wings dry. Add vegetable oil to frying pan over medium heat and fry wings until golden. Place in a casserole as they are done. Fry meatballs in the same fat and remove to the casserole. Pour tomato sauce, lemon juice, and brown sugar over all, and stir until meats are coated. Cover and simmer 20 minutes over low heat.

Stir in cabbage, cover pot again, and simmer another 20–30 minutes, until cabbage is quite tender. Serve with cooked rice or plain boiled potatoes.

Chicken Wings Grand-Mère

THIS IS ONE OF MY FAVORITE RECIPES, AND IT'S SO EASY AND TASTY I'VE SERVED IT AT FAMILY MEALS FOR YEARS. THE BACON AND POTATOES GIVE SUBSTANCE TO THE DISH, AND THE TOMATO PASTE AND HERBS PROMOTE A FINE BALANCE OF FLAVORS. I CAN'T ACCURATELY REMEMBER WHETHER THIS PARTICULAR GRAND-MÈRE WAS SO PARSIMONIOUS AS TO USE CHICKEN WINGS RATHER THAN PARTS FOR HER LOVELY DISH, OR WHETHER I FIRST PINCHED THE PENNIES FOR HER WITH A FROZEN BAG OF WINGS ON HAND, BUT I'VE NEVER BEEN TEMPTED TO FIDDLE WITH HER SUCCESS.

SERVES 4

12 *chicken wings*
flour
salt and freshly ground
  pepper
2 *tablespoons olive oil (or*
  vegetable oil)
2 *tablespoons butter*
1 *medium onion, chopped*
1 *clove garlic, minced*
1 *cup chicken stock*
¼ *pound mushrooms,*
  quartered
1 *tablespoon tomato paste*
½ *teaspoon dried thyme*
½ *teaspoon dried tarragon*
1 *bay leaf*
6 *slices bacon, cut in*
  ¼-inch strips
2 *medium potatoes, peeled*
  and cut in ¼-inch cubes
minced parsley

Cut off tips of chicken wings and use for making stock. Shake wings in flour seasoned with salt and pepper. Heat olive oil and 1 tablespoon of butter in a frying pan. Sauté wings over medium heat until lightly golden on both sides, then remove from pan.

Cook onion and garlic in the fat left in the pan until onion is transparent, then add wings, chicken stock, mushrooms, tomato paste, and herbs. Simmer, covered, 30 minutes.

While the wings cook, place bacon and remaining tablespoon of butter in another frying pan and cook over medium heat until bacon is lightly brown but not crisp. Scoop out with a slotted spoon and drain on paper towels. Add bacon to wings. Fry potato cubes in bacon fat and butter until crisp and golden—about 10 minutes.

When wings are done, stir in potatoes, divide into portions on dinner plates, and sprinkle with parsley. Serve immediately.

Chicken Livers with Sage

I LOVE ANY SAUCY THING OVER CRISP CROUTONS, AND THESE ARE AMONG THE VERY BEST. THEY ARE ALSO GREAT WITH A SPRIG OF ROSEMARY AND A CLOVE OF GARLIC, RATHER THAN THE SAGE, OR WITH A SLOSH OF MARSALA INSTEAD OF VINEGAR. SOMEHOW I THINK THEY SHOULD BE SERVED JUST AS IS RATHER THAN WITH A VEGETABLE—WHY NOT MAKE SOME KIND OF COLD VEGETABLE FOR A FIRST COURSE, THEN END THE MEAL WITH A FRUIT DESSERT?

SERVES 4

8 *slices home-style white bread*
olive oil
1½ *pounds chicken livers*
3 *slices bacon, cut in small strips*
2 *tablespoons butter*
1 *teaspoon dried crumbled sage* (*not powdered*)
salt and freshly ground pepper
2 *tablespoons red wine vinegar*
minced parsley (*or grated Parmesan cheese*)

Preheat oven to 325°. Stack bread and trim crusts so you have a square. Cut these diagonally like a sandwich. Brush these on both sides with olive oil and lay in a baking dish or on a cookie sheet. Bake 10 minutes, turn over, and bake another 5 minutes or more, until croutons are crisp and golden. Keep warm with oven door open.

To cook livers, cut them in two through the small connecting fiber. Put bacon and butter in a frying pan and cook over medium heat until bacon is done but not crisp. Add livers and sage, and cook, tossing now and again, 4–5 minutes. They should be brown on the outside but still a little pink inside. Sprinkle with salt and pepper as you cook them.

Lift livers out with a slotted spoon onto the croutons. Turn up heat and add wine vinegar to pan juices. Stir and scrape to loosen all the little bits, and pour over livers. Serve sprinkled with parsley.

A SIMPLE BUT TASTY DISH. I LIKE TO SERVE IT WITH RICE WITH ZUCCHINI (PAGE 311) FOR A VERY QUICKLY PUT-TOGETHER MEAL.

Chicken Livers Provençal

SERVES 4

1 *pound chicken livers*
flour
salt and freshly ground
  pepper
3 *tablespoons olive oil (or*
  butter)
1 *clove garlic, minced*
½ *cup chopped canned*
  tomatoes, drained
¼ *cup minced parsley*

Cut livers in half between connecting fiber. Shake in a bag with flour seasoned with salt and pepper. Heat olive oil in a frying pan and sauté livers a couple of minutes over medium-high heat. Stir in garlic, and after a half minute stir in tomatoes. Cook another 3 minutes, turning now and again so mixture cooks evenly. Stir in parsley and serve.

Turkey Parts

A whole turkey can be cut up as one would prepare a chicken, though it takes a whiz with a knife and cleaver to accomplish it. For only a few pennies more in the market, turkey parts are convenient and beckoning for recipes. The breast can be baked with or without traditional stuffing, slices can be marinated for grilling or pan-frying, and chunks can be stewed in the manner of veal with a sunset of saucings. Plain and cooked ahead it can stand in for any of the old-time chicken salads, a tetrazzini or curry, or creamed as a filling for crepes. The rest—thighs and wings I can handle, but stringy legs I can't, and turkey tails I won't. I have a friend who likes to barbecue the legs, and I've seen recipes for them deviled, and even one that made a kind of *ossobuco* by sawing them in slices after pulling out the wiry tendons with pliers, but though I usually prefer dark meat to white in roast turkey, I draw the line at the legs.

THIS IS USEFUL FOR A SMALL GATHERING, AND FOR AN EVEN SMALLER GROUP YOU CAN ROAST A HALF BREAST IN THE SAME MANNER TO SERVE 4–6. IF YOU LIKE STUFFING AS I DO, THE TURKEY CAN BE COOKED ON TOP OF ANY STUFFING YOU WISH, OR IT CAN BE BAKED IN A SEPARATE DISH.

Roast Turkey Breast

SERVES 8–12

1 *whole turkey breast (8–9 pounds)*
salt and freshly ground pepper
¼ *teaspoon dried thyme*
5 *tablespoons butter, melted*
¼ *cup dry white wine*

Preheat oven to 350°. Rub turkey with salt, pepper, thyme, and about 2 tablespoons of butter. Combine remaining butter with wine. Place turkey on a rack in a roasting pan. Bake 20 minutes a pound, or until a meat thermometer registers 165°. Baste during roasting with the butter-wine mixture. Slice and serve with your favorite bread stuffing and a green vegetable.

THIS IS A SPIN-OFF FROM THAT GLORIOUS SUMMER ITALIAN DISH OF COLD ROAST VEAL SLICES SMOTHERED IN TUNA SAUCE CALLED VITELLO TONNATO. BUT YOU DON'T HAVE TO APOLOGIZE FOR THE TURKEY, FOR IT IS JUST AS ELEGANT AND TASTY, IF NOT AS RUINOUSLY EXPENSIVE, AS VEAL. IT MAKES, OF COURSE, A PERFECT DISH FOR HOT SUMMER PARTIES, ACCOMPANIED BY A RICE SALAD AND A BOTTLE OF CHILLED WHITE WINE.

Turkey Tonnato

SERVES 6–8

½ *turkey breast (3–4 pounds)*
1 *can anchovies*
1 *large clove garlic, cut in slivers*
3 *tablespoons butter, melted*
3 *tablespoons dry white wine*
1 *6½-ounce can tuna packed in oil, drained*
juice of ½ lemon (or more)
2 *tablespoons capers*
2 *cups mayonnaise (preferably homemade)*
sprigs of parsley (optional)

Preheat oven to 350°. Loosen skin of turkey by slipping your fingers under it, then tuck 5 fillets of anchovies under it. Make incisions through skin into meat with a small knife and poke in each a sliver of garlic. Roast 20 minutes a pound, or until a thermometer registers an internal heat of 165°. Combine butter and wine and use to baste turkey as it cooks. Remove from oven and let cool to room temperature.

Put tuna in a bowl with lemon juice, capers, and 2 anchovies, and mash as finely as possible (or whirl in a blender). Combine with mayonnaise, and taste: it should be salty enough from the anchovies, and adjust for lemon juice—it should be a little tart.

Cut turkey meat in thin slices and slather each with tuna mayonnaise. Place on a platter and refrigerate 1 hour or more. Serve garnished with more whole capers, if you like, and perhaps sprigs of parsley.

EVERY BIT AS GOOD AS VEAL SCHNITZEL, AND I LIKE THEM TO BE
SERVED WITH A MOUNTAIN OF CREAMY MASHED POTATOES.

Turkey Schnitzel

SERVES 4

4 *slices turkey breast*
juice of 1 lemon
flour
salt and freshly ground
  pepper
1 *egg, beaten*
bread crumbs
vegetable oil
4 *tablespoons butter*
1 *teaspoon paprika*

Cut slices from a partially frozen turkey breast (this makes
slicing easier). Make them about ¼ inch thick and pound
lightly between sheets of waxed paper with a rolling pin.
Sprinkle with half the lemon juice and let marinate for 30
minutes in refrigerator.

Dredge each slice in flour seasoned with salt and pepper,
dip in egg, and then into bread crumbs. If there is time, let
coating set by placing coated slices in refrigerator another
30 minutes.

Heat vegetable oil in a frying pan—only about ⅛ inch.
When it is quite hot, fry slices 2–3 minutes a side, or until
crisp and golden. Remove to warm plates. Heat butter with
remaining lemon juice and paprika, and pour sizzling over
schnitzels. Serve immediately.

AH, THIS IS DOWNRIGHT WONDERFUL, WITH A TASTE MORE AKIN TO
FINE LAMB THAN TURKEY. TURKEY THIGHS MAKE A GREAT SUNDAY
ROAST SERVED WITH CARROTS WITH GARLIC (PAGE 279) AND RICE
WITH ZUCCHINI (PAGE 311).

Turkey Thighs Baked in Red Wine

SERVES 4

2 *turkey thighs*
2 *cloves garlic, peeled and sliced*
4 *small sprigs of fresh rosemary (or 1½ teaspoons dried)*
1 *cup dry red wine*
2 *tablespoons olive oil*
salt and freshly ground pepper
sprigs of parsley (or watercress) (optional)

Remove skin from thighs. With a small sharp knife cut out bone underside by slitting meat on either side of the bone, then cutting under and around the ends. Spread the thighs out flat and sprinkle with garlic and rosemary. Fold back over and place in a small baking dish. Pour wine over and marinate 4–5 hours, turning once.

Preheat oven to 350°. Pour out some of the marinade and reserve it, then brush meat with olive oil. Sprinkle with salt and pepper. Bake 50 minutes, basting several times in the process. If they get dry, add more marinade. Lift thighs out of the pan and cut into neat slices. Serve them fanned out on a plate, perhaps with a few sprigs of parsley or watercress as garnish.

THIS IS MORE LIGHT AND DELICATE THAN THE PRECEDING RECIPE AND MORE TURKEYEY, IF THAT IS POSSIBLE TO SAY. THEY CAN BE SERVED WITH STUFFING, RICE OR, BETTER YET, BAKED YAMS.

Turkey Thighs with Orange and Sage

SERVES 4

2 *turkey thighs*
1 *large orange*
½ *teaspoon dried crumbled sage (not powdered)*
⅓ *cup vegetable oil*
freshly ground pepper
salt

Skin and bone thighs as in preceding recipe. Place in a bowl with juice from orange and ½ teaspoon of grated orange rind. Add sage, vegetable oil, and pepper to taste. Marinate 4–5 hours.

Preheat oven to 350°. Place thighs in a baking dish, smooth side up and rolled back as if they still had a bone, with about half the marinade. Bake 50 minutes, basting several times as they cook. When done, they will have started to brown on top. Serve sliced and fanned out on the plate. Salt lightly.

Classic stringing up need not bother us here, just think of it as a package to wrap and tie securely, and make it a little loose because stuffing expands. This is one place toothpicks won't do, and you have to have plain old-fashioned cotton string, making a good stiff knot every few inches.

Turkey Thighs Stuffed with Tarragon Mushrooms

SERVES 4

2 turkey thighs
½ cup dry white wine
¼ cup vegetable oil
freshly ground pepper
2 tablespoons butter
¼ cup chopped onion
½ pound mushrooms, thinly sliced
2 tablespoons minced parsley
1 teaspoon dried tarragon
1 cup fresh bread crumbs
salt

Skin and bone thighs as for Turkey Thighs Baked in Red Wine (page 181). Spread them flat and place between sheets of waxed paper. Pound lightly but soundly with a rolling pin (or bottle) until nearly twice the size and about ½ inch thick. Place in a bowl with wine, vegetable oil, and some pepper. Marinate for several hours.

Preheat oven to 350°. Put butter in a saucepan and sauté onion several minutes, then add mushrooms, parsley, and tarragon, and stir over medium heat until mushrooms start to exude liquid. Stir in bread crumbs and salt and pepper to taste. Set aside.

Remove turkey from marinade and reserve liquid. Pat the thighs dry with paper towels. Divide stuffing between thighs and smooth with your fingers. Roll each up like a jelly roll, starting from the longest side, then tie well with lengths of string. Place in a baking pan, add some marinade, then bake 50 minutes, spooning marinade over them every 10 minutes. If the pan gets dry, add more marinade. When they are done, they should be springy to the touch and glazed golden.

Remove from oven and let sit 5 minutes. Snip off the string and cut into rounds.

WHAT MORE CAN I SAY BUT THAT THIS TAKES THOSE STRINGY WINGS AND TURNS THEM TO CREOLE MAGIC? TREAT IT TO A BED OF RICE AND STREW THEM WITH TOASTED SLIVERED ALMONDS IF YOU ARE FLUSH.

Turkey Wings Creole

SERVES 4

4 *turkey wings*
1 *small onion, sliced*
1 *bay leaf*
¼ *teaspoon thyme*
salt and freshly ground
  pepper
1 *tablespoon vegetable oil*
2 *cups chopped onion*
1 *clove garlic, minced*
½ *cup chopped green*
  pepper
2 *cups chopped canned*
  tomatoes, drained
½ *cup beer*
¼ *cup raisins*

Put turkey wings in a large pot with water to cover and sliced onion, bay leaf, thyme, and salt and pepper to taste. Bring to a boil, cover, turn heat down, and simmer 1½ to 2 hours, or until very tender. Remove wings and strip meat from bones, discarding skin and bones. The stock may be used for soup or to cook rice to be served alongside this dish.

While turkey cooks, put vegetable oil in a saucepan and sauté chopped onion and garlic until onion softens. Add green pepper, tomatoes, and beer. Simmer 30 minutes. Add turkey flesh and raisins, and cook another 15 minutes.

Turkey Wing Pot Pie

I WILL ALWAYS REMEMBER MISS DOROTHY'S GREAT CHURCH SUPPER CHICKEN POT PIE, WHICH SHE STOPPED MAKING BECAUSE ALL THE CHICKEN FAT FROM THE PLUMP HEN BEGAN TO GIVE EVEN *HER* GALL BLADDER ATTACKS. IT WAS PROBABLY THE RICHEST AND MOST GREEDILY CONSUMED POT PIE IN THE WHOLE OF GEORGIA AND WELL BEYOND (FOR GUESTS CAME FROM ALL OVER). BUT SINCE I DO NOT WISH TO BE ACCUSED OF ADVOCATING ALL THAT CHICKEN FAT, HERE IS A RECIPE FOR LEAN TURKEY WINGS THAT RECREATES SOME OF HER SECRETS.

SERVES 4

- 5 tablespoons butter
- 1 large onion, coarsely chopped
- 4 turkey wings
- 2 carrots, pared and cut in slices
- 2 celery stalks, sliced with part of leaves
- 2 cloves garlic
- 4 sprigs of parsley
- 1 bay leaf
- ¼ teaspoon dried thyme
- ¼ teaspoon dried crumbled sage (not powdered)
- salt and freshly ground pepper
- 3 tablespoons flour
- 1 biscuit recipe (or 2 cups biscuit mix, prepared according to directions)
- 2 tablespoons melted butter
- ¼ cup minced parsley

Put 2 tablespoons of butter in a large pot over medium heat. Add onion and cook until it softens, then add wings, carrots, celery, garlic, parsley sprigs, herbs, and salt and pepper to taste. Add water to cover, put a lid on the pot, and simmer 1½ hours.

Preheat oven to 375°. Lift wings from pot and cool, then remove flesh and set aside. Discard bones and skin. Strain stock and measure out 4 cups (reducing it at a high boil if necessary). Discard cooking vegetables and scraps. Put remaining 3 tablespoons of butter in a saucepan, stir in flour, and cook 3–4 minutes. Add stock and stir until sauce thickens and is smooth. Taste for seasoning, then add turkey. Place mixture in an 8-inch by 8-inch casserole.

Prepare biscuits and roll dough out about ⅓ inch thick. Brush with melted butter and sprinkle evenly with parsley. Roll up like a jelly roll and cut in ½-inch slices. Place these on top of turkey. Bake 30 minutes, or until biscuits begin to brown and the pot is bubbly.

Pasta, Polenta, and Pizza

I didn't grow up with pasta, but I hope to grow old on it. As a student, and years after, I understood it was dashing and Bohemian to serve spaghetti bolognese, for you needed only a few cushions for guests, an herb or two, a large pot, a pound of ground beef, a foil-wrapped loaf of bread sliced and slathered with garlic butter and left in a warm oven, a jug of wine, and a tossed salad that firmly refused to become wilted.

Now I admire pasta that tastes of itself, cooked until tender yet still firm, tossed with butter or good olive oil, then perhaps a little cheese and some of its intended sauce. And only one ladle of sauce, not a lake. This to be laced in as you eat, but it should be the pasta you summon from the fork. The cookbooks will tell you this is only a course before fish or meat or fowl, though most Italians know pasta or a bowl of hearty soup can be the focus, the reason for any meal, and on a plate of it a day—particularly with garlic—you thrive. I fully concur.

MOST TOMATO SAUCES FOR PASTA ARE RATHER DISPIRITING, AND THE CANNED ONES ARE DOWNRIGHT MUDDY. THIS HAS A FRESH ZING TO IT (EVEN MORE SO IF YOU GROW YOUR OWN TOMATOES, RIPE AND BURSTING WITH FLAVOR), HOW-

Home-Style Tomato Sauce

EVER, I THINK IT IS FINE ENOUGH TO SERVE AS A SIMPLE MEATLESS MEAL NOW AND AGAIN. I START OFF WITH SOMETHING LIKE SWISS CHARD SALAD (PAGE 284) AND A FRESH LOAF OF FRENCH OR ITALIAN BREAD, AND HAVE A SOUND INEXPENSIVE BOTTLE OF RED WINE AT HAND. FOLLOWED BY A FAVORITE SIMPLE DESSERT, NOBODY COMPLAINS—AT LEAST IF YOU DON'T TRY TO PULL IT OFF MORE THAN ONCE A MONTH.

SERVES 4

1 *tablespoon butter*
1 *tablespoon olive oil*
1 *large onion, finely chopped*
1 *clove garlic, minced*
salt and freshly ground pepper
⅛ *teaspoon dried oregano*
1 *teaspoon dried basil*
1 *tablespoon minced parsley*
pinch of crushed dried red pepper (optional)
1 *strip orange peel (optional)*
¼ *teaspoon fennel seeds (optional)*
1 *large can (1 pound 12 ounces) tomatoes (preferably Italian plum)*
pinch of sugar
1 *pound tagliarini (or fettuccine, spaghetti, or other pasta)*
freshly grated Parmesan cheese (or Romano)

Heat butter and olive oil in a saucepan (a rather large one because the sauce will spatter) and sauté onion and garlic over medium-low heat. Cook about 10 minutes, or until onion starts to turn golden. Toward the end start adding salt, pepper, herbs, red pepper, orange peel, and fennel seeds if you use them.

Put tomatoes, juice and all, through a food mill set atop onion mixture. (A food mill is best because it removes the seeds.) Taste, and add a little sugar just to cut the acidity of tomatoes.

Bring to a boil and lower heat, then simmer, uncovered, 30 minutes. By this time the sauce has reduced to serving consistency. Unlike tomato sauces made with tomato paste, this should not cook a long time—about 30 minutes is just right for a fresh and lively-tasting sauce.

Cook pasta in a large pot of boiling salted water according to label directions. Taste and test as it cooks, and drain immediately in a colander when it still has a little bite to it, you don't want it mushy. Toss pasta with some sauce and serve portions with a little more sauce on top and sprinkled with Parmesan cheese.

Spaghettini Estivi

I'M NOT A FAN OF NEW-FANGLED PASTA SALADS, USUALLY OVER-ELABORATE BUT STILL NOT MUCH MORE THAN OLD-FASHIONED MACARONI SALAD. MOST ITALIANS WOULD SHUDDER TO THINK OF EATING SOME OF THESE, BUT THEIR "SUMMER SPAGHETTI," WITH DELICATE HOT PASTA TOSSED WITH BUTTER AND TOPPED WITH A SURPRISING COLD TOMATO SAUCE, IS DELIGHTFUL ON HOT DAYS, ESPECIALLY WHEN YOU HAVE SUN-RIPENED TOMATOES ON THE VINE. STORE TOMATOES ARE NOT GOOD ENOUGH HERE SO MAKE THIS ONLY AT THE HEIGHT OF THE TOMATO SEASON.

SERVES 4

6 *medium garden ripe tomatoes*
2 *tablespoons minced parsley*
2 *tablespoons minced fresh basil (or 1 teaspoon dried)*
¼ *cup lemon juice*
3 *tablespoons olive oil*
2 *cloves garlic, minced*
salt and freshly ground *pepper*
1 *pound spaghettini*
2 *tablespoons butter*

Put tomatoes in boiling water for about 15 seconds, then remove with a slotted spoon and slip off skins. Chop coarsely, place in a strainer over a bowl, and drain 1 hour or so.

Combine tomatoes with parsley, basil, lemon juice, olive oil, garlic, and salt and pepper to taste.

Cook spaghettini until just tender, then drain in a colander and return to the pot. Stir with butter and then with some of the sauce. Divide into serving portions and ladle sauce over. Serve immediately.

THIS SAUCE HAS BECOME SO COMMON THE LAST FEW YEARS WE EVEN SEE IT FROZEN IN THE SUPERMARKET. IT IS ALWAYS BETTER HOMEMADE, HOWEVER, AND IT IS SO EASY IN A BLENDER, WHY NOT? NOTHING IS SO FRESH AND LIVELY ON PASTA (USUALLY LINGUINI) BUT PESTO ALSO MAKES A SUPERB SAUCE FOR BOILED POTATOES, A LIVELY ACCENT STIRRED INTO A BLAND SOUP AT THE LAST MOMENT, AND A HEAVENLY TOPPING FOR BROILED TOMATO HALVES.

Pesto in a Blender

SERVES 4

2 *cups loosely packed fresh basil leaves*
½ *cup olive oil*
3 *tablespoons pine nuts (or walnuts)*
2 *cloves garlic, peeled*
1 *teaspoon salt*
½ *cup freshly grated Parmesan cheese (or Romano or a mixture)*
3 *tablespoons butter, at room temperature*
1 *tablespoon boiling water from cooking pasta*

Put basil, olive oil, nuts, garlic, and salt in a blender and reduce to a paste at high speed. Scrape down ingredients as you do this to make sure it smooths evenly. Scrape into a bowl and stir in Parmesan cheese and then butter. Just before serving, add tablespoon of pasta water before tossing with drained pasta.

(If you freeze Pesto, leave out cheese and butter, and incorporate it into thawed sauce, while the pasta cooks.)

Pasta with Tuna and Anchovy Sauce

WHEN I WAS AN UNDERGRADUATE IN NEW YORK CITY, A POET FRIEND AND I WERE INVITED TO DINNER BY AN OUT-OF-WORK ACTOR. WE LOOKED AROUND THE KITCHEN AS A JUG OF WINE WAS BEING POURED AND SAW ONLY A PACKAGE OF SPAGHETTI, A CAN OF ANCHOVIES, AND A HEAD OF GARLIC. WE WERE POOR ENOUGH, BUT THIS LOOKED GRIM EVEN FOR THE FRINGES OF THE THEATER—AND IT WAS. THIS IS THE WAY I'D MEET THAT SITUATION TODAY. MANY ITALIANS AUTOMATICALLY REACH FOR A CAN OF TUNA AND A CAN OF ANCHOVIES WHEN THEY WANT A QUICK AND EASY SEAFOOD SAUCE FOR PASTA, AND THEY MORE OR LESS GO ABOUT IT THIS WAY. SOMETIMES TOMATOES ARE ADDED, SOMETIMES CAPERS, BUT THE SIMPLEST WAY IS WONDERFUL. THEY ALSO DON'T BELIEVE IN CHEESE FOR SEAFOOD PASTA, SO I'VE TAKEN A TIP FROM THE SICILIANS AND TOP IT WITH CROUTONS.

SERVES 4

1 *pound spaghetti (or fettuccine)*
4 *slices home-style white bread*
2 *tablespoons olive oil*
3–4 *tablespoons butter*
2 *cloves garlic, minced*
1 *can flat anchovies, drained and chopped*
1 *6½-ounce can tuna (packed in oil)*
¼ *cup minced parsley*
salt

Put a large pot of water to boil. While it heats prepare remaining ingredients. Trim bread of crusts and cut into dice. Heat olive oil in a frying pan and add bread. Toss quickly to coat with oil, then continue tossing over medium heat until cubes are golden. Drain on paper towels and keep warm.

Wipe out pan and add 3 tablespoons of butter. Cook garlic 1–2 minutes over medium-low heat, then add anchovies. Turn up heat a bit and cook another minute or so. Add tuna, oil and all, and break up pieces with a fork. After a minute, stir in parsley. Some tuna has more oil than others, so if the sauce looks dry, add remaining tablespoon of butter. Turn heat off.

When water comes to a boil, add some salt and cook pasta until it is done but still has a little bite to it. Drain, toss with sauce, and divide among plates. Sprinkle with croutons and serve.

Spaghetti Carbonara

THE ROMANS USUALLY COOK THIS DISH WITH AN UNSMOKED BACON CALLED *PANCETTA*, BUT I LIKE IT WITH PLAIN AMERICAN BACON. INDEED, IT'S ONE OF THE BEST WAYS TO SERVE BACON AND EGGS EVER DEVISED. THOUGH IT IS USUALLY PREPARED WITH SPAGHETTI, RIGATONI IS ALSO ESPECIALLY FINE, AND REALLY ANY PASTA WILL DO.

SERVES 4

8 *slices bacon*
2 *tablespoons butter*
3 *eggs*
3 *tablespoons minced parsley*
½ *cup grated Parmesan cheese (or Romano)*
salt and freshly ground pepper
1 *pound spaghetti*

Put bacon and butter in a small frying pan. Cook over medium-high heat until bacon starts to crisp, then turn off heat. Crack eggs into a bowl large enough to toss pasta in later, then beat them lightly with parsley, Parmesan cheese, and salt and pepper to taste (this dish should have rather a lot of pepper).

Boil spaghetti in a large pot of salted water until done but still with a little bite to it. Drain through a colander and immediately put into the bowl with eggs. Toss pasta with 2 forks until completely coated with eggs—the heat of the pasta will cook the egg slightly. Heat up bacon and pour over spaghetti, tossing it into the pasta well. Serve on warm plates, and pass more cheese.

THERE'S NOTHING WRONG WITH PASTA TOSSED WITH PLENTY OF GARLIC SAUTÉED IN OIL OR BUTTER, THEN SPRINKLED WITH CHEESE, BUT THIS IS MORE SUBTLE AND NEARLY AS EASY. THE GARLIC CAN BE COOKED AT ANY TIME WHEN YOU HAVE A DISH IN THE OVEN, AND LIKE BAKED POTATOES CAN BE DONE AT ANY TEMPERATURE. IT CAN THEN BE STORED IN THE REFRIGERATOR IN ITS PACKET UNTIL YOU NEED IT. IN FACT, IT'S FINE TO HAVE SOME AROUND FOR SEASONING DISHES SUCH AS STEWS, OR SIMPLY TO SPREAD ON TOAST.

Mario's Garlic Pasta

SERVES 4

- 1 *whole head of garlic*
  olive oil (or vegetable oil)
- 2 *tablespoons butter*
  salt
- 4 *green onions, minced with part of tops*
- ¼ *cup minced parsley*
- 1 *pound spaghetti (or tagliarini)*
- ¼ *cup grated Parmesan cheese (or Romano)*

Preheat oven to 350°. Separate cloves from the head of garlic and place on a sheet of foil. Sprinkle with a little olive oil and turn to coat them, then fold up in foil to make a secure packet. Bake 30–45 minutes, or until cloves are completely soft. Remove from oven and cool to room temperature. Squirt flesh from garlic cloves into a small bowl. Mash thoroughly with butter, add salt to taste, then stir in onions and parsley.

Cook pasta in plenty of boiling salted water until done, but still with a little bite to it. Drain and put back into the pot with the garlic mixture. Toss well with 2 forks and divide into portions on warm plates. Serve sprinkled with Parmesan cheese.

Pasta with Harlot's Sauce

SELDOM MENTIONED IN GENTEEL COOKBOOKS, IT IS SAID THAT THIS IS THE WAY NEAPOLITAN PROSTITUTES PUT TOGETHER A CHEAP AND HASTY MEAL BETWEEN CUSTOMERS. THE SAUCE ALSO CAN BE PERKED UP WITH A FEW CHOPPED ANCHOVIES IF YOU HAVE THEM, AND ONE VERSION THROWS IN SOME CAPERS. THE SAUCE COULD ALSO BE MADE WITH A CAN OF ITALIAN PLUM TOMATOES PUT THROUGH A FOOD MILL RATHER THAN THE WATER AND TOMATO PASTE. THIS TAKES A LITTLE LONGER, BUT THE RESULT IS A PURER, FRESHER TASTE. THE CROUTONS ARE SOUTHERN ITALIAN, A SUBSTITUTE FOR EXPENSIVE PARMESAN CHEESE, AND GIVE THE PASTA A PLEASANT CONTRAST IN TEXTURE. I SPLURGE AND USE BOTH.

SERVES 4

7 *tablespoons olive oil*
1 *large onion, chopped*
2 *cloves garlic, minced*
4 *tablespoons tomato paste*
1 *cup water*
20 *Italian olives (or Greek), pitted and sliced*
¼ *teaspoon dried oregano*
½ *teaspoon dried basil*
½ *teaspoon dried red pepper flakes (or regular black pepper)*
3 *slices white bread, trimmed of crust and cut in dice*
salt
1 *pound spaghetti (or other pasta)*
minced parsley
grated Parmesan cheese (optional)

This is a quick sauce, so put on a kettle of salted water to boil and have all the ingredients at hand.

Put 4 tablespoons of olive oil in a saucepan and sauté onion and garlic over medium heat until onion wilts. Add tomato paste, water, olives, herbs, and pepper. Bring to a boil, lower heat, and simmer 10 minutes. Taste for salt—the olives should have salted it almost enough.

Heat remaining 3 tablespoons of olive oil in a frying pan and sauté bread cubes over medium heat, tossing until crisp and golden all over. Lift out onto paper towels and sprinkle lightly with salt. Keep warm.

Cook pasta until done but still with a little bite to it—what the Italians call *al dente,* then drain and toss with sauce. Divide into serving portions and sprinkle with croutons and parsley. Pass Parmesan cheese separately if you use it.

Rigatoni with Cream and Ham

THIS IS ADAPTED FROM A POPULAR PASTA SERVED AT GEORGE'S IN ROME, WHERE IT IS PREPARED WITH THE FINEST PROSCIUTTO. IT IS SO GOOD, THOUGH, THAT IT'S STILL TASTY WITH THE LAST OF A HOME-COOKED HAM, WITH TINY CREAMY BITS LODGING IN THE HOLES OF THE LARGE PASTA.

SERVES 4

1 *pound rigatoni*
6 *tablespoons butter*
1 *cup thinly sliced ham,*
   cut into tiny strips
2 *egg yolks*
⅔ *cup heavy cream*
salt
freshly grated nutmeg
½ *cup grated Parmesan*
   cheese (or *Romano*)

Put pasta to boil in plenty of salted water. As it cooks, melt butter in a frying pan and sauté ham a few minutes. When rigatoni is done to taste, drain and put back in the cooking pot. Toss with ham.

Beat egg yolks, cream, a bit of salt, and nutmeg in a small bowl, then stir into the rigatoni. Cook, stirring gently, 1 minute or so over low heat, just enough to heat through and thicken—any more will curdle egg yolks.

Place on plates and sprinkle with Parmesan cheese.

Hole-in-the-Wall Chicken with Pasta

SOME YEARS AGO A MAN WROTE A LETTER TO *GOURMET* MAGAZINE AND INCLUDED THIS LONG-REMEMBERED RECIPE FROM A TINY RESTAURANT OF HIS BROOKLYN CHILDHOOD. IT WAS WELL REMEMBERED, IN SPITE OF THAT SUSPICIOUS-LOOKING CAN OF TOMATO SAUCE, BECAUSE THE RESULT IS INEFFABLE. I'VE TRIED USING HOMEMADE SAUCE, ADDING OTHER HERBS, GARLIC, AND RED PEPPER FLAKES, BUT IT IS REALLY BEST JUST THIS WAY. PERHAPS IT IS ALL THOSE GOLDEN ONIONS?

SERVES 4

1 *chicken, cut up into pieces*
flour
salt and freshly ground pepper
⅓ *cup olive oil*
3 *cups chopped onion*
1 *15-ounce can tomato sauce*
1 *teaspoon dried basil*
½ *teaspoon sugar*
1 *pound seashell pasta (or ziti or rigatoni)*
grated Parmesan cheese (or Romano)

Shake chicken pieces in flour seasoned well with salt and pepper. Heat olive oil in a large frying pan and sauté chicken until lightly golden on both sides. Remove pieces to an oven-top casserole.

Sauté onions in the same oil until golden—this will take about 15 minutes over medium-low heat. Add tomato sauce to onion with basil, sugar, and salt and pepper to taste. Pour over chicken, toss well, and cook, covered, 30 minutes over low heat. Uncover pot and cook another 30 minutes.

Cook pasta until done but still with a little bite. Drain, toss with a little tomato sauce, and serve beside chicken pieces, sprinkled with Parmesan cheese.

SATISFYING WITHOUT A SCRAP OF MEAT, THIS IS A PASTA FOR THOSE WHO LIKE A ROBUST SAUCE AND PLENTY OF IT.

Sicilian Eggplant Spaghetti

SERVES 4

3 cups eggplant, peeled
  and cut in ½-inch cubes
salt
½ cup olive oil
½ cup chopped onion
2 cloves garlic, minced
1 cup chopped green
  pepper
3 cups chopped canned
  tomatoes, drained
1 teaspoon dried basil
freshly ground pepper
6 anchovies, minced
1 tablespoon capers
½ cup black olives
  (preferably dry oil-cured)
¼ cup minced parsley
1 pound spaghetti (or
  other pasta)
grated Parmesan cheese
  (optional)

Place eggplant in a colander, salt liberally, and leave to sweat 30 minutes or more. Before using, squeeze cubes with your hands to wring out as much moisture as possible, then dry on paper towels.

Heat olive oil in a large saucepan and sauté onion and garlic until onion wilts. Add green pepper and cook a few more minutes, then add eggplant. Stir and toss another few minutes, then add tomatoes, basil, and pepper to taste. Cook sauce, covered, 30 minutes over low heat.

Uncover, add anchovies, capers, and olives, and cook another 10 minutes. Taste for salt—usually the salt on the eggplant and in the anchovies and olives is enough. Finally, stir in parsley. Boil spaghetti in plenty of salted water until done but still with a little bite to it, then drain. Toss with some sauce, then place on plates and top with more sauce. Grated Parmesan cheese may be served over it, if you like, but it's not really necessary.

Beans and Sausage with Pasta

ITALIANS MOSTLY COMBINE BEANS AND PASTA IN A SOUP, BUT OCCASIONALLY THEY DO IT "DRY" ON A PLATE. THIS IS A CALIFORNIA VERSION USING KIDNEY BEANS, BUT YOU COULD USE LARGE WHITE BEANS OR CANNED *CANNELLINI*, TO BE MORE AUTHENTICALLY ITALIAN. IT MAKES A HEARTY DISH, VERY SIMPLE AND ECONOMICAL, AND KIDS LOVE IT.

SERVES 4

1 *tablespoon olive oil*
1 *medium onion, chopped*
1 *clove garlic, minced*
1 *small green pepper, cut in strips*
2–3 *Italian sausages (sweet or hot)*
1 *tablespoon tomato paste*
½ *cup dry red wine*
½ *teaspoon dried basil*
salt and freshly ground pepper
1 *1-pound can kidney beans (preferably without sugar)*
¾ *pound small shell pasta (or macaroni)*
2 *tablespoons butter*

Put olive oil in a saucepan and wilt onion, garlic, and green pepper over medium-low heat. Peel casings off the sausages, crumble them, and cook with onion until the meat loses all its pinkness. Stir in tomato paste, wine, basil, and salt and pepper to taste. Finally, add beans, bring to a boil, cover pan, and cook slowly 45 minutes to 1 hour over low heat.

Cook pasta in plenty of boiling salted water until done. Drain, toss with butter, and place on warm plates. Ladle sauce over and serve.

Tortellini with Cream

QUITE A FEW MANUFACTURERS ACROSS THE COUNTRY NOW MAKE SURPRISINGLY EXCELLENT TORTELLINI AT VERY REASONABLE PRICES. A PACKAGE OR TWO IN THE FREEZER CAN MEAN YOU WILL BE ABLE TO TURN OUT A FAST AND ECONOMICAL MEAL AT ANY TIME WITH FLAIR AND EASE. THOUGH IN ITALY THIS DISH WOULD BE ONLY A COURSE PRECEDING THE ENTREE, IN THE MOOD OF NEW LIGHTER DINING THE TORTELLINI ITSELF COULD BE THE ENTREE, PRECEDED BY AN ANTIPASTO AND ACCOMPANIED BY A LOAF OF BREAD.

SERVES 2

2 *cups chicken stock (or water)*
1 *10-ounce package tortellini (fresh or frozen)*
1 *cup heavy cream*
2 *tablespoons butter*
freshly grated nutmeg
grated Parmesan cheese (or Romano)

Heat oven to 350°. Bring stock to a boil in a saucepan. Drop in tortellini and simmer 5 minutes for fresh, or 8 minutes for frozen. Place cream in another saucepan and heat it. When tortellini are done, lift out with a slotted spoon, or carefully drain through a colander, into hot cream. Cover pan and let sit 10 minutes to soak in the cream.

Butter a shallow casserole or individual ramekins and lift out tortellini with a slotted spoon into the baking dish. Add butter and a little nutmeg to the cream, then cook down over high heat until it thickens to a sauce. Pour this over tortellini, sprinkle with Parmesan cheese, and place in the oven. Heat only 5 minutes or so—just enough to warm through and melt the cheese. Serve immediately.

THIS IS NEARLY AS GOOD AS LASAGNA OR PASTITSIO, AND MUCH EASIER TO PREPARE. IT IS A BOON FOR THE COOK WHO NEEDS A PASTA DISH PUT TOGETHER IN ADVANCE, WITH NO LAST-MINUTE FUSS. BOTH FAMILY AND COMPANY WILL ENJOY IT, SERVED WITH FRESH BREAD, A TOSSED SALAD, AND A GLASS OF RED WINE. IF YOUR MEAL IS FOR LESS THAN SIX, CUT UP THE REMAINDER, WRAP IN FOIL, AND FREEZE FOR AN EASY LUNCH OR SUPPER ANYTIME.

Baked Mostaccioli with Italian Sausage

SERVES 6

1 *recipe Home-Style Tomato Sauce (page 189)*
1 *cup ricotta cheese*
½ *teaspoon salt*
freshly grated nutmeg
pinch of sugar
1 *teaspoon dried basil*
1 *tablespoon minced parsley*
freshly ground pepper
4 *sweet Italian sausages*
1 *pound mostaccioli*
grated Parmesan cheese (or Romano)

Make tomato sauce. In a small bowl, combine ricotta cheese with salt, nutmeg, sugar, basil, parsley, and rather a lot of pepper. Set aside. Split sausage casings and brown insides in a frying pan, mashing down as it cooks so it crumbles. When sausage begins to brown, lift out with a slotted spoon onto paper towels to drain.

Preheat oven to 375°. Prepare mostaccioli according to package directions. When the pasta is done—but still with a little bite to it—drain in a colander. Pour half the tomato sauce into the bottom of a 13-inch by 9-inch lasagna pan, spread half the pasta over, then the sausage. Spread the ricotta mixture over that, then layer on the remaining pasta, topping with the rest of the tomato sauce. Sprinkle liberally with Parmesan cheese.

This can be done 1 hour or so in advance, if need be, just cover with foil or plastic wrap to keep it from drying out. To cook, bake, uncovered, 20 minutes, or until bubbly.

Pastitsio for Eight (or One)

A few years ago I moved into a different San Francisco neighborhood and was barely unpacked before I saw a large street banner proclaiming a Greek church festival and dinner just around the corner. I knew a little about Greek restaurant food, but never having visited Greece, I knew less than little about the warmth, largesse, and frugality of Greek home cooking.

I ate at the church and learned quickly, and now cook many dishes at home, and every year take friends back for the four days of convivial dining and dancing—a far cry from the Presbyterian church suppers of my youth.

I discovered nearby a tiny Greek shop that sells inexpensive large cans of fruity olive oil, a good selection of olives and feta cheeses, sheets of phyllo, fragrant bunches of dried oregano, and large plump capers for a fraction of what they cost at the supermarket. You may not be so blessed, but you can prepare Pastitsio as I learned it from the church ladies without any exotic ingredients at all. It is best certainly with lamb and ziti, but it does very well with plain hamburger and elbow macaroni.

Classic Pastitsio

SERVES 8

1 *pound ground lamb (or beef)*
1 *cup chopped onion*
1 *clove garlic, minced*
1 *cup chopped canned tomatoes, drained*
½ *cup dry white wine*
salt and freshly ground pepper
¼ *teaspoon ground cinnamon*
¼ *teaspoon ground allspice*
1 *bay leaf*
¼ *teaspoon dried basil*
2 *tablespoons minced parsley*
½ *cup butter*
½ *cup flour*
4 *cups milk, heated*
pinch of nutmeg
2 *cups grated* Parmesan cheese
1 *pound ziti, broken up (or elbow macaroni)*
3 *eggs, separated*
bread crumbs
2 *tablespoons melted butter*

PASTITSIO IS ABOUT THE FINEST WAY I KNOW TO SERVE A PARTY OF EIGHT ON ONE POUND OF MEAT. IT MAKES A WELCOME, SOOTHING DISH, ACCOMPANIED BY A LARGE BOWL OF GREEK SALAD—A TOSS OF LETTUCES, FETA CHEESE CRUMBLED, GREEK OLIVES, TOMATOES, SMALL PICKLED PEPPERS, RADISHES (PERHAPS), AND CAPERS—AND A COUPLE OF LOAVES OF CRUSTY BREAD AND A JUG OF DRY RED WINE.

HOWEVER, I ALSO FIND IT MAKES A SUPERB DISH FOR ANY SMALL FAMILY, OR EVEN ONE PERSON ALONE, SINCE IT CAN BE FROZEN IN FOIL PACKETS AND HEATED UP FOR A MEAL ANYTIME. I KNOW I WILL ALWAYS EAT WELL (AND GRACIOUSLY) WHEN THERE IS A SUPPLY IN MY FREEZER.

Pastitsio is constructed from a meat sauce, a white sauce, and a large pot of pasta, and you will need about 1 hour to put it all together.

To make the meat sauce: put ground lamb in a saucepan and stir with a fork over high heat until crumbly and starts to brown. Pour out all fat the meat releases, then add onion and garlic. When the onion is soft, add tomatoes, wine, salt, pepper, cinnamon, allspice, and bay leaf. Cook, covered, 15 minutes over low heat, then uncover pan and cook another 15 minutes, adding basil and parsley toward the end. All the juices should cook away by the time it is done.

To make the white sauce, cook butter and flour several minutes in another saucepan. Add hot milk and cook, stirring, until sauce is smooth and thickened. Add salt and nutmeg to taste, then set aside.

Finally, cook the pasta in lots of boiling salted water until done, but still with a little resistance when you bite into it. Drain in a colander.

Separate eggs, putting 1 white in one bowl and 2 in another. Beat egg yolks into the white sauce. Lightly whip 1 egg white and stir it into meat sauce, lightly whip the other 2 and toss into cooked pasta. Stir 1 cup of Parmesan cheese into white sauce and ¾ cup into pasta. Now assemble dish.

Preheat oven to 350°. Butter a 13-inch by 9-inch lasagna pan and sprinkle with bread crumbs to coat. Layer in half of the pasta, smooth half of the white sauce over, then spoon on all of the meat sauce. Top with remaining pasta and then remaining white sauce. Sprinkle with ¼ cup of Parmesan cheese, then some more bread crumbs. Dribble melted butter over top.

Bake, uncovered, 40–45 minutes, or until golden and bubbly. Remove from oven and let sit about 15 minutes before slicing in squares and serving.

HERE IS ANOTHER SALAD THAT PARTNERS PASTITSIO WELL. THIS
GIVES US EVERYTHING WE NEED EXCEPT FOR THE FRAGRANT RETSINA
WINE, THE STEAMING LITTLE CUPS OF STRONG MURKY COFFEE, AND
THE DANCING, THE
DANCING!

Greek Tomato Salad with Feta

SERVES 1

3 tablespoons olive oil
salt and freshly ground
   pepper
⅛ teaspoon dried oregano
¼ pound feta cheese,
   crumbled
2 medium tomatoes, peeled
   and sliced
red wine vinegar

Mix olive oil, salt and pepper to taste, oregano, and feta
cheese in a bowl. Let sit 10–15 minutes. Slice tomatoes,
place on a plate, and pour dressing over. Have a cruet of
wine vinegar on the table to sprinkle as desired over salad.

My Lasagna, or How to Make Ten Servings from One Pot Roast

Anyone who has tasted lasagna prepared with homemade pasta will never again be satisfied with store-bought noodles, for this is the one place pasta you make yourself really counts. May I also submit the suggestion that a sauce with shredded pot roast is far superior to any ground meat concoction. Now, this is a long, laborious process, but like homemade bread, well worth every minute. If prepared for only one or two, rather than a family or a lasagna party, roast a smaller cut of meat or freeze portions of the larger piece for a series of future glorious feasts. This is how I make the pot roast.

Italian Pot Roast

1 *4-pound chuck (or rump) beef roast*
2 *tablespoons vegetable oil*
1 *cup chopped onion*
2 *cloves garlic, minced*
1 *cup chopped canned tomatoes*
1 *cup sliced mushrooms*
1 *cup beef stock*
1 *cup dry red wine*
1 *bay leaf*
1 *teaspoon dried basil*
¼ *teaspoon dried thyme*
1 *strip orange peel (optional)*
½ *teaspoon fennel seeds (optional)*
salt and freshly ground pepper

Pat meat dry with paper towels. Heat vegetable oil in a large oven-top casserole and sear meat on all sides over high heat. Lower heat to medium, add onion and garlic, stir, and cook several minutes, then add all the rest of the ingredients, including salt and pepper to taste. Cover pot, turn heat down low, and simmer 2½–3 hours, or until the meat is very tender.

Serve 4 slices of meat with some of the sauce poured over, for one meal. Shred the rest into remaining sauce, for making lasagna: you will need 3 cups. The shredded meat can be frozen, if necessary, until you need it.

For this book I've never suggested anything but the most minimal equipment (such as a pressure cooker that saves not only time but gas). But for making pasta, I think it is a wise investment to go out and purchase a machine roller. Some cookbooks toll the glories of hand-rolled pasta, but that takes practice to turn out, as well as hours of elbow grease. The new electric pasta machines are quick, expensive, and not altogether reliable, but the old reliable roller, which all Italian cooks I know use (they simply call it the *machina*), not only quickly rolls out pasta but also does most of the preparatory kneading.

And this is how I go about lasagna—I make spinach pasta here because it is just as easy as regular egg pasta, and much prettier.

Spinach Pasta

½ *package frozen leaf*
    spinach (or 1 bunch
    fresh)
salt
1½ *cups flour*
    (approximately)
 2 *large eggs*

If using frozen spinach, cook according to package directions, then drain and cool. If using fresh spinach, trim stems, wash through several waters, and cook 10 minutes in a little salted water before draining and cooling. For either, squeeze out water with your hands until it is as dry as you can make it. Chop the spinach finely.

Place flour on a work surface, make a kind of well in the middle, and put eggs and spinach in it. Beat eggs and spinach with a fork and add flour from edges gradually. Work the mixture together, adding as much flour as needed to make a stiff mixture. When the whole mass sticks together well, set up pasta machine.

The first setting, where the rollers are widest apart, will help you knead the dough. Pull off a fistful of dough (always keeping the rest covered with plastic wrap or a damp towel so it doesn't dry out) and put through the rollers about a dozen times, or until dough is smooth and elastic, and spinach is an even green. After each roll, double dough before putting it through again. If it remains sticky, dust with flour. Repeat this process for all the dough, keeping already-worked dough covered.

Finally, take the dough sections and, starting at widest setting, go through all the settings without doubling dough until you get to the next-to-last (lasagna does not need the very finest). Cut strips the length of the lasagna pan and place on a towel. Any smaller pieces can be used to patch the lasagna as you build it.

Bring a large pot of salted water to boil. Have ready a bowl of cold water at the side. Drop 3 or 4 strips at a time into boiling water. Cook 10 seconds, then remove to the cold water with a slotted spoon. Wring each strip lightly with your hands and lay out on the towel while completing the dish.

Have the meat sauce warm and ready, and make the Béchamel.

Béchamel for a Lasagna

SERVES 10

6 *tablespoons butter*
4½ *tablespoons flour*
3 *cups milk, heated*
salt
freshly grated nutmeg

Heat butter in a saucepan, and when it sizzles, stir in flour. Stir 3–4 minutes, then add milk and stir until you have a smooth silky sauce. Season to taste with salt and a little nutmeg.

Now everything should be ready for the lasagna. Prepare about 1 cup of freshly grated Parmesan cheese, and 2 tablespoons melted butter.

To assemble: smear bottom of a 9-inch by 13-inch lasagna pan with a little meat sauce, preferably from the top where there is a bit more fat. Place a single layer of pasta in the pan. Overlap a little and piece if necessary, but don't prop up pasta ends or sides, or it will become tough as it cooks. Spread some meat sauce over pasta and dribble with Béchamel, then sprinkle with Parmesan cheese. Repeat for about 6 layers, being a little sparing at first with the sauces so you will have enough at the end. Save enough really pretty strips of pasta for the top so it will look nice. Coat the top with the last of the Béchamel, strew it with cheese, then dribble butter over the top. This can be made ahead, covered with foil, and refrigerated if necessary, but bring to room temperature before cooking.

Heat oven to 450°. Bake lasagna 10–15 minutes, or until lightly golden on top and bubbly below. Allow to settle about 10 minutes before cutting. Serve on warm plates.

Now you have something to crow about! My only advice is don't be too stingy using the Béchamel and if necessary make another cup for the top.

Potato Gnocchi

I USED TO SHY AWAY FROM THESE BECAUSE I'D EATEN SOME INDIFFERENT (AND RATHER TOUGH) ONES IN ITALY, BUT VARIOUS COOKS CONVINCED ME THAT GNOCCHI MADE WITHOUT EGG ARE LIGHT AND DELICIOUS. THEY ARE ALSO VERY EASY ONCE YOU GET THE HANG OF IT, AND PROBABLY WHAT TAKES THE LONGEST IN THE WHOLE PROCESS IS BOILING THE POTATOES. THE ITALIANS, OF COURSE, EAT THEM AS ONE COURSE DURING THE MEAL, AND THEY ARE RIGHT. BUT ALSO REMEMBER THEM FOR A LUNCH DISH OR A LATE SUPPER. THEY CAN TAKE ANY SAUCE BUT A HEAVY ONE, AND ONE OF THE BEST IS SOME GRAVY FROM A POT ROAST, IF YOU HAVE SOME ON HAND.

SERVES 4

1½ *pounds boiling potatoes*
(4 medium or 3 large)
½ *teaspoon salt*
freshly grated nutmeg
1 *cup flour*
(approximately)
Home-Style Tomato Sauce
(page 189) or Pesto
(page 191)
grated Parmesan cheese (if
not using Pesto)

Boil potatoes with skins on. When tender, drain and peel as soon as they are easy to handle. Put through a ricer into a bowl. Add salt and a little nutmeg, then stir in ¾ cup of flour. Turn onto a lightly floured board and knead gently, adding as much flour as necessary to make a soft smooth dough. If trying this for the first time, test a pinch of it in boiling water to see if it holds together. If it does not, add a little more flour.

Pinch off a handful of dough at a time and with floured hands roll into lengths about as thick as your thumb. Cut these in ¾-inch pieces. Take each piece and press it lightly into the tines of a fork with your index finger (the depression the poke makes ensures easier cooking, and the imprint of the tines traps the sauce). These should be flicked off the fork onto the board as you make them. They can sit, covered with a towel, 1 hour or so.

To cook, bring a large pot of salted water to a boil and warm sauce (unless you use Pesto). Drop gnocchi into simmering water in batches of a couple of dozen. When they rise to the top, cook about 10 seconds, then remove to a bowl with a slotted spoon. Add a little sauce, stir, and repeat for the other batches. When all are done, toss with the rest of the sauce and some grated Parmesan cheese. Serve immediately.

Spinach Gnocchi

I'VE COOKED THESE PLUMP, MELTINGLY TENDER LITTLE BEAUTIES FOR YEARS, SOMETIMES AS A LUNCH OR SUPPER, SOMETIMES AS A FIRST COURSE FOR SIX. IN FACT, I HAVE A STANDING ORDER FROM ONE FRIEND TO PREPARE THEM FOR ANY MEAL SHE COMES TO. THEY ARE ITALIAN, BUT THEY GO BEAUTIFULLY WITH MANY ANOTHER CUISINE—CONSIDER THEM, FOR INSTANCE, AS A SIDE DISH FOR A LAMB CHOP OR BROILED CHICKEN.

SERVES 4

1 *package frozen leaf spinach*
2 *tablespoons butter*
1 *cup ricotta cheese* (or *sieved dry cottage cheese*)
grated Parmesan cheese
2 *eggs*
2 *tablespoons flour*
6 *tablespoons melted butter*
salt and freshly ground pepper
freshly grated nutmeg

Cook spinach according to package directions, then drain in a sieve and run cold water over it. Squeeze with your hands until you get out as much of the liquid as possible. Chop very finely. Add 2 tablespoons of butter to a small saucepan and cook spinach several minutes over medium-low heat or until it dries out and starts to stick to the pan bottom. Remove from the heat.

Mix ricotta cheese, ¼ cup of Parmesan cheese, eggs, and flour, then mix in spinach. Stir in 1 tablespoon of melted butter, salt and pepper to taste, and a little nutmeg. Cover with plastic wrap and refrigerate several hours or overnight.

Take a little of the mixture, roll it in flour, then drop into a barely simmering pot of lightly salted water. If it holds together and rises to the top after about 5 minutes, you're ready to go. If not, add a little more flour to the mixture and proceed.

Spread flour onto a smooth, clean work surface, and lightly roll mixture out in ropes about ¾ inch thick. Cut them in 2-inch lengths, rolling well in flour. Drop in batches into barely simmering pot—there should be plenty of room for them to cook. They are done when they rise to the top—about 5 minutes. With some melted butter lightly grease a shallow casserole large enough to hold them all, or individual ramekins and sprinkle lightly with a little Parmesan cheese. Remove gnocchi with a slotted spoon to casserole as they cook. When they are all done, dribble with remaining melted butter and sprinkle with Parmesan cheese.

These may sit, covered well, 1 hour or so. To cook, heat oven to 375° and bake 10 minutes, until hot through.

Polenta

Most recipes call for ordinary American cornmeal for this, but for me, the point of eating polenta is the texture you feel by using coarse-milled Italian meal that turns creamy rather than mushy, with little granules rather like the ones in tapioca pudding. It can be found in any Italian market, of course, at unbelievably low prices, and if none is that handy, sometimes it can be found in health food stores. It's worthwhile laying in a supply, for polenta is every bit as good as pasta, and much more easily prepared.

Many recipes these days seem to call for cooking it in chicken stock or milk, both of which are absolutely unnecessary. At the most, polenta needs only a bit of cheese to perk up the flavor. However, there are variations that are sometimes fine to try. You can pour the polenta in layers, with Parmesan, Romano, or a creamy cheese such as Fontina in the middle. This can be set aside and reheated in a 350° oven until the top begins to take a little color and the cheese melts in the middle. Sautéed mushrooms may also be used as a filling.

In Italy, they often deliberately make too much polenta so it can be cooled in a pan of any shape, then cut in wedges and fried the next day. This is particularly pleasing, and either butter or olive oil can be used. I learned the easy wonders of polenta years ago and certainly cook it as much as pasta. Here are some of my favorite ways to serve it.

Basic Polenta

SERVES 4

¾ *cup coarse milled polenta*
4 *cups water*
salt
3–4 *tablespoons grated Parmesan cheese* (*optional*)

Combine polenta and water in a large saucepan, turn on heat, and bring to a boil, stirring now and again. As it begins to thicken stir steadily so that no lumps are formed. Turn heat to low until the polenta makes just a gentle *plop plop* as it cooks. (You will see the need for a large saucepan at this time because some of these plops can be volcanic.)

Stir every 5 minutes or so, and if the polenta seems too thick and begins to stick to the sides of the pan, add a little more water. Cook 30–45 minutes, depending on the mill of the meal used. Polenta is done when it's a thick and creamy mass with individual particles still with a little bite to them. Toward the end, add salt to taste and Parmesan cheese if you wish a little added flavor.

In Italy, the polenta is poured out on a slab, usually marble, and cooled slightly, then cut with a thread into wedges. This is not necessary—I use 2 pie pans that have been lightly wetted, and cut with a knife.

Fontina Polenta

SERVES 4

1 *recipe for Basic Polenta*
 (see above)
1 *cup sliced Fontina cheese*
 (or Swiss, Jack, or
 Cheddar)
2 *tablespoons butter,*
 melted
grated Parmesan cheese
Home-Style Tomato Sauce
 (page 189)

THIS, A WONDERFULLY RICH DISH, AT ITS BEST WITH FONTINA CHEESE, CAN BE MADE WITH ANY BITS AND PIECES OF CHEESE AT HAND AS LONG AS THEY MELT WELL AND DO NOT BECOME STRINGY (AS MOZZARELLA TENDS TO DO). BITS OF SAUSAGE, COOKED MUSHROOMS, OR ROAST MEATS MAY BE INCLUDED, AND OF COURSE IT IS VERY GOOD WITH LEFTOVER BEEF GRAVY IN PLACE OF THE TOMATO SAUCE. FOR VERY LITTLE, IT MAKES A COZY WINTER MEAL.

Prepare polenta. Preheat oven to 375°. Use some of the butter to grease a 9-inch cake pan and layer half the polenta, while still warm, smoothly into the pan. Lay Fontina cheese over, sprinkle with a little more butter, then layer remaining polenta on top. Sprinkle with Parmesan cheese and dribble remaining butter on top.

Bake 15 minutes, or until the top is bubbly and has started to become golden. Serve in wedges on a pool of tomato sauce.

THIS WILL GIVE YOU SOME IDEA HOW LITTLE MEAT IS NECESSARY, AS LONG AS IT IS TASTY AND HAS SOME SAUCE, WHEN THERE IS A STEAMING SLAB OF POLENTA ON THE PLATE.

Polenta with Sage Chicken Wings

SERVES 4

1 *recipe for Basic Polenta (page 214)*
12 *chicken wings*
2 *tablespoons butter*
2 *tablespoons vegetable oil*
4 *bacon slices, cut in small strips*
salt and freshly ground pepper
1 *cup dry white wine*
½ *teaspoon dried crumbled sage (not powdered)*

Prepare polenta. Keep covered in a warm place until needed. While it cooks, cut tips off chicken wings and pat dry with paper towels. Melt butter and vegetable oil in a large frying pan over medium-high heat. When it sizzles, add wings and bacon, and fry until wings are golden on both sides.

Salt and pepper to taste, add wine, and let it bubble up. Add sage, then turn heat down to a simmer. Cover pan and cook 20 minutes, or until wings are tender.

Pour out polenta on a board or plate, cut in wedges, and serve each with 3 wings and some pan juices poured over.

Sparerib Sauce for Polenta

THE FIRST TIME YOU MAKE THIS WONDERFUL SAUCE YOU WILL BE TEMPTED TO ADD SOME ONION, A LITTLE GARLIC, MAYBE A PINCH OF BASIL, AS YOU WOULD TO ANY OTHER SAUCE. BUT PLEASE TRY IT SIMPLY THIS WAY FIRST, FOR IT IS SURELY ONE OF THE MOST FLAVORFUL SAUCES IN THE WORLD JUST AS IS. IT CAN BE USED WITH PASTA, BUT IT'S PERFECT FOR POLENTA.

SERVES 4

1½ pounds spareribs, cut in 3-inch lengths
2 tablespoons olive oil
1 cup dry red wine
1 28-ounce can Italian plum tomatoes
¼ teaspoon red pepper flakes
salt and freshly ground pepper

When buying the ribs have the butcher cut them down the center—you can cut them into single rib sections at home. Heat olive oil in a frying pan and sauté ribs until golden all over. Remove them and place in a stove-top casserole. Stir wine into frying pan to loosen any bits, then add it to ribs. Place tomatoes in the pan, juice and all, and mash them with a potato masher. Add to the rib pot with red pepper flakes and salt and pepper to taste.

Simmer the pot, uncovered, about 2 hours, or until you have achieved a rich dark sauce. Serve ribs at the side of polenta wedges, with sauce poured over polenta.

REMEMBER THIS RECIPE WHEN YOU HAVE ONLY A FEW KIDNEYS TUCKED AWAY IN THE FREEZER AND NEED A QUICK AND EASY MEAL FOR PENNIES.

Lamb Kidneys, Italian Sausage, and Polenta

SERVES 4

1 *recipe for Basic Polenta (page 214)*
4 *lamb kidneys*
2 *sweet Italian sausages*
4 *green onions*
¼ *cup dry vermouth (or white wine)*
⅓ *cup heavy cream*
salt and freshly ground pepper

Prepare polenta. Keep covered in a warm place until needed.

Slice kidneys in half lengthwise. Cut out all white knobs and cut each half in slices. Cut sausages in ¼-inch slices. Mince white part of the onions, then separately mince about 2 inches of green tops for garnish.

Put sausages in a frying pan and cook over medium heat until they release fat and start to brown. If too much fat accumulates, tip out all but a couple of tablespoons. Add kidneys, turn heat up high, and toss 2–3 minutes, or until they lose their pinkness. Add onions, stir another few minutes, then scoop sausages and kidneys onto a warm plate with a slotted spoon.

Add vermouth to the pan and cook over high heat until it reduces by half, then add cream and cook until sauce begins to thicken slightly. Add salt and pepper to taste. Serve meats at the side of a warm wedge of polenta, with sauce poured over both and a sprinkle of green onion on top.

Salt Cod and Swiss Chard with Polenta

SERVES 4

1 *pound salt cod*
1 *recipe Fontina Polenta
   (page 215), cooked with
   Romano cheese*
flour
¼ *cup olive oil*
2 *cloves garlic, minced*
2 *shallots, minced*
1 *bunch Swiss chard*
½ *cup chopped canned
   tomatoes, drained*

A GOOD FRIEND BROUGHT THIS ADMIRABLE DISH BACK WITH HIM FROM A CHICAGO VISIT, AND TOLD ME HOW TO COOK IT. THE NORTHERN ITALIAN HOUSEHOLD FROM WHENCE IT COMES INDICATED THAT SWISS CHARD IS SOMETIMES OMITTED, AND MUSHROOMS OR TINY BROWN BARI OLIVES ARE USED INSTEAD—BUT THEY ALWAYS USE THE FINEST PECORINO ROMANO IN THE POLENTA. IT IS A FABULOUS TREAT!

Soak cod at least 4 hours in a large bowl of water, changing water every hour. Taste a piece, and if it is still salty, change water and soak until it seems right (though you don't want to leach out *all* the salt). The length of time will depend on the kind of cod you get—some pieces hard as a bone will take nearly 12 hours.

Prepare polenta with Romano cheese, cover, and keep warm until needed. Skin and bone cod, if necessary, then cut into serving portions and dust lightly with flour. Put olive oil in a large frying pan and sauté cod 3–4 minutes a side over medium heat, then lift out onto a plate. Add garlic and shallots to the pan and cook several minutes.

Wash Swiss chard well and cut out stems (reserve them for a salad or soup), then chop leaves in coarse shreds. Add to the pan and cook several minutes, until they begin to wilt, then stir in tomatoes. Put cod back in, cover the pan, and cook 5 minutes over low heat. Serve over wedges of polenta.

Oxtails with Celery and Polenta

Oxtails with a rich, meaty sauce are also perfect partners with polenta. I first had this dish in Rome's Trastevere district, where it is famous. They were the first oxtails I'd ever eaten, and I found them so delicious I not only dug up this recipe, with its fine contrast of the soft and rich meat with the tender-crisp sweet celery, but also began a long file of other oxtail recipes.

SERVES 4

3 *pounds oxtail, cut in pieces*
1 *tablespoon vegetable oil (or lard)*
2 *slices bacon (or some salt pork), cut in small strips*
1 *medium onion, chopped*
1 *clove garlic, minced*
1 *carrot, chopped*
1 *tablespoon minced parsley*
salt and freshly ground pepper
1 *cup dry white wine*
3 *tablespoons tomato paste*
8 *celery stalks, cut in 1-inch pieces*
1 *recipe for Basic Polenta (page 214)*

Pat oxtails dry with paper towels. Heat oil in a large frying pan and sauté oxtails over high heat until seared on all sides. Lower heat and remove to an oven-top casserole with a slotted spoon. Add bacon, onion, garlic, carrot, and parsley to frying pan and cook slowly several minutes, then add to the oxtails. Sprinkle with salt and pepper to taste.

Add wine and tomato paste to frying pan and cook several minutes, scraping up bits left in the pan, then pour over oxtails. Add enough water to come up almost to the top of the meat, cover pot, and simmer 4 hours, or until meat is almost falling off the bone. (I use a pressure cooker for this, with no added water, and cook 2 hours.)

Toward the end of this cooking time, prepare polenta. Cover and keep in a warm place until needed. When meat is tender, add celery pieces and cook, uncovered, 10–15 minutes, or until done but with still a little crispness to them. Serve with wedges of polenta.

Home Pizza

I admire pizza as much as anyone (and doesn't everyone?), but I used to think of it as impossible to make at home, that it took unglazed tiles and a special paddle, that only an expert could shape it, that it could never be as good as a restaurant's. Nonsense: It takes the simplest equipment, a regular oven, a bit of stretching here and there, and you can have something better than most of what you order out for. Best of all, pizza can be topped with practically anything, using up leftovers ranging from meat to dried-up cheese to vegetables, and you have a meal that costs practically nothing.

I'll give three recipes for crusts, but you really don't need a recipe for toppings. Though there are several things to keep in mind as you construct. First, the crust should be brushed with either oil or tomato sauce (or both) to lubricate the bread and keep it crisp and flavorful. But remember that the tomato sauce—homemade or canned—should be thick. In fact, nothing on the crust should be soupy, or the result will be a soggy pizza.

Second, the cheese. Everybody thinks you need mozzarella for pizza, but it's practically impossible in this country to find fresh mozzarella, and what is available is usually pretty tasteless and melts to strings. The humble Monterey Jack is better, but any cheese that melts well (and some that don't melt at all, such as feta) can be used. Parmesan, even, is not absolutely necessary, though I think it melds the whole together.

Third, I like to sauté any vegetables, such as onion, garlic, or green peppers, just slightly to avoid their being underdone. But vegetables may be cut very thinly and placed on top, and still come out well. Garden ripe tomatoes rather than tomato sauce can be sliced and used, but they should be drained before so they won't make the crust soggy.

Fourth, all toppings should be out in array before you roll out the dough. Never make a topping more than ½ inch thick, and remember, you don't have to use the whole refrigerator every time. In fact, the more you make pizza, the more you find that simplest is often best. I used to be invited to pizza parties by a writer in Carmel, and she made mountainous and indigestible pizzas, delighting in odd combinations. After the one with pickles, anchovies, and bananas (yes, bananas!), I refrained from attending another party there.

One of the finest toppings is a spread of olive oil, some Pesto sauce, a sprinkle of good black olives, and then some Parmesan cheese. Neither does the topping have to be Italian. Californians stick in their famous avocados, and a Greek lady I know makes one with feta, Kalamata olives, and anchovies. In the Southwest there is no reason not to use red chile sauce, minced fresh coriander and jalapeños, Monterey Jack cheese, and maybe even a bean or two. Why not?

Fifth, any pan can be used. The recipes here are all enough to make one 12-inch round pizza, and that can fit on a regular baking sheet. A double recipe, though, may be fit up to the edges of a jelly roll pan (11 inches by 17 inches) and be cut into squares rather than wedges. The sheet should be oiled lightly and does not need a dusting of cornmeal—though this gives character to the pizza.

Sixth, the dough should rise at least once, but it isn't something that has to be timed to the minute. It can rise a second time, and that second time can be in the refrigerator. You can, for instance, let it rise as long as possible in the evening, cover it well with plastic wrap, then refrigerate it for next evening's meal. If so, the dough should be punched down and let sit for an hour or so before rolling out.

With that in mind, here are three different crusts.

Basic Pizza Dough

1 *teaspoon granulated
    yeast*
⅔ *cup warm water*
2 *tablespoons olive oil*
¾ *teaspoon salt*
1½ *cups flour (or more)*

Dissolve yeast in water in a warm bowl. When it starts to bubble up, stir in olive oil, salt, and flour. Turn out onto a floured surface and knead 5 minutes or more. Add flour as necessary, but unlike bread, this dough should be as softly sticky as possible, so add only enough to make it behave.

Place the dough in a lightly oiled bowl, turn to coat with oil, cover with plastic wrap, and let rise until doubled, about 2–3 hours.

Preheat oven to 475°. Punch dough down and roll out on a lightly floured surface to a 12-inch circle, pinching out the edges to make them slightly thicker. (If the dough seems recalcitrant, let it rest a few minutes and try again.)

Place on a baking sheet, brush with oil, add toppings, slightly dribble a little more oil over, and bake about 20 minutes on the upper rack of the oven. Cook only until the edges and bottom are golden. Remove, let sit a few minutes, then cut into serving pieces.

Semolina Pizza Dough

This should be made exactly as the Basic Pizza Dough, but it will need a bit more yeast—about 1¼ teaspoons per pizza. Semolina flour (not the breakfast cereal) can be found at Italian markets and is the hard wheat flour used to make superior pasta. It also makes a wonderfully crusty pizza.

Whole Wheat Pizza Dough

This substitutes ½ cup of whole wheat flour for ½ cup of regular flour, and like Semolina Pizza Dough needs 1¼ teaspoons of yeast per pizza. It also gives a more crusty, nutty flavor.

My Antipasti

No one knows why some Italian cookbooks skimp on their starters. At any Italian inn the visitor finds a whole array of mysterious tidbits swimming in bowls of sauce or tempting from a shiny plate, bread to break, and sunlight in the wine. But hard to come by are the recipes for what glistens in these bowls and on these platters. Here, then, is a small collection of pleasures I've found over the years, little out of pocket.

Think about it. You go out and purchase prosciutto to wrap around the breadsticks or sliced melon, buy two or more cheeses and sausages, maybe green and black olives both wrinkled and smooth, some anchovies to crisscross over those bottled red peppers, and maybe some marinated fancy artichoke hearts, too. Already you've spent more than the whole meal put together. With very little work, you can instead serve something company and family will appreciate even more, and complete the meal with some pasta or polenta dish, then some such fruit dessert as Custard Apples (page 342) or Italian Glazed Oranges (page 346) with coffee.

First lay out the plates on your counter. Make a base of lettuce, or better yet raggedy chicory leaves. On them put piles of contrasting colors and texture, then shave a little Parmesan or Romano cheese over, if you have some. Tuck in a pickled pepper or cherry tomato. Finally, dribble a little extra olive oil around, just bless with vinegar. Crostini or Focaccia are extras for the lucky, and to be passed separately.

FOR THOSE ABLE TO GET FENNEL, THIS IS NOT ONLY A GREAT
ADDITION TO ANTIPASTI BUT IT ALSO MAKES A FINE SALAD ANYTIME.
FENNEL IS SO FRESH AND LIVELY TASTING YOU DON'T NEED A
FULL-SCALE VINAIGRETTE HERE, ONLY A LITTLE MOISTENING.

Fennel and Radish Salad

SERVES 4–6

1 *bulb fennel*
1 *tablespoon white wine
   vinegar*
2 *tablespoons olive oil (or
   vegetable oil)*
1 *bunch radishes*

Trim fennel bulb and cut vertically into thin slices. Cut
each slice into julienne strips and place in a bowl. Toss
with wine vinegar and olive oil, and refrigerate 30 minutes
or more. Somehow I don't think this needs salt or pepper,
but you might.

Clean and trim the radishes, and cut into thin slices. Toss
with fennel and serve either cold or at room temperature.

Tuscan Beans and Tuna

THE BEANS USED IN TUSCANY ARE ELUSIVE IN THIS COUNTRY, BUT THEY ARE NOT NECESSARY FOR THIS FAMOUS FLORENTINE ANTIPASTO. I'VE GIVEN THE SIMPLEST VERSION HERE—OTHER VERSIONS SEASON THE BEANS WITH HERBS SUCH AS BASIL AND OREGANO, AND MAY TOSS IN A FEW TOMATOES, CHOPPED GARLIC, MINCED PARSLEY, ANCHOVIES—YOU NAME IT.

SERVES 4–6

¾ *cup dried white beans*
  (small or large)
 1 *clove garlic, peeled*
 1 *sprig of fresh rosemary*
  (or ½ teaspoon dried)
salt
½ *cup minced green onions*
  including part of tops
⅓ *cup olive oil*
 1 *tablespoon white wine*
  . *vinegar*
freshly ground pepper
 1 *6½-ounce can chunk*
  tuna (packed in oil)

Soak beans in plenty of water overnight. The next day, bring to a boil, add garlic and rosemary, lower heat, cover, and simmer until nearly soft. This will take 2–3 hours. Add salt to taste, cook another 15 minutes or so, then drain and place in a bowl. Stir in onions, olive oil, wine vinegar, and freshly ground pepper to taste. Let sit in the refrigerator for 1 hour or so to gather flavor.

To serve, drain tuna and cut into rather large chunks. Toss lightly into beans and serve cold or at room temperature.

A TRUSTY DISH THAT MAKES AN EASY PICKLE FOR A PLATTER. ANOTHER I LIKE TO SERVE, THOUGH IT IS NOT ITALIAN, IS ZUCCHINI JOSEPHINE (PAGE 315).

Marinated Zucchini

SERVES 4–6

4 *medium zucchini*
2 *tablespoons olive oil*
¼ *cup parsley*
1 *teaspoon dried basil (or
   1 tablespoon fresh)*
2 *cloves garlic*
*salt and freshly ground
   pepper*
½ *cup red (or white) wine
   vinegar*

Wash and trim zucchini, then cut into ¾-inch pieces. Heat olive oil in a frying pan and cook zucchini in batches over medium-high heat until lacy golden on each side. This will take about 3 minutes a side—don't overcook, the zucchini should be resilient to a fork rather than mushy.

Place in a bowl. Mince parsley, basil, and garlic together and add to the bowl. Gently simmer wine vinegar 5 minutes, then add to the bowl and toss all together. Cover with plastic wrap and refrigerate, retossing now and again so zucchini marinates evenly. This is best after 24 hours.

THIS SOUTHERN ITALIAN SPECIALTY IS AS FINE TO EAT AS IT IS PRETTY
TO LOOK AT—SQUID CUT IN THIS MANNER CURLS UP INTO LITTLE
BUNDLES, IN A VINAIGRETTE SWIMMING WITH PURPLE TENTACLES.
HOW COULD YOU RESIST?

Marinated Squid

SERVES 4–6

  2 *pounds squid*
  3 *cups water*
½ *cup red wine vinegar*
½ *lemon, quartered*
  1 *bay leaf*
salt
½ *cup vegetable (or olive)*
   oil
  3 *garlic cloves, slightly*
   flattened and peeled
freshly ground pepper
¼ *teaspoon dried oregano*
  1 *tablespoon minced*
   parsley

Clean squid (page 69). Cut body sacs in half lengthwise, then cut tentacles so each is a separate strand. Put water, ¼ cup of wine vinegar, lemon, bay leaf, and a pinch of salt in a saucepan and simmer 5 minutes. Drop in squid bodies and tentacles and cook 30 seconds, then drain and place in a bowl.

Beat remaining ¼ cup of wine vinegar with vegetable oil, garlic, salt and pepper to taste, oregano, and parsley. Pour over squid, toss well, then cover with plastic wrap and refrigerate at least 2 hours before serving.

Crostini Ines Pirami

RUMORED TO HAVE THE BEST CROSTINI IN THE UNITED STATES, I TELEPHONED A FRIEND'S MOTHER FOR THIS. YOU CAN TALK ALL YOU WANT ABOUT CHOPPED LIVER, BUT TRY THESE AND MELT. THE CROUTONS NEED NOT BE HOT, AND THE LIVER CAN BE REFRIGERATED IF YOU LIKE BUT SHOULD BE BROUGHT BACK TO ROOM TEMPERATURE BEFORE SPREADING.

MAKES 18

½ pound chicken livers
3 tablespoons olive oil
salt and freshly ground
  pepper
1 teaspoon anchovy paste
  (or finely chopped
  anchovies)
1 tablespoon coarsely
  chopped capers
½ teaspoon white wine
  vinegar
18 thin slices French (or
  Italian) bread (or 9 slices
  cut in half if a large loaf)

Push livers through a sieve or whirl in a blender. Put 1 tablespoon of olive oil in a small frying pan over medium heat. Add livers and stir until they lose their pinkness, seasoning with salt and pepper as you stir—not too much salt because the anchovies and capers are salty.

Remove from heat. Stir in anchovies and capers, then put back on the heat, and mash and stir until as smooth as possible, adding remaining oil as you work. This should take only a few minutes. Finally, add wine vinegar and remove from heat.

Heat oven to 350°. Put bread slices in a baking pan and cook about 10 minutes, turning once, until golden and crispy. Spread liver paste on them and serve immediately.

San Francisco *Focaccia*

THIS GENOESE SPECIALTY SEEMS TO HAVE TAKEN FIRM ROOT IN SAN FRANCISCO WHERE I FIRST SAMPLED IT. FOCACCIA LOOKS LIKE A NUDE PIZZA, BUT DON'T LET THAT FOOL YOU, FOR IT MAKES A SPLENDID SAVORY BREAD TO SERVE WITH ANTIPASTI (OR EVEN TO MAKE A SAND-WICH). SOMETIMES I PICK UP A SLICE FROM THE MARKET, WARM IT A LITTLE IN THE OVEN, AND MAKE A LUNCH OF IT WITH OLIVES AND A TOMATO SALAD. IN GENOA, OTHER SEASONINGS ARE USED, SUCH AS ROSEMARY OR A STREW OF BLACK OR GREEN OLIVES, EVEN LITTLE SPECKS OF GORGONZOLA CHEESE—ALL POKED INTO DIMPLES IN THE DOUGH. BUT WHATEVER YOU USE, REMEMBER THAT THESE ARE SPARE SEASONINGS, NOT TO BE HEAPED UP LIKE PIZZA, AND MOST OF THE FLAVOR SHOULD COME SIMPLY FROM THE OLIVE OIL AND SALT. IF NEED BE YOU CAN LET THE DOUGH RISE THE SECOND TIME IN THE REFRIGERATOR SLOWLY, THEN TAKE IT OUT BEFORE THE MEAL AND LET REST FOR AN HOUR, BEFORE FORMING AND COOKING.

SERVES 2–4

1 *package granulated yeast*
⅔ *cup warm water*
2½ *cups unbleached all-purpose flour*
olive oil
1½ *teaspoons salt*
½ *cup green onion tops, sliced in ¼-inch pieces (or 10–12 fresh sage leaves chopped, or 1 teaspoon dried crumbled sage leaves)*
coarse sea salt (or Kosher salt)

Dissolve yeast in water. Put 1½ cups of flour in a bowl. When the yeast starts to puff, add it to the flour with 2 tablespoons of olive oil and salt. Stir to combine, dump out onto a floured board, and knead in as much flour as necessary to make a good stiff dough. Knead for 5 minutes or more, or until dough is elastic.

Place in a warm bowl that has been greased with a little olive oil and turn to coat the ball of dough. Cover with plastic wrap and let rise in a warm place until it doubles in volume. This will take 2 hours or so.

Punch dough down and let rise again until double—only about 1 hour this time. Punch dough down again and roll out to a 12-inch circle. Slip onto a floured piece of stiff cardboard. Sprinkle evenly with onion tops or sage and punch pieces down well into the dough with your fingers. Dribble 2 tablespoons of olive oil over, then sprinkle lightly with coarse sea salt.

Cover dough with plastic wrap. Heat oven to 400°. For best cooking you will need four 6-inch unglazed quarry tiles. (They are inexpensive and available at almost any tile store, they will give the focaccia the best crust.) Lay tiles in a square on the top rack of the oven and let them heat 30 minutes or so.

In a warm kitchen the focaccia should have puffed up by

the time the tiles are heated, if not, leave until it is as puffed as pizza dough. Slip it from the cardboard onto the tiles. Bake 20 minutes, or until the top starts to turn pale golden. Remove from the oven with a spatula and let cool 15–20 minutes before serving. It can also be served at room temperature.

Beanfests

E ven with bad press from Greek philosophers and modern quips from Don Marquis that there will be no beans in the Almost Perfect State (one suspects he had eaten only those of Boston), anyone with a head on his shoulders can figure out that dried beans and grains, along with some herbs of the field strewed over, are a mainstay to well-being when times are lean or winter blows outside the door.

With more and more dietary know-how, we've come to learn that "complex carbohydrates"—grains, nuts, seeds, and legumes—combined with each other or with dairy products, offer a complete protein with fewer saturated fats than meats, and the bonus of natural fiber. This translates to "they're good for you," and certainly inexpensive.

All colors stripes speckles shapes and flavors—I happen to like beans as beans, and am proud to say so, too. Sandwiched in affection somewhere between France's great Cassoulet and our own Southern Hoppin' John on New Year's Day is a stack of recipes I hanker for, recipes which rescue the sad reputation of the bean, recipes to be passed on, served up, recipes to please.

A MOUND OF WELL-SEASONED BEANS AND RICE, CURRIED BANANAS CURLING AROUND—WHAT MORE COULD YOU ASK FOR AS SUSTENANCE IN PARADISE . . . PERHAPS A SHAKE OF HOT SAUCE?

Kidney Beans Caribbean

SERVES 4

1 *cup dried kidney beans*
¼ *pound salt pork (or bacon), cut in ¼-inch dice*
2 *tablespoons vegetable oil*
1 *large onion, chopped*
2 *cloves garlic, minced*
1 *green pepper, chopped*
salt and freshly ground pepper
½ *teaspoon dried thyme*
1 *cup long-grain rice*
4 *bananas (not too ripe)*
4 *tablespoons butter*
½ *teaspoon curry powder*

Wash and pick over beans, then put them to soak overnight in plenty of water. The next day, add salt pork or bacon, bring beans to a boil, skim off any foam, then reduce heat and simmer, covered, a couple of hours—or until beans are just tender.

Put vegetable oil in a saucepan, add onion, garlic, and green pepper, and sauté over medium heat until onion starts to turn golden. Add salt and pepper to taste and thyme, and stir into the beans. Add rice and simmer, covered, 20 minutes.

Peel bananas and slice lengthwise. Heat butter in a large frying pan over low heat. Sauté bananas, cut side down, until starting to turn golden (about 2 minutes), then turn and cook another 2 minutes, sprinkling with curry powder as they cook.

Serve beans and rice in a mound on a plate with banana slices curving around it.

This is the original "rib-sticking dish," the one for which you should break out the homemade cornbread and slaw for, along with a keg of beer.

Spareribs with Red Chile Beans

SERVES 4

2 *cups dried kidney beans*
salt
2 *pounds pork spareribs*
2 *tablespoons vegetable oil*
1 *large onion, chopped*
3 *cloves garlic, minced*
2 *tablespoons chili powder*
freshly ground pepper
1 *8-ounce can tomato sauce*

Wash and pick over beans for small stones, then put to soak overnight in plenty of water. The next day, bring to a boil, skim off any foam, then reduce heat and simmer, covered, a couple of hours—or until beans are just tender. Add salt to taste and cook another 15 minutes or so.

Preheat oven to 350°. Cut ribs into one-rib sections. Put vegetable oil in a large frying pan and sauté ribs over high heat until brown and crusty. Remove to a plate, lower heat, and sauté onion and garlic in the same fat, until onion wilts. Return ribs to the pan and sprinkle with chili powder and salt and pepper to taste. Toss well and place in a baking dish.

Drain beans, saving their cooking liquid. Put beans over ribs and onions, top with tomato sauce, and add enough cooking liquid to moisten them well. Cover with foil or a lid and bake 1 hour and 15 minutes. When done most of the liquid should be absorbed, and the ribs will give off a wonderful aroma.

Bruschetta with Kidney Beans

BRUSCHETTA AT ITS MOST SPARTAN USES A SALTLESS TUSCAN BREAD OF A ROUGH COUNTRY CAST. GARLIC IS RUBBED WELL INTO IT AFTER BEING TOASTED OVER SMOKY FIRE, THE BEST VIRGIN GREEN OLIVE OIL IS THEN DRIBBLED OVER FROM A CRUET. A FEW GREEN OLIVES, A GLASS OF CHIANTI, A SUNNY TERRACE, AND YOU HAVE A TASTE OF A LIFETIME. THRIFTY TUSCANS ALSO MAKE A SIMPLE MEAL OF THIS WITH A TOPPING OF SEASONED BEANS AND SWISS CHARD STIR-FRIED WITH MORE GARLIC OR, AS IN THIS CASE, WITH CHEESES. EVEN WITHOUT THE MOST AUTHENTIC BREAD, A GLOWING GRILL OR FIREPLACE EMBER, THIS MAKES A SUPERB ROBUST SUPPER, NEEDING ONLY SOME SALADRY AND A GLASS OF WINE (CHIANTI OR NOT).

SERVES 4

1 *cup dried kidney beans*
salt
¼ *cup salt pork*
cloves garlic
2 *tablespoons parsley*
¼ *teaspoon dried basil*
¼ *teaspoon dried oregano*
1 *cup chopped canned tomatoes, drained*
8 *1-inch slices French bread, cut at a diagonal*
olive oil
1 *cup grated mozzarella cheese (or Fontina)*
¼ *cup grated Parmesan cheese*

Sort and cook beans according to preceding recipes, or you can use 2 cups of canned beans if you can find the Italian ones with no sugar. If you cook the beans, drain off any extra cooking liquid—they should just be covered with it—and add salt toward the end of cooking.

Chop salt pork, 1 clove of garlic, and parsley finely and add to beans with herbs and tomatoes. Simmer, covered, 30 minutes.

The Italians toast the bread over a grill or fireplace embers, but lacking these, it can be toasted under an oven broiler—just until crusty outside but still soft in the middle. Cut some garlic cloves and rub into bread, using as much as you like. Sprinkle lightly with olive oil.

Place in a shallow casserole, top with beans, sprinkle with mozzarella and Parmesan cheeses, then broil until cheeses melt. Serve immediately.

WHAT IS THERE TO MAKE THIS DISH SO GOOD IT COULD STRETCH WELL OVER SIX, ON A BED OF RICE? IS IT THE LARD, THE PAPRIKA, OR THAT FINAL SPLASH OF WINE VINEGAR? MAYBE IT IS ALL THREE.

Hungarian Bean Goulash

SERVES 4

1 *pound dried red beans*
2 *ham hocks*
1 *carrot, peeled and chopped*
1 *large onion, chopped*
2 *cloves garlic*
6 *sprigs of parsley*
½ *teaspoon dried thyme*
1 *bay leaf*
3 *tablespoons lard (or butter)*
½ *cup chopped onion*
2 *cloves garlic, minced*
3 *tablespoons flour*
2 *tablespoons paprika*
½ *cup minced parsley*
2 *tablespoons red (or white) wine vinegar*
salt and freshly ground pepper
Tabasco
sour cream

Wash beans and pick over, then soak in plenty of water overnight. The next day, add ham hocks, carrot, and onion. Also add, tied in a cheesecloth bag, garlic, parsley, thyme, and bay leaf. Bring to a boil, skim off any foam, then lower heat and simmer 2–3 hours, until tender. When soft, drain beans and measure liquid. There should be 2 cups, but if not add enough water to make it up. Shred meat from the hocks and return it to the beans.

Add lard to a large saucepan and cook chopped onion and minced garlic until wilted. Stir in flour and cook several minutes, stirring, then take off the heat and stir in paprika. Add bean liquid and stir until you have a smooth thickened sauce. Add beans and simmer 10 minutes. Finally, add minced parsley, wine vinegar, and salt and pepper to taste. Add a squirt of Tabasco—the beans should be faintly hot and tart. Serve with dollops of sour cream on top.

THE FRENCH NEARLY ALWAYS ACCOMPANY THEIR ROAST *GIGOT* WITH WHITE BEANS TO ABSORB THE COOKING JUICES, FOR THEY ARE NEAR PERFECT COMPANIONS. HERE, BOTH SHARE A POT FOR MAXI-

White Beans with Breast of Lamb

MUM SUC-CULENCE, AT LITTLE EXPENSE, IN ONE OF MY FAVORITE BEANFESTS. IF THERE'S ANY LEFT OVER, IT MAKES QUITE A LIVELY SOUP THE NEXT DAY WITH A BIT OF STOCK.

SERVES 4

1 *pound white beans (small or Great Northern)*
salt
1 *3-pound lamb breast*
2 *tablespoons vegetable oil*
1 *medium onion, chopped*
2–3 *cloves garlic, minced*
1 *teaspoon dried thyme*
¼ *teaspoon dried basil*
¼ *teaspoon dried summer savory*
6 *whole cloves*
1 *cup chicken stock*
½ *cup dry white wine*
salt and freshly ground pepper

Wash and pick over beans, then soak overnight in plenty of water. The next day, bring to a boil, skim off any foam, and simmer 2–3 hours, depending on beans, until just tender. Add salt to taste during last 15 minutes of cooking.

Cut any fell, and as much fat as possible, from lamb. Cut into rib sections. Put vegetable oil in a frying pan and cook ribs over high heat until crusty brown. Don't skimp on this procedure, for you need to get them to render out as much fat as possible. Remove them to a plate and pour all but 1 tablespoon of fat from pan.

Sauté onion and garlic in the fat for several minutes over low heat. When the onion is soft, scrape it into a large pot, then add herbs, cloves, chicken stock, wine, ribs, and salt and pepper to taste. Drain beans (reserving cooking liquid) and add to the pot. Add enough liquid just to moisten contents of the pot.

Cover and simmer about 1 hour over very low heat. If they dry out, add a little more liquid. When done the lamb should be fork tender and the beans will have absorbed most of the liquid.

NOTHING RESEMBLES THE SENSUOUS TRUE CASSOULET, WITH THE RANGE OF MEATS AND GOOSE FAT ALL MELTING TOGETHER IN INEFFABLE FLAVOR, BUT THIS STURDY LITTLE DISH HAS ENOUGH SAVOR TO RECOMMEND IT FOR A FAMILY MEAL NOW AND AGAIN. IF IT HAS NO COMPLEXITIES, IT HAS A FORTHRIGHT FLAVOR AND THE VELVET TEXTURE OF GOOD BEANS TO RECOMMEND IT. I MUST ADMIT, TOO, THAT I KEEP GOOSE FAT IN THE REFRIGERATOR TO SNEAK IN.

Poor Man's Cassoulet

SERVES 4

1 *pound Great Northern beans (or other dried white beans)*
1 *large onion, chopped*
2 *cloves garlic, minced*
2 *tablespoons bacon fat (or butter)*
1 *cup tomato sauce (Home-Style Tomato Sauce, page 189, or canned)*
salt and freshly ground pepper
¼ *teaspoon dried thyme*
½ *teaspoon dried basil*
1 *pound Polish sausage, sliced ⅛-inch thick*
minced parsley

Wash and pick over beans for stones, then soak overnight in plenty of water. The next day, bring to a boil, skim off any foam, then reduce heat and simmer 2 hours or more, until done. Drain beans of all but about ½ cup of cooking liquid.

Sauté onion and garlic in fat until soft, and add to beans, along with tomato sauce, salt and pepper to taste, and herbs and sausage. Cook covered, 30–45 minutes over low heat, or until rich and tasty. Taste for seasoning as it cooks because the beans are cooked without salt at first, and they will take some time to absorb it. You may find you have undersalted.

Serve sprinkled with parsley.

I LEARNED THIS RECIPE FROM A BRITISH COOK LONG AGO AND HAVE CONTINUED USING HER SECRET BIRDS WITH THE PALE GREEN STUFFING, JUST SLIGHTLY FRAGRANT WITH NUTMEG AND CINNAMON—UNMISTAKABLE YET HARD TO PUT A FINGER ON.

Haricot Beans with Bacon "Birds"

SERVES 4

 2 *cups small white beans*
12 *slices bacon*
½ *cup minced parsley*
 1 *clove garlic, minced*
freshly grated nutmeg
ground cinnamon
freshly ground pepper
salt (optional)

Wash and pick over beans, then soak overnight in plenty of water. The next day, bring to a boil, skim off any foam, and simmer until just beginning to get tender. Drain beans, saving the cooking liquid, and put them in a casserole.

Heat oven to 325°. Lay out bacon slices and sprinkle with parsley minced with garlic, then sprinkle with a little nutmeg, cinnamon, and pepper. Don't have a heavy hand with the cinnamon—only a whisper. Roll up bacon, fasten each "bird" with a toothpick, and lay rolls on top of the beans. Pour enough bean liquid to come just to the top of the beans.

Cover with foil or a lid and bake 3–4 hours, checking every now and again to make sure liquid has not all cooked away. If so, add some more bean juice or a little stock or water. During the last hour of cooking, uncover to let bacon brown.

Most bacon is salty enough to season the beans well, but check for salt during the last hour.

Remove toothpicks from bacon rolls and serve on top of heaped beans.

Midwestern Butter Beans and Onions

DURING THE DEPRESSION, MY MOTHER USED TO SERVE A DISH SIMILAR TO THIS, LADLED OVER A SLICE OF GOOD WHEAT BREAD TO SOAK UP THE JUICES. I STILL LIKE IT THAT WAY, THOUGH THESE DAYS I CONSUME IT WITH A GLASS OF WINE OR FULL-BODIED ALE, NEITHER OF WHICH WERE TO BE FOUND IN MY DRY KANSAS CHILDHOOD.

SERVES 6

1 *pound large dried lima beans*
1 *ham bone with meat* (or 2 *meaty ham hocks*)
4 *large onions, thinly sliced*
¼ *teaspoon dried thyme*
3 *bay leaves*
pinch of powdered cloves
pinch of powdered allspice
salt and freshly ground pepper
1 *cup minced parsley*

Wash and pick over beans, then soak overnight in water. The next day, bring to a boil, skim off any foam, then simmer 20 minutes. Add ham, onions, herbs, and spice, and enough water to come just to the top.

Simmer until beans are soft. This may take as little as 30 minutes or much longer, depending on freshness of the beans. Both the beans and the onions ought to retain their shape and not become mushy. Remove bone or hocks and shred the meat. Return this to the pot, season to taste with salt and pepper, and let sit until ready to serve.

Finally, stir in the parsley, heat gently, and ladle onto warm plates.

Sagebrush Beans

SOME FOLKS, WHEN THEY FIND OUT THAT I COOK, WONDER IF I'VE A RECIPE OR TWO FOR CASSEROLES. I REPLY THAT I KNOW MANY EASILY COOKED DISHES, IF THAT'S WHAT THEY WANT, BUT HARDLY ANY CASSEROLES AS SUCH. SO HERE IS AN HONEST-TO-GOD CASSEROLE, AND A VERY FINE ONE, TOO.

SERVES 4

  2 *cups dried lima beans*
     (*small or large*)
salt
  2 *tablespoons butter*
  2 *medium onions, thinly*
     sliced
freshly ground pepper
  1 *teaspoon dried crumbled*
     sage (*not powdered*)
  1 *cup grated Cheddar*
     cheese
  ½ *cup heavy cream*
  4 *slices bacon*

Wash and pick over beans, then soak overnight in plenty of water. The next day, bring to a boil, skim off any foam, then lower heat and simmer 2 hours or more, until tender. Add salt toward the end of cooking.

Preheat oven to 350°. Lightly grease a shallow casserole about 8 inches in diameter. Put butter in a frying pan and sauté onions until limp. Add a layer of half the beans, sprinkle with a little black pepper and half the sage, then top with onions. Cover with remaining beans, some more pepper, and remaining sage. Sprinkle with Cheddar cheese, pour cream over, and top with bacon slices.

Bake, uncovered, 30 minutes, or until bacon crisps.

USUALLY BEANS ARE COOKED WITH HAM, BUT FRESH PORK GIVES
ANOTHER SAVOR ALTOGETHER. IT CAN BE MADE WITH FOUR FRESH
HOCKS, BUT I LIKE THE SLIGHTLY GELATINOUS QUALITY THE FEET GIVE
WHEN I'M ABLE TO FIND THEM. A FULL TROTTER
WITH THE HOCK IS ABOUT A FOOT LONG, AND
YOU SHOULD HAVE YOUR BUTCHER CUT IT IN
2-INCH SECTIONS, THEN SAW THE FEET DOWN
THE MIDDLE.

Lima Beans with Fresh Pork Hocks

SERVES 4

1 *pound dried lima beans (large or small)*
2 *fresh pig's feet with hocks, split in half by butcher*
1 *large onion, chopped*
1 *green pepper, seeded and chopped*
3 *stalks celery, chopped*
3 *cloves garlic, minced*
1 *8-ounce can tomato sauce*
1 *bay leaf*
1 *teaspoon ground cumin*
salt and freshly ground
   pepper

Wash and pick over beans, then soak overnight in plenty of water. The next day, drain and reserve soaking water. Place pig's feet in a large kettle with water to cover and bring to a boil. Lower heat, skim off any foam that rises, then simmer about 1 hour.

Add drained beans and all the other ingredients, with salt and pepper to taste, and enough of the bean soaking liquid to cover ingredients by 1 inch. Simmer, covered, 1 hour, or until beans begin to get tender. Check for salt and pepper, and simmer, uncovered, another 30–45 minutes, or until beans are very tender.

Remove meat from hocks and serve it shredded alongside beans.

Chile Pasado

I WAS FIRST ATTRACTED TO THIS DISH BY ITS SIMPLE HONESTY IN THE MIDST OF A LADIES' CLUB CASSEROLE POTPOURRI, WHERE THE MAGIC IS USUALLY SUPPLIED BY PACKAGES OF DRIED ONION SOUP MIX, CANS OF CONCENTRATED MUSHROOM SOUP, GRAVY MIXES, AND GARLIC SALT GALORE. ANYONE ELSE, I FELT, WOULD HAVE JUST DUMPED IN A COMMERCIAL CHILI POWDER AND LET IT GO AT THAT. INSTEAD, WE HAVE A DISH COMPOSED OF ALL THE THINGS INCLUDED IN A CHILI POWDER, BUT EACH ADDED SEPARATELY AND WITH THE CARE ONE FINDS IN GOOD INDIAN COOKING WHEN EACH SPICE IS INDIVIDUALLY GROUND.

THE LARGE RED CHILES MAY BE THE COMMON NEW MEXICO, OR *ANCHO* OR *PASILLA,* IF THEY ARE AVAILABLE. THE ORIGINAL RECIPE CALLED FOR *CHILE TEPINA,* WHICH I INTERPRET AS ANY LITTLE RED ONES SUCH AS *SERRANOS* OR *CHILE DE ARBOL*—YOU COULD EVEN USE MINCED FRESH CHILES HERE. WHAT CAME OUT OF THE POT, AS IT COOKED, WAS A LOVELY PERFUME. AND WHEN TASTED, IT HAD A LIVELY FLAVOR OUT OF PROPORTION TO THE SIMPLE INGREDIENTS, WITH A HOTNESS THAT LINGERED SLIGHTLY ON THE TONGUE WITHOUT SEARING THE THROAT—A WONDER!

THE CHILE CAN BE SERVED IN BOWLS BY ITSELF OR LADLED OVER RICE ON A PLATE. IN EITHER CASE YOU WILL WANT TO HAVE AN ARRAY OF GARNISHES FOR IT: SHREDDED LETTUCE, SLICED RADISHES, CHOPPED GREEN ONION, SLICED AVOCADO, GRATED CHEESE, LIME WEDGES, AND SO FORTH. IT'S ALSO GOOD TO HAVE A STACK OF FRESH TORTILLAS STEAMED IN FOIL, WITH BUTTER TO SPREAD OVER THEM. IN ADDITION TO SERVING THE CHILE THIS WAY I FIND ANY LEFTOVERS EVEN BETTER THE NEXT DAY (OR MONTH, IF YOU FREEZE THEM) AS A TACO FILLING OR THE BASE FOR A TOSTADA, OR EVEN AS THE FILLING FOR A PUFFY TAMALE PIE. PORK IS ALSO FINE IN PLACE OF BEEF, THOUGH IT WILL NEED TO BE VERY LEAN OR THE STEW WILL BE TOO GREASY.

SERVES 8

1 *pound dried pinto beans*
4 *large dry red chiles*
1½ *pounds lean beef, cut in ½-inch cubes*
vegetable oil
2 *cloves garlic, minced*
1 *cup chopped onion*
1 *teaspoon dried oregano*
1 *teaspoon powdered cumin*
2 *small dry red peppers, crushed*
¼ *cup minced fresh coriander (optional)*
salt

Wash and pick over beans, then put in a large pot with enough water to come 2 inches over their top. Bring to a boil, cover pot, and boil 2 minutes, then turn heat off and let sit, covered.

Put large red chiles in a saucepan with 4 cups of water and cook 30 minutes over low heat. Drain, reserving cooking water. Remove stems and seeds from chiles, then scrape pulp from the skins into the chile cooking water.

Dry beef with paper towels and sauté in a large frying pan smeared with a little vegetable oil. These should be done in batches over high heat so the pieces sear and brown well. Remove to a plate as you cook the beef cubes. When done sauté garlic and onion in the pan in a little oil until the onion wilts.

Add the chile pulp water to the beans along with beef, garlic and onion, oregano, cumin, and crushed small chiles.

Simmer, covered, until beans start to soften—2 hours or so. Add coriander and salt to taste and cook, uncovered, another 2 hours or more. When done, most of the liquid will be cooked away, the beef will be very soft, and the beans will have started to disintegrate.

A SIMPLY-PUT-TOGETHER CASSEROLE WITH A GOOD ZING TO IT FROM THE BIT OF RED PEPPER, THE TOOTHSOME CHICK-PEAS, AND A FEW UNEXPECTED RAISINS. IT CAN BE STRETCHED TO SERVE SIX IF YOU SERVE IT ON A BED OF RICE.

Beef, Eggplant, and Chick-Pea Casserole

SERVES 4–6

1 *medium eggplant, peeled and cut in cubes*
salt
¼ *cup vegetable oil*
1 *large onion, chopped*
¾ *pound ground beef*
freshly ground pepper
½ *teaspoon red pepper flakes*
½ *teaspoon ground allspice*
1 *large can tomatoes, drained and chopped*
1 *large can chick-peas, drained*
2 *tablespoons raisins*
water or stock
1 *tablespoon red wine vinegar*
minced parsley

Put eggplant in a colander and sprinkle well with salt. Place over a bowl and let eggplant drain 1 hour, then rinse off under water and pat dry with paper towels. Heat vegetable oil in a frying pan and sauté eggplant 5 minutes, then lift out into a casserole.

Preheat oven to 400°. Add a little more oil, if necessary, and sauté onion in frying pan until soft. Place in the casserole as well. Add hamburger, turn up heat, crumble it with a fork as it cooks, and cook until all trace of pink is gone. As it cooks season to taste with salt and pepper, red pepper, and allspice. Put this in the casserole and stir in tomatoes, chick-peas, and raisins. Add about ¼ cup of water or stock.

Cover casserole and bake 30 minutes. Uncover and bake another 15 minutes, then stir in wine vinegar and taste for seasoning. Serve sprinkled with parsley.

Moors and Christians

THIS CUBAN DISH MAKES THE MOST OF TWO WORLDS; INDEED, IF ONE CONSIDERS THE CLOUDS OF SOUR CREAM AS HEAVEN, AND THE GREENERY TUCKED AROUND THE EDGE AS THE EARTH, IT BECOMES AN ALMOST COSMOLOGICAL DISH. BLACK BEANS CAN BE FOUND IN ALMOST ANY SPANISH MARKET AND MANY LARGE SUPERMARKETS, AND THEY ARE WORTH LOOKING OUT FOR. THEY REALLY DO HAVE SUCH A RICH TASTE AS TO ALMOST PRECLUDE ANY NEED FOR MEAT. FOR ACCOMPANIMENT BEER IS BETTER THAN WINE, AND YOU WILL NEED A FRESH LIGHT SALAD. DESSERT SHOULD ALSO BE LIGHT—BANANAS IN RUM (PAGE 345) WOULD BE PERFECT.

SERVES 4–6

- 2 *cups dried black beans*
- ¼ *cup diced salt pork (or bacon)*
- 1 *cup chopped onion*
- 2 *cloves garlic, minced*
- 2 *tablespoons minced fresh coriander*
- 2 *teaspoons chili powder*
- 2 *bay leaves*
- *salt and freshly ground pepper*
- 1 *cup beef stock*
- 2 *tablespoons chutney*
- *cooked rice*
- *sour cream*
- *sprigs of coriander*

Pick over beans and wash them well. Soak overnight in plenty of water. The next day, turn up heat, skim foam off the top when it comes to a boil, then turn heat low and cook, covered, 2 hours or so—just until they start to become tender. Drain beans.

Add salt pork, onion, garlic, coriander, chili powder, bay leaves, and salt and pepper to taste. Then add stock and enough water to just cover beans. Bring to a boil, turn down heat, and simmer, covered, another 2 hours. After 1 hour check beans, and if they have a lot of liquid, uncover pot. Add chutney, minced if it has large pieces like Major Grey's. When done, the beans will have started to disintegrate, so the pot is part whole, part creamy beans, and all the liquid should be absorbed.

To serve, cook ½ cup of rice in 1 cup of salted water for each person. On each plate make a ring of rice (the Christians) and ladle the Moors into the middle. Place a dollop of sour cream on top of the beans and garnish with sprigs of coriander. Extra chutney can be passed if you wish.

Picadillo *with* Beans and Rice

FROM BRAZIL, THIS IS DEFINITELY A PARTY, A COMPANY, DISH. YES, EVEN WITH BEANS AND GROUND MEATS. SPICY DISHES, I THINK, SHOULD BE SERVED WITH BEER RATHER THAN WINE. IF THEY'RE GOING FOR LITTLE AT THE MARKET, SLICED AVOCADOS OVER TENDER LETTUCE MAKES A FINE SALAD, AND YOU WILL WANT YOUR MOST FESTIVE DESSERT TO SERVE WITH COFFEE (FROM BRAZIL).

SERVES 6

1 *cup dried black beans*
salt
1 *tablespoon vegetable oil*
1½ *cups chopped onion*
1 *large green pepper, chopped*
3 *cloves garlic, minced*
½ *pound ground beef*
½ *pound ground pork*
1 *cup canned tomatoes, drained*
2 *tablespoons red wine vinegar*
pinch of sugar
½ *teaspoon ground cinnamon*
¼ *teaspoon ground cumin*
pinch of ground cloves
2 *tablespoons chili powder*
1 *bay leaf*
½ *cup raisins*
cooked rice
6 *bananas*
3 *tablespoons butter*

Wash and pick over beans, then soak overnight in plenty of water. The next day, bring to a boil, skim, turn down heat, and cook until soft, adding salt the last 15 minutes. Drain off most of the liquid.

Put vegetable oil in a saucepan and sauté ½ cup of onion, ¼ cup of green pepper, and 1 minced clove of garlic. Mix this with the beans and taste for seasoning.

Heat a frying pan over high heat and add meats. Stir to crumble them and cook until there is no more pink showing. Add remaining minced onion, green pepper, and garlic. Stir until onion is tender, then add tomatoes, wine vinegar, sugar, spices, bay leaf, and salt to taste. Cover and cook 30 minutes over low heat. If mixture becomes too dry, add a little stock or water. Add raisins, uncover pan, and cook another 10 minutes. When done the mixture should have absorbed all liquid.

Cook rice in your favorite manner—about ½ cup of uncooked rice per person should be enough. While it cooks peel bananas and slice them in half lengthwise. Sauté lightly in butter, just until golden on both sides. Keep warm.

To serve, place a mound of rice on each plate, put banana halves around the rice, flat side up, top with Picadillo, then put beans over top as a sauce.

IN INDIA, COOKS USE SEVERAL KINDS OF LENTILS AS WELL AS OTHER KINDS OF BEANS FOR "DAL." THIS RECIPE IS FROM AN OLD BRITISH COOKERY TEXT THAT CALLS FOR "BLACK-EYED BEANS." I DON'T KNOW WHETHER THIS TRANSLATES TO OUR "PEAS," BUT IT CERTAINLY MAKES A VERY FINE VEGETARIAN CURRY. IF YOU DON'T HAVE ALL THESE SPICES THAT MAKE IT SO SPRIGHTLY ON THE SHELF, GO AHEAD AND USE CURRY POWDER TO TASTE, WITH NO APOLOGIES TO THE PURISTS. THE DISH CAN BE SERVED WITH ANY CURRY ACCOMPANIMENTS YOU WISH, BUT YOU SHOULD CERTAINLY USE THE REST OF THAT PLAIN YOGURT TO MAKE A "RAITA" WITH GRATED CUCUMBER, MINCED GARLIC AND MINT, AND SALT AND PEPPER TO TASTE.

Curry of Black-Eyed Peas

SERVES 4

1½ *cups dried black-eyed peas*
salt
2 *tablespoons butter*
1 *large onion, thinly sliced*
1 *teaspoon turmeric*
1 *teaspoon ground ginger*
1 *teaspoon ground red chile*
½ *teaspoon ground cumin*
2 *teaspoons ground coriander seeds*
3 *tablespoons plain yogurt*
cooked rice

Pick over beans and wash them. Put in a pot with plenty of water, turn up heat, and let come to a boil. Cook 2 minutes, turn off heat, cover, and let stand 1 hour. Add more water if necessary to cover beans by 2 inches, turn up heat, let come to a simmer, then cook until tender—black-eyed peas need only about 30–45 minutes. Add salt to taste during last 5 minutes of cooking. Drain beans and reserve 2 cups of cooking liquid.

Heat butter in a large frying pan and sauté onions over medium-low heat until they start to turn golden. This will take about 15 minutes. Stir in all the spices and cook 5 minutes, then add beans, reserved cooking liquid, and yogurt. Taste for salt and simmer, uncovered, 10 minutes. Serve over cooked rice.

Spareribs and Black-Eyed Peas

AT THE MARKET ASK THEM TO CUT THE RIBS IN HALF, DOWN THE MIDDLE, THEN AT HOME YOU CAN KNIFE THEM INTO RIBLETS. THIS MAKES A HEARTY SAVORY STEW FOR BLUSTERY NIGHTS AND IS NOT AS MESSY AS IT SOUNDS BECAUSE BY THE END OF COOKING THE MEAT IS ALMOST FALLING OFF THE BONES, SO THEY DON'T HAVE TO BE PICKED UP BY HAND AS USUAL. WITH THE ADDITION OF A CRISP SLAW AND COLD BEER, THIS MAKES A MEAL YOU'LL WANT TO TRY AGAIN AND AGAIN.

SERVES 4

2 *cups dried black-eyed*
  peas
1 *medium onion*
4 *cloves*
salt
2 *pounds spareribs, cut in*
  3-inch lengths
2 *tablespoons vegetable oil*
2 *large onions, chopped*
2 *cloves garlic, minced*
½ *teaspoon dried red*
  pepper flakes
¼ *teaspoon dried crumbled*
  sage (not powdered)
¼ *cup tomato paste*
1 *cup beer*
pinch of sugar
½ *teaspoon wine vinegar*
freshly ground pepper

Pick over beans and wash them. Put in a kettle with plenty of water, turn up heat, and let come to a boil. Cook 2 minutes, cover, turn off heat, and let stand 1 hour. Add more water if necessary to cover beans by 2 inches, turn up heat, add onion stuck with cloves, and simmer, covered, until tender—about 30 minutes. Near the end of cooking add salt to taste.

In a large frying pan brown spare ribs in vegetable oil over high heat. Remove to the bean pot and sauté onions and garlic over medium heat until onion wilts. Add mixture to beans, along with red pepper, sage, tomato paste, beer, and sugar. Stir well, cover pot, turn heat low, and let simmer 45 minutes to 1 hour.

Peek every now and again to see there is enough liquid; if not, add some hot water—but not too much, for by the end all the liquid should be absorbed into the beans. Add vinegar and pepper to taste.

THIS DELIGHTFUL RECIPE WAS GIVEN TO ME BY PRINTER GLEN TODD (OR RATHER, I DRAGGED IT OUT OF HIM AFTER SEEING A JAR OF THE COLORFUL BEAN MIXTURE IN HIS KITCHEN.) IT IS CHOCK-FULL OF INEXPENSIVE FLAVOR, AND THOUGH IT IS CONSIDERED MORE A SIDE DISH IN TEXAS, IT MAKES A SPECIAL MEAL ON ITS OWN, WITH BEER AND EITHER TORTILLAS OR CORNBREAD TO ROUND IT OUT.

Texas Nine-Bean Chili Stew

SERVES 4

2 *cups basic mixture (equal parts white pea beans, small red beans, black beans, pinto beans, black-eyed peas, Great Northern beans, lentils, split peas, and pearl barley)*
2 *ham hocks (or a meaty ham bone)*
1 *medium onion, chopped*
2 *cloves garlic, minced*
1 *cup chopped canned mild green chiles*
½ *teaspoon dried oregano*
salt and freshly ground pepper
Tabasco
1 *cup chopped canned tomatoes, drained*
¼ *cup chopped green onions*
2 *tablespoons minced fresh coriander*
1 *tablespoon red wine vinegar*
1 *tablespoon vegetable oil*

Wash and pick over beans, then soak with plenty of water overnight. Next day, bring to a boil, skim off any foam, then simmer, covered, with ham, onion, and garlic until the largest beans are almost tender. Add chiles, oregano, and salt, pepper, and Tabasco to taste. Remove ham hocks and chop the meat, then return it to the pot. Cook another 30 minutes.

Combine tomatoes, green onions, coriander, wine vinegar, and vegetable oil, and salt and pepper to taste. Let sit 30 minutes to gather flavor.

Serve stew with some of the tomato-onion relish on top.

In a Pinch

When the bank account is low and you are worrying how to squeeze another meal from it, how do you put dinner on the table and still feel well fed? Asking around, I found different personal solutions to this. My own would be to lay out everything for a pot of pinto beans with all the southwestern trimmings— tortillas, cheese, chiles, lettuce, fresh coriander—for I never tire of the subtle variations to be pulled from that particular hat. Another person I know invests in a bag of brown rice and a load of vegetables from the farmer's market, and if her children grumble, at least they look bright and shiny.

Then there's my friend, the stand-up comic Paul Chopak, who believes The Refrigerator will always provide. "Like what," I ask. "Well, tonight I rendered some cubes of salt pork I discovered in the freezer. When they were crisp I took them out and stir-fried a bunch of Swiss chard in the fat, along with some fresh ginger, then I served that over rice sprinkled with the pork bits and a dash of soy sauce." I would never have thought of that.

The U.S. Department of Agriculture has a pamphlet available for the asking entitled "Making Food Dollars

255

Count, Nutritious Meals at Low Cost." But their reci-
pes! Consider Vegetable Fried Rice that stir-fries celery,
onion, and a package of frozen peas and carrots, and
then sprinkles the rice with Worcestershire sauce, garlic
powder, and salt and pepper. I would rather dine on
Paul's Dish any day.

KOSHERI, I'M TOLD, IS TRADITIONALLY SERVED BY STREET VENDORS
FOR A QUICK NUTRITIOUS MEAL. IT IS SURPRISINGLY TASTY, WITH A
LITTLE KICK FROM THE CHILES AND VINEGAR. I LIKE TO SERVE A
COLORFUL PLATTER OF IT, TO BE PUT IN PITA
POCKETS WITH A LITTLE CHOPPED LETTUCE.

Egyptian Kosheri

SERVES 4

¾ *cup dried lentils*
1 *cup long-grain rice*
¾ *cup elbow macaroni*
salt
3 *tablespoons vegetable oil*
1–2 *small fresh chiles (or 1–2 teaspoons dried chile flakes)*
½ *cup chopped green pepper*
1 *cup tomato sauce (homemade or canned)*
½ *cup water*
2 *tablespoons vinegar*
2 *cups chopped onions*

Cook lentils, rice, and macaroni separately in salted water until done: the lentils will take about 1 hour, the rice about 20 minutes, and the macaroni 12–15 minutes. Drain and reserve each at room temperature.

While they cook place 1 tablespoon of vegetable oil in a small frying pan and sauté chilies and green pepper 5 minutes over medium heat. Stir in tomato sauce, water, and vinegar. Simmer 15 minutes over low heat. Reserve and keep warm.

Heat remaining 2 tablespoons of oil in a medium frying pan and sauté onions over medium heat until tender and starting to turn golden—about 12 minutes. Salt lightly.

Combine lentils, rice, and macaroni, and stir together carefully. Serve in portions sprinkled with onions and topped with tomato sauce. Or you can put the mixture in a large bowl, turn it out on a platter, then sprinkle with onions and coat with tomato sauce.

Risotto Valtellina

FROM THE LOMBARDY REGION OF ITALY, THIS RECIPE MAY SOUND STODGY ON THE PAGE, BUT IT IS A MASTERPIECE OF HUMBLE INGREDIENTS AVAILABLE EVERYWHERE THROUGH THE WINTER. THOUGH CALLED A RISOTTO IT ISN'T COOKED LIKE ONE AND DOESN'T NEED FANCY ARBORIO RICE. TRULY A PEASANT FOOD, POETS MAY FEAST THEREON.

SERVES 4

¾ *cup dried red kidney beans*
salt
1 *small cabbage (1 pound)*
1½ *cups long-grain rice*
6 *tablespoons butter*
1 *sprig of sage (or ¼ teaspoon dried crumbled sage)*
grated Parmesan cheese

Soak beans overnight, then simmer until almost tender. Add salt to taste and finish cooking until done. These can be prepared at any time and reheated for the completed dish. Canned beans may be used, but they should be an Italian brand that does not include sugar.

Cut cabbage in quarters and knife out the cores. Drop in a pot of boiling salted water and cook 2 minutes. Drain and cut into coarse shreds. Add rice to a pot of boiling water and cook 5 minutes. Add cabbage and cook 15 minutes at a lively boil. Drain cabbage and rice, and mound on a platter. Surround with a ring of beans and keep warm in the oven.

Melt butter in a small pan and cook sage over low heat until it turns golden—the butter should not brown. If you don't have fresh sage, add the dried and let the butter just bubble up. Pour this over rice and beans and sprinkle generously with Parmesan cheese.

Jansson's Temptation

SERVES 4

I'VE NEVER READ WHO JANSSON WAS, BUT THIS SCANDINAVIAN DISH IS CERTAINLY JOHNSON'S TEMPTATION. THOSE WHO DON'T THINK THEY LIKE ANCHOVIES WILL FIND THEM SO MELLOW HERE THAT THEY MIGHT THINK TWICE—AND OF COURSE THEY CAN ALWAYS USE THE PICKLED HERRING. IT MAKES A FINE SIMPLE FAMILY SUPPER, WITH A TOSSED SALAD AND A GLASS OF WHITE WINE OR FROSTY BEER.

4 *large potatoes, peeled and*
 cut as for french fries
1 *large onion, very thinly*
 sliced
1 *can flat anchovies (or 1*
 8-ounce jar pickled
 herring)
1 *cup heavy cream*
salt and freshly ground
 pepper
2 *tablespoons butter*

Preheat oven to 275°. Layer half the potatoes in a buttered baking dish. Add a layer of onion, a layer of anchovies or herring, then remaining potatoes. Mix cream with salt and pepper to taste (not too much salt, as the anchovies are salty) and pour over. Dot with butter and sprinkle with anchovy oil. Bake, covered, 1 hour, then continue baking, uncovered, 30 minutes.

Pig's Hocks and Feet with Sauerkraut

NOT AN ELEGANT DISH, CERTAINLY, AND NOT FOR EVERYONE. BUT I LIKE IT, WITH THE SAVORY, PORKY SAUERKRAUT AND CRISP GRISTLY FEET TO GNAW ON—ONE CAN ALMOST HEAR BESSIE SMITH SINGING IN THE BACKGROUND ABOUT THAT PIG'S FOOT AND BOTTLE OF BEER. IT WILL NEED PLAIN BOILED POTATOES, AND OF COURSE THAT BOTTLE OF BEER. . . .

SERVES 4

4 *pig's feet with hocks*
1 *pound sauerkraut (fresh or canned)*
1 *12 oz. bottle of beer*
½ *teaspoon caraway seeds*
salt and freshly ground pepper
bread crumbs
3 *tablespoons melted butter*
mustard

If you are able to get hocks with the feet attached, as I do, ask the butcher to cut the hocks away from the foot. Wash the feet, then tie them up in cheesecloth (this prevents the skin from breaking as they cook). Put sauerkraut in a colander and run cold water over it until a little of the sharp brine taste is gone but it still retains some tang.

Put hocks and feet in a large kettle, cover with sauerkraut, add beer and caraway seeds, and then enough water almost to cover. Cover kettle and simmer about 3 hours. Remove hocks and feet to cool. If the dish looks very watery, let it boil down until there is just a little liquid.

Remove flesh from hocks, tear it into shreds, and return to the pot. Taste for salt and pepper—if the sauerkraut is fresh, it probably won't need any salt at all.

Unwrap feet and split them vertically with a large knife. Salt and pepper them, roll in bread crumbs, and dribble with butter. Put under a broiler (about 5 inches) and turn them until golden all over.

Serve sauerkraut-hock mixture on a platter surrounded with crispy pig's feet. Pass a jar of mustard for the feet (and napkins, because they are eaten by hand).

FOR THIS RIB-STICKER YOU NEED SOME PLAIN BOILED POTATOES TO SHARE IN THE GOODNESS.

Transylvanian Casserole

SERVES 4

½ *cup long-grain rice*
salt
1 *pound ground pork*
2 *medium onions, chopped*
2 *cloves garlic, minced*
1 *tablespoon paprika*
freshly ground pepper
1 *pound sauerkraut (fresh or canned)*
1 *cup sour cream*
4 *slices bacon*

Cook rice in boiling salted water 12–15 minutes, then drain and reserve. While it cooks add pork to a frying pan and cook, stirring to break it up, until no pink shows. Add onions and garlic, and cook until soft. Add paprika and salt and pepper to taste. Remove from heat.

Preheat oven to 325°. Place sauerkraut in a colander and run water over it to leach out some of the salt. Taste it—it should still have some tang. Squeeze out the water with your hands. Mix sour cream with cooked rice.

Grease a casserole lightly and make layers of sauerkraut, then pork, then rice, ending with a layer of sauerkraut. Top with bacon and bake, covered with a lid or foil, 1 hour. Remove cover and bake another 30 minutes. Serve hot.

IF NOT AS PRETTY TO LOOK AT AS PLUMP ROLLS OF STUFFED CABBAGE, THIS STILL HAS ALL OF THEIR FLAVOR AND IS VERY EASILY PUT TOGETHER. IT CAN BE STRETCHED WITH A LITTLE MORE RICE, AND IF YOU HAVE THREE OR FOUR SAUSAGES RATHER THAN THE SPARE TWO, AND IF THE BOTTLE OF DRIED THYME IS AT HAND, OR A BAY LEAF. . . .

Unstuffed Cabbage

SERVES 4

1 *large onion, chopped*
1 *clove garlic, minced*
2 *tablespoons butter*
2 *Italian sausages*
½ *cup long-grain rice*
salt and freshly ground
    pepper
1 *small cabbage, coarsely*
    chopped
2 *tablespoons tomato paste*
½ *cup white wine (or beer)*
chicken stock
4 *slices bacon*

Preheat oven to 350°. Set a frying pan over medium heat and sauté onion and garlic in butter until wilted. Remove casings from sausages and mash them down into the onion-garlic mixture. Stir and mash until there is no more pink in the sausage meat. Meanwhile, cook rice in boiling salted water 20 minutes, then drain.

Layer ingredients in a casserole—first some cabbage, then some meat, then rice, with a sprinkle of salt and pepper as you go. End with a layer of cabbage. Mix tomato paste and wine, and pour it over, then add enough stock to come almost to the top. Place bacon slices over.

Cook, covered, 1 hour, or until most of the stock has been absorbed. Serve on warm plates.

A DELICIOUS PEASANT DISH, LIKELY TO MAKE A FAMILY MEAL IN
ALSACE WHEN PARTNERED WITH SMALL POTATOES BOILED IN THEIR
SKINS. IT CAN ALSO BE ENHANCED WITH WEDGES OF HARD-BOILED

French Wilted Cabbage Salad

EGGS IF YOU LIKE.
MOST OFTEN THE CAB-
BAGE IS TOSSED IN THE
COOKED BACON UNTIL IT WILTS, BUT THIS METHOD RECOMMENDED
BY RICHARD OLNEY IS BOTH EASIER AND MORE DEPENDABLE.

SERVES 3–4

1 *medium cabbage
(about 2 pounds)*
8–10 *ounces slab bacon (or
thick-cut)*
½ *cup olive oil*
*salt and freshly ground
pepper*
¼ *cup white wine
vinegar*

Remove any limp outer leaves of cabbage, cut into wedges,
cut out core, and slice in thin shreds as for slaw. Place in a
bowl and pour boiling water over—enough to come to the
top of the cabbage. Cover with a lid or plate and let steep
about 10 minutes.

If you have slab bacon, trim off its rind and cut into
¼-inch strips. (Thick-cut or regular bacon need only be cut
into strips.) Place in a frying pan with a little olive oil and
cook over medium-low heat until crisp and golden.

Drain cabbage through a colander, wipe out warm bowl,
and return cabbage to bowl. Season with salt and rather a
lot of pepper, pour bacon and its fat over, and toss with
wine vinegar and remaining oil. Serve on warm plates.

Amish Washday Dinner

THIS IS A DOUR-SOUNDING LITTLE DISH—AMISH COOKS USED TO MAKE IT ON HEAVY WASHDAYS SINCE IT ALMOST COOKS ITSELF. BUT IT REALLY IS PRETTY GOOD IF YOU USE FINE POLISH SAUSAGE AND MAYBE TUCK IN A BAY LEAF.

SERVES 4

2 *tablespoons butter,*
  melted
1½ *pounds onions, sliced*
¾ *pound smoked sausage,*
  thinly sliced
1½ *pounds potatoes, sliced*
2 *tablespoons flour*
salt and freshly ground
  pepper
2 *cups tomato juice*
boiling water

Preheat oven to 300°. Butter a 1½-quart casserole lightly with some butter. Make layers of onions, sausage, and then potatoes. Sift flour over and add salt and pepper to taste. Pour tomato juice over, then add boiling water to cover potatoes. Dribble remaining butter on top.

Bake, uncovered, 3 hours. Every hour or so check to make sure the top layer isn't too dry—if so, spoon some cooking juices over. If it starts to brown too much, cover with foil.

Brabant Poor Boy Sandwich

CHEAP, FILLING, AND TASTY, THIS IS A NEW ORLEANS SPECIALTY BASED ON THEIR GARLICKY BRABANT POTATOES. IT IS NOT FOR EVERYONE—NOT FOR THOSE WHO SHUDDER AT THE "STARCH ON STARCH" OF BRITISH "CHIPS" SANDWICHES, OR EVEN MRS. BEETON'S TOAST SANDWICH FOR INVALIDS (TOAST BETWEEN TWO SLICES OF UNTOASTED BREAD, AN ADVENTURE IN TEXTURES). BUT SOME DOTE ON THIS POOREST OF POOR BOYS, AND WHY EVER NOT IF ALL YOU CAN AFFORD IS A HANDFUL OF POTATOES AND A FRESH CRUSTY LOAF?

SERVES 2

2 *large potatoes*
vegetable oil for frying
salt and freshly ground
    pepper
3 *tablespoons butter*
1–2 *cloves garlic, minced*
3 *tablespoons minced*
    parsley
1 *medium loaf French*
    bread
mayonnaise

Peel potatoes and cut into ½-inch dice. Drop into a bowl of cold water to wash off starch, then drain and dry on paper towels.

Preheat oven to 175°. Add about 1 inch of vegetable oil to a medium frying pan over high heat. When oil begins to shimmer, test a cube in it—the potato should sizzle up immediately and cook in earnest. Add all the potatoes and fry until golden. Turn once and again as they cook so they brown evenly. When done, lift out with a slotted spoon onto paper towels and sprinkle with salt and pepper.

Put butter in a small saucepan, add garlic, and cook over medium heat until garlic starts to turn light golden. Place potatoes in a baking dish and pour garlic butter over through a sieve, discarding the garlic. Toss with parsley and more salt and pepper if you wish.

Cook potatoes in the oven 15–20 minutes. Meanwhile, split loaf of bread and warm it in the oven during the last few minutes of cooking. Remove and spread with a thin coat of mayonnaise on both sides, then put potatoes on the bottom half, cover with the top half, and cut into serving portions.

Onion Rarebit

THIS SIMPLE MIDNIGHT SUPPER WAS TAUGHT TO ME BY THE LATE LONDON ARTIST BARBARA JONES, THOUGH HEAVEN KNOWS IT COULD BE SERVED ANYTIME, ANYWHERE. ITS SIMPLICITY OUGHT NOT TO BE TAMPERED WITH MUCH, THOUGH PERHAPS IT BENEFITS FROM A PINCH OF THYME ADDED TO THE ONION. ANY BREAD OR CHEESE MAY BE USED, BUT THE CHEESE SHOULD BE A MELTABLE ONE, NOT STRINGY. BARBARA USED TO SERVE THIS WITH GUINNESS, BUT HERE WE MUST MAKE DO WITH BEER.

SERVES 1

1 *medium onion, thinly sliced*
1 *tablespoon butter*
1 *slice bread (preferably whole wheat)*
salt
1 *slice cheese (sharp or mild)*
paprika

Preheat oven to 300°. Put onion in a bowl and cover with boiling water. After 4–5 minutes, drain and pat dry with paper towels. While onion sits, melt half of butter in a frying pan over medium heat. Turn bread slice so butter soaks in evenly, then fry until golden on both sides and starting to crisp. Keep warm on a plate in the oven.

Add remaining butter to pan and cook onion until pale gold, adding salt to taste as it cooks. Place onion on top of bread, top with cheese and a sprinkle of paprika, and put back in the oven until cheese melts.

Preziosini

SERVES 4

½ loaf French bread (about
    ½ pound)
 4 eggs
grated Parmesan cheese
 2 tablespoons fresh basil (or
    dried basil chopped with
    parsley)
salt and freshly ground pepper
olive oil (or vegetable oil)
tomato sauce, heated

THESE "LITTLE PRECIOUSES," SO CRISP AND LIGHT THEY ALMOST FLOAT OFF A PLATE, ARE A SPLENDID ITALIAN WAY TO USE UP A LOAF OF BREAD FROM THE NIGHT BEFORE, EVEN IF YOU'RE NOT DOWN TO YOUR LAST CENT. ANY KIND OF BREAD MAY BE USED, CRUSTED OR CRUSTLESS AS YOU CHOOSE, AND DON'T WORRY ABOUT THE OLIVE OIL BECAUSE REGULAR COOKING OIL TASTES JUST AS GOOD HERE.

Cut bread in pieces, put in a bowl, and cover with warm water from the tap. Let soak until tender, about 15 minutes. Squeeze water from bread with your hands, getting out as much liquid as possible. Measure it—you should have 3 cups of bread.

Put bread, eggs, 3 tablespoons of Parmesan cheese, basil, and salt and pepper to taste in a bowl and beat until quite smooth. (It can also be put through a food mill or whirled in a blender.)

Pour olive oil in a frying pan to a depth of about ¼ inch and heat until nearly smoking. Drop batter by a large spoon onto the hot fat and fry cakes 2–3 minutes on each side, or until crisp and brown. (There should be about 16 cakes, 2½ inches in diameter.) Drain on absorbent paper and keep warm.

Serve in a pool of tomato sauce sprinkled with more Parmesan cheese.

My Chick-Pea and Swiss Chard Dish

THIS CHICK-PEA SAUCE I LEARNED FROM A TUSCAN FRIEND WHO USES IT OVER PASTA—A VARIATION ON THE COMMON *PASTA E FAGIOLI* FOUND ALL OVER ITALY. AFTER MAKING A BATCH ONE DAY I HAD HALF OF IT LEFT OVER WITH NO PASTA ON HAND, AND I CAME UP WITH THIS DISH THAT I THINK SHOWS THE SUCCULENT SAUCE TO EVEN GREATER ADVANTAGE. MY APOLOGIES TO TUSCANY, BUT ANY DISH CAN BE IMPROVED UPON! AND I KNOW OF FEW WAYS I COULD DINE SO WELL ON SOMETHING LIKE TWENTY-FIVE CENTS A SERVING.

SERVES 4

1½ *cups dried chick-peas*
olive oil
　1 *medium onion,*
　　chopped
　2 *cloves garlic, minced*
　½ *teaspoon chopped*
　　dried rosemary (or 1
　　teaspoon fresh)
　2 *tablespoons tomato*
　　paste
salt and freshly ground
　　pepper
　4 *slices home-style white*
　　bread (or 8 slices
　　French bread)
1–2 *cloves garlic, slightly*
　　flattened and peeled
　1 *bunch Swiss chard*
　1 *tablespoon red wine*
　　vinegar (or lemon
　　juice)
grated Parmesan cheese

Soak chick-peas overnight in plenty of water. The next day, put in a pot, cover with water, bring to a boil, skim if necessary, then simmer until tender—a matter of some 3 hours. When done, drain, save cooking juices, and puree half of the beans by putting through a sieve, food mill, processor, or in a blender with some cooking juices.

Add ⅓ cup of olive oil to a saucepan, and when it sizzles over medium-low heat, add onion, minced garlic, and rosemary. Stir now and again to make sure they don't cook too quickly. Cook around 15 minutes, or until onion starts to turn golden. Add whole and pureed chick-peas, stir in tomato paste, and salt and pepper to taste. Simmer 30 minutes, adding a little of the cooking juices from time to time if necessary. The sauce ought to be stewlike, not runny.

Heat oven to 350°. Brush bread lightly with some olive oil, place on a baking sheet, and bake about 20 minutes, turning once. The bread should be crisp and starting to turn golden. Rub bread well with flattened garlic and keep warm.

Wash Swiss chard thoroughly and cut out stems. Slice these diagonally in 1-inch pieces and boil in salted water 5 minutes, then drain and run cold water over. Cut Swiss chard leaves in large shreds. Heat 2 tablespoons of olive oil in a large frying pan. Add stems, toss, and cook 1 minute. Add leaves to pan, tossing until just wilted—about 2 minutes. Toss with wine vinegar or lemon juice.

Serve sauce over the croutons, with Swiss chard arranged around. Sprinkle with Parmesan cheese and serve.

Mexican Ropa Vieja

Ropa Vieja is named for its likeness to old clothes. Tattered it is, but still very tasty. Its pound of beef could be any small roast you find on sale. And the recipe—alongside spicy beans topped with shredded cheese and lettuce, fresh hot salsa, radish slices, and so forth—feeds a small army.

SERVES 6–8

1 *pound beef chuck roast (or other inexpensive cut)*
salt
6 *peppercorns*
bay leaf
vegetable oil
1 *large onion, chopped*
1 *clove garlic, minced*
4–6 *jalapeño peppers (fresh or canned), seeded and minced*
1 *15-ounce can tomatoes, drained and chopped (juice saved)*
1 *teaspoon dried oregano*
1–2 *tablespoons red wine vinegar*
1 *cup red wine*
2 *large potatoes, peeled and cut in cubes*
2 *carrots, scraped and sliced*
minced fresh coriander (optional)
1 *dozen corn tortillas*

Put beef in a pot with water to cover, a strew of salt, peppercorns, and bay leaf. Turn heat high, and when it begins to bubble, lower to the merest simmer. Skim any foam off the top. Cover and cook about 2 hours, or until very tender when tested with a fork. Remove from heat and let come to room temperature. Lift meat out (reserving stock for soup sometime) and shred it with a fork and fingers to clumps about 1½ inches long.

Clean pot, and add 2 tablespoons of vegetable oil. Stir in onion and cook over medium heat, until softened, then stir in garlic and peppers. Add tomatoes, oregano, wine vinegar, wine, potatoes, and carrots, including some juice of tomatoes. Simmer, uncovered, about 20 minutes, or until potatoes and carrots are cooked. If it gets dry, add more tomato juice. Taste for vinegar and hotness, then adjust as you choose. Add beef and coriander, then heat through.

Stack tortillas and cut in half. Cut each of these half moons into ½-inch ribbons. Heat 1 inch of oil in a heavy frying pan until very hot and fry these strips until crisp, lifting out onto paper towels to drain as you cook a batch. Don't crowd them in the pan. Salt lightly as they drain.

To serve, sprinkle a layer of tortillas over a plate and top with a crown of Ropa Vieja.

Eggplant Parmigiana

THIS IS PROBABLY MY FAVORITE MEATLESS MAIN DISH. EARLY ON I COOKED IT AS ALL COOKBOOKS DIRECT, AND THOUGH IT TASTED WONDERFUL, MY NIGHTS WERE PREY TO INDIGESTION. SO I DEVISED THE METHOD BELOW OF PARBOILING THE EGGPLANT SO IT DOESN'T SPONGE UP CUPS AND CUPS OF OIL. THE PROCESS ALSO ELIMINATES ANY NEED FOR SALTING THE EGGPLANT TO LET IT SWEAT OUT ANY BITTERNESS. IT'S NOT AUTHENTIC, BUT YOU HAVE ALL THE FLAVOR AND NONE OF THE PAINS. ALSO, ALTHOUGH ALL RECIPES CALL FOR MOZZARELLA, IT IS A TASTELESS CHEESE IN THIS COUNTRY, ENTIRELY DIFFERENT FROM THAT OF ITALY, AND IT MELTS TO RUBBER BANDS (ALSO INDIGESTIBLE). I SUBSTITUTE BEL PAESE, FONTINA, OR EVEN THE MUSKY PROVOLONE. IT MAY SOUND HERETICAL, BUT A NATURAL MONTEREY JACK, LESS EXPENSIVE THAN ANY OF THE ABOVE, MAKES A SPLENDID SUBSTITUTE.

SERVES 4

2 *medium eggplants*
flour
salt and freshly ground pepper
olive oil
2 *cups Home-Style Tomato Sauce (page 189)*
½ *pound whole milk mozzarella cheese (or other mild, meltable cheese) grated*
½ *cup grated Parmesan cheese*

Preheat oven to 350°. Peel eggplants and slice in ⅓-inch rounds. Bring a large pot of water to a boil, put in eggplant slices, cover pot, and cook 1 minute. Immediately drain in a colander and pat dry. Dredge slices in flour seasoned with salt and pepper.

Put a thin film of olive oil in a large frying pan. Sauté slices over medium-high heat until pale gold on each side. Remove to a plate as they cook or drain on paper towels. Add more olive oil to pan as needed.

Coat a large shallow casserole lightly with olive oil. Spread some tomato sauce in the bottom, then make layers of eggplant, tomato sauce, mozzarella, and Parmesan cheese. If necessary, some slices of eggplant can be cut to make an even layer. Finally, dribble a little olive oil over the top layer of Parmesan cheese and bake, uncovered, 20–30 minutes, or until hot and bubbly. Serve hot or warm.

Brother Ricardo's Chicken Pudding, or How to Dine a Dozen on a Shoestring

BROTHER RICARDO BELDEN WAS THE LAST SURVIVING MEMBER OF THE HANCOCK, MASSACHUSETTS, CHAPTER OF SHAKERS. TO THE LAST, HE REPAIRED CLOCKS AND NEIGHBORS' SEWING MACHINES, AND PRODUCED HIS RICH AND TASTY PUDDING FOR VISITORS. USING EVERY SCRAP WAS HIS SECRET. THIS RECIPE NEEDS FOUR DIFFERENT OPERATIONS, BUT THEY ARE EASY. FIRST, YOU BOIL THE FOWL, MAKING STOCK AND FAT TO BE USED LATER, THEN YOU MAKE A BREAD DRESSING, PREPARE A THICK SAUCE AND TOPPING, AND ASSEMBLE IT AS A CASSEROLE TO BE BAKED.

WE DO NOT KNOW WHAT BROTHER RICARDO SERVED WITH THIS IN THE DECLINE OF HANCOCK VILLAGE, BUT WHO COULD GO WRONG WITH A CRANBERRY SAUCE, A SIMPLE GREEN VEGETABLE, AND A TOSSED SALAD, WITH COMPANY ON THE WAY AND LITTLE SPARE HARD CASH? YOU COULD ALSO MAKE THIS WITH A HALF TURKEY BREAST, THOUGH YOU WON'T HAVE THE FAT TO USE—FOR THAT I'D SUBSTITUTE ½ CUP OF BUTTER AND ½ CUP OF VEGETABLE OIL. LIKE MOST DISHES OF THIS SORT, YOU DON'T HAVE TO HAVE A DOZEN PEOPLE TO FEED, FOR WRAPPED IN FOIL, IT FREEZES WELL FOR FUTURE MEALS.

SERVES 12

COOKING THE CHICKEN

1 *5–6-pound stewing hen (or 2 regular market chickens)*
salt
1 *large onion, cut up*
1 *bay leaf*

Put the hen in a pot with water to cover, a little salt, and onion and bay leaf. Set aside giblets for later. Cover and simmer until meat flakes off the bones—about 2 hours for an old fowl, 1 for regular chicken (halve this in a pressure cooker). When done, let cool to room temperature in the pot, then drain and refrigerate or freeze the stock. Debone and shred chicken flesh and save skin. When the stock is cold, remove and save fat on top and reduce stock to 5 cups.

DRESSING

chicken giblets (excluding liver)
12 *cups white bread, trimmed of crust and cut into cubes*
½ *cup butter*
1 *medium onion, chopped*
2 *stalks celery, chopped*
1 *teaspoon dried crumbled sage (not powdered)*
salt and freshly ground pepper
1 *cup stock (approximately)*

Put giblets to cook in some salted water for about 20 minutes, then drain and chop finely. Put bread in a bowl and toss with giblets. Put butter in a saucepan and cook onion and celery over medium heat until softened, then toss with bread, along with sage, and salt and pepper to taste. The dressing ought to be a little peppery. Toss with stock until just moistened. The dressing ought not to be too heavy with moisture, and very light breads will not need as much as a cup. Set aside.

SAUCE

1 *cup chicken fat*
1 *cup flour*
4 *cups stock, heated*
1 *cup milk*
4 *eggs, beaten (optional)*
chicken skin

Put fat in a saucepan over medium heat, and when it bubbles, add flour, stirring for several minutes. Add stock, stir vigorously until smooth, then add milk. Stir until you have a smooth thickened sauce. At this point Brother Ricardo stirred in eggs, though I think these are unnecessary. Put skin through a grinder or whirl in a blender with some sauce, and stir it into the sauce.

CASSEROLE

1 *cup bread crumbs*
¼ *cup butter, melted*

Preheat oven to 400°. Lightly grease a large casserole or a 9-inch by 14-inch lasagna pan, or 2 8-inch-square baking pans. Put a layer of half the dressing, then cover it with half the sauce. Strew shedded chicken over, then remaining dressing, the last of the sauce. Toss bread crumbs with melted butter and sprinkle on top. Bake, uncovered, 30 minutes, or until lightly brown and bubbly.

Stretchers and Side Dishes

B eyond the precincts of Mashed, Fried & Boiled there are fascinating suburbs and by-ways among the cheapest staples. Any cook needs a potato surprise or a way to turn an old vegetable dish new. How many times can you trot out mashed potatoes, buttered rice, or the same old boiled zucchini without causing the family to revolt? It is quite pleasing as well, to be asked for a recipe for carrots, say, rather than your devil's food cake that you know very well lies in a Joy of Cooking.

So I've combed my files for such humble tricks. No asparagus tips wrapped in prosciutto here, no artichokes dripping lemony Hollandaise, no snow peas with crisp water chestnuts, and certainly no radicchio, arugula, or mâche! Ah, no potatoes melting with Gruyère. . . . But let us keep chins up and wallets in shape, for surely money is not necessary for delight, the palate needs no truffle a day to keep in tune, and even the prolific and dull zucchini might amaze if we set ourselves about it.

Asparagus Stems, Pea-Style

IT'S POSSIBLE TO FEAST ON ASPARAGUS ONE DAY, AND BUDGET THE NEXT WITH THEIR STEMS. THE DISH IS MODELED ON THE WAY THE FRENCH COOK TINY PEAS WITH A LITTLE ONION AND SHREDDED LETTUCE, AND IT IS EVERY BIT AS GOOD, SURPRISINGLY DELICATE. ANOTHER SAVING— HERE IT'S ACTUALLY BEST TO USE THOSE OUTER LETTUCE LEAVES THAT PERHAPS SEEM TOO TOUGH OR UNLOVELY FOR A SALAD.

SERVES 2

stems from 1 pound
  asparagus
2 tablespoons water
2 green onions, minced
  with part of tops
1 tablespoon minced
  parsley
2 cups shredded lettuce
1 tablespoon butter
salt and freshly ground
  pepper

Cut asparagus tips in about 5-inch lengths and reserve for another meal. Peel stems remaining with a vegetable peeler and cut off tough white parts at the ends. Cut green part into ¼-inch sections. Place in a saucepan with water and remaining ingredients. Cover and cook 4–5 minutes over medium heat, or until asparagus is tender. Stir well together and serve hot.

AH, NEVER THROW ANYTHING AWAY, UNLESS YOU HAVE PIGS OR RABBITS TO FATTEN! CAREFULLY PEELED DOWN TO THE INNER STEM, THESE HAVE A FLAVOR EVERY BIT AS GOOD AS THE FLORETS.

Sauté of Broccoli Stems

SERVES 2

stems from 1 bunch broccoli
 1 tablespoon butter
¼ teaspoon lemon juice
freshly grated nutmeg
salt and freshly ground
  pepper
canned pimiento strips

Peel stems carefully, then cut in 2-inch lengths. Cut these into ¼-inch strips. Place in a bowl of cold water to crisp 30 minutes or more.

Drain and drop in a pot of boiling salted water. Let water return to a boil and cook 2 minutes. Immediately drain and run under cold water. At this point the stems can be held several hours before cooking.

To serve, melt butter in a saucepan and toss stems 3–4 minutes over medium heat. As they cook add lemon juice, a little nutmeg, and salt and pepper to taste. Serve in piles garnished with pimiento strips.

FIAMMIFERO MEANS MATCHSTICKS, AND THIS DISH MAKES VERY PRETTY ONES—RIGHT DOWN TO THE TOMATO'S SMALL FLAMES. IT MAKES A FINE EVERYDAY SALAD OR A DELIGHTFUL PART OF AN ANTIPASTO PLATTER.

Fiammifero

SERVES 4

stems from 1 bunch broccoli
1 large tomato, peeled, seeded, and chopped
1 clove garlic, minced
¼ teaspoon salt
2 teaspoons lemon juice
1 teaspoon red wine vinegar
¼ cup olive oil (or vegetable oil)
3 tablespoons grated Parmesan cheese
freshly ground pepper
lettuce leaves

Trim stems well with a vegetable peeler and cut in 2-inch lengths, then slice these into matchsticks. Place in a bowl and toss with tomato. Mash garlic and salt well together in a small bowl. Whisk in lemon juice, wine vinegar, and olive oil. Pour over broccoli sticks and toss well, then toss with Parmesan cheese and pepper to taste.

Cover and chill 1 hour or more. Serve on crisp lettuce leaves.

THIS, FROM MY FRIEND DOROTHY NEAL, IS MY FAVORITE WAY TO LIVEN UP THE CARROT, RATHER THAN THE USUAL GLAZING WITH SUGAR. I LIKE TO PARTNER THEM WITH AN EQUALLY EASY INVENTION OF MY OWN, RICE WITH ZUCCHINI (PAGE 311), FOR CONTRAST IN COLOR, TEXTURE, AND FLAVOR.

Carrots with Garlic

SERVES 4

1 *pound carrots*
2 *cloves garlic, slightly flattened and peeled*
1 *tablespoon butter*
1 *tablespoon olive oil (or vegetable oil)*
1 *bay leaf*
2 *tablespoons water*
salt and freshly ground pepper
2 *tablespoons minced parsley (optional)*

Trim and scrape carrots, then cut diagonally in ½-inch slices. Place in a saucepan with garlic, butter, olive oil, bay leaf, water, and salt and pepper to taste. Bring to a boil, cover pan, turn heat low, and cook about 10 minutes. Every few minutes lift the lid, stir, and check on progress. When done, the water will have cooked away, the carrots should have started to brown a little and they will be done but not soft. If the water is not cooked away, cook, uncovered, a few minutes over a higher heat, stirring so the carrots color evenly.

To serve, discard garlic and bay leaf, toss with parsley, and place on warm plates.

ANYONE WOULD EAT CARROTS THIS WAY, AND THEY ARE NOT ONLY TASTY BUT ALSO ALL SHADES OF GOLD AND ORANGE SO THEY ALMOST GLOW ON A PLATE. I LIKE THEM PARTICULARLY WITH LAMB, BUT THEY ARE ALSO GOOD WITH A PORK CHOP.

Curried Carrot Fritters

SERVES 4

½ *cup flour*
¼ *teaspoon salt*
 1 *egg, slightly beaten*
vegetable oil
½ *cup flat beer*
 1 *teaspoon curry powder*
 1 *egg white*
½ *pound carrots, scraped*
    and coarsely grated

Combine flour, salt, egg, 1 tablespoon of vegetable oil, and beer to make a smooth batter. Cover with plastic wrap for several hours at room temperature, the longer the better (it can also be refrigerated overnight).

Stir in curry powder. Beat egg white until stiff and fold it into the batter. Gently fold in carrots. Drop large spoonfuls of mixture into hot oil (375°) and cook about 1 minute on each side. (The oil doesn't need to be more than 1 inch in depth for this.) Remove with a slotted spoon and let drain on paper towels. Serve hot.

French Marinated Carrots

I HAVE USED THIS RECIPE FOR YEARS IN ALL KINDS OF SITUATIONS. THEY ARE GOOD FOR PARTIES, RATHER THAN JUST HAVING A CARROT STICK TO DIP INTO SOMETHING, AND I USED THEM CONSTANTLY IN CATERING. IN MY RESTAURANT WE SERVED THEM AND *CORNI-CHONS* WITH THE SLICE OF PÂTÉ. THEY CAN BE PART OF A SALAD IF ANY ARE LEFT OVER, OR THEY CAN NESTLE IN A LETTUCE LEAF AS A SALAD OR VEGETABLE COURSE. AND BEST OF ALL THEY ARE CHEAP AND EASY TO PREPARE!

SERVES 6–8

1 *pound carrots*
¾ *cup water*
¾ *cup dry white wine*
¼ *cup white wine vinegar*
½ *cup olive oil (or vegetable oil)*
1 *teaspoon salt*
1 *teaspoon sugar*
pinch of cayenne pepper (optional)
¼ *teaspoon dried thyme (or several sprigs of fresh)*
several sprigs of parsley
1 *bay leaf*
1 *clove garlic, slightly flattened and peeled*
1 *teaspoon dry mustard (or 1 tablespoon Dijon-style mustard)*

Peel carrots and slice off tips and stem ends. Cut in about 2½-inch lengths. The thickest lengths can be cut into 8 sticks, the middle ones in 4, and the slender just cut in half. Don't worry much about this, you want to have sticks approximately all the same size and length, but that's it.

Place in a saucepan with all ingredients except mustard. Bring to a boil and cook, uncovered, 15–20 minutes over medium-high heat. After 15 minutes bite into one and see. They should still have some bite to them, not limp. Let them sit in the marinade until cool, then lift with a slotted spoon into a bowl. Discard bay leaf, parsley and thyme sprigs, and garlic. Whisk mustard into the marinade and pour over carrots.

Serve chilled or at room temperature.

Shaved Carrots

THESE ARE INTERESTING BECAUSE OF THEIR UNEXPECTED FORM, FOR THEY TURN OUT A KIND OF WEIGHT-WATCHER PASTA WITH A GREAT DEAL OF FRESH FLAVOR. EVEN OLD CARROTS MAY BE USED THIS WAY, PERKED UP WITH A FEW DROPS OF LEMON JUICE AND A WHISPER OF NUTMEG.

SERVES 4

1 *pound carrots*
2 *tablespoons butter*
salt and freshly ground
  pepper
¼ *cup minced parsley*

Top and peel carrots. With a vegetable peeler, shave each one down on all sides from top to bottom until you reach the inner yellow core. Reserve cores for flavoring stews or soups.

Put butter in a large frying pan over medium heat. Toss long shavings, adding salt and pepper to taste, and cook about 10 minutes, just until they are limp. Toss with parsley and serve.

Pima Peelings Fry

AN AMERICAN INDIAN DISH TO REMEMBER WHEN YOU ARE PREPARING VEGETABLES FOR A ROAST, THE PEELS CAN BE KEPT IN A PLASTIC BAG TO USE THE NEXT DAY AS A SIDE DISH, OR THEY CAN BE MADE INTO A COCKTAIL NIBBLE BEFORE DINNER. OF COURSE EITHER POTATOES OR CARROTS MAY BE COOKED ALONE, AND IN ANY PROPORTION.

SERVES 4

peels from 6 large carrots
peels from 6 medium
*   potatoes*
2 tablespoons vegetable oil
salt

Cut peels in 2-inch strips. Place oil in a frying pan over medium heat. Add peels and fry, stirring frequently, 10–12 minutes, or until peels are crisp and golden. Drain on paper towels and salt lightly.

Swiss Chard Salad

SERVES 2–3

1 *bunch Swiss chard (red or white)*
¼ *cup olive oil*
2 *tablespoons red wine vinegar*
1 *clove garlic, minced*
¼ *teaspoon dried oregano (or basil)*
salt and freshly ground pepper

WHEN YOU ARE TIRED OF THE SAME OLD TOSSED SALAD, THIS MAKES A WONDERFUL CHANGE OF PACE WITH MANY DIFFERENT KINDS OF MEALS. IT LOOKS PRETTY, TOO, ESPECIALLY WITH RED SWISS CHARD. REMEMBER THAT THE METHOD CAN ALSO BE USED FOR BEETS AND THEIR GREENS, OR WITH FRESH SPRING DANDELION GREENS (GARNISHED, THESE, WITH HARD-BOILED EGG SECTIONS).

Cut stems off Swiss chard and cut diagonally in 1-inch pieces. Either steam or cook in a little salted water until just tender. This will take only 5–6 minutes, and they should still have a little bite to them. Quickly run cold water over them to stop their cooking.

Cut leaves into bite-size pieces, wash to remove any grit, and either steam or cook in a little salted water just until they wilt. Run cold water over them and pat dry with paper towels.

Combine olive oil, wine vinegar, garlic, oregano, and salt and pepper to taste. Place stems and leaves in separate bowls and toss with dressing, using a little more for leaves than for the stems. Let marinate 1 hour or so, either in the refrigerator or at room temperature.

To serve, place leaves on a salad plate and top with stems.

Cracked Wheat (Bulgur) Pilaf

BULGUR IS A STAPLE OF MIDDLE EASTERN COOKING AND WITH ITS NUTTY TASTE AND TEXTURE MAKES A PLEASANT ALTERNATIVE FROM POTATOES AND RICE. IT IS EASILY FOUND IN HEALTH FOOD STORES OR MIDDLE EASTERN GROCERIES. SOMETIMES THE RICE-SHAPED PASTA ORZO IS COOKED ALONG WITH IT, MAKING YET ANOTHER VARIATION.

SERVES 4

2 *tablespoons butter*
2 *tablespoons minced onion*
1 *cup medium-grind cracked wheat*
salt and freshly ground pepper
2 *cups chicken stock*

Melt butter in a saucepan and sauté onion several minutes. Add cracked wheat and stir to coat grains. Add salt and pepper to taste, and stock. Bring to a boil, lower heat, cover, and simmer 15 minutes, or until liquid is absorbed and wheat is tender.

THIS IS ONE OF MY FAVORITE SUMMER DISHES, FOR IT COMBINES STARCH AND SALAD IN A PLEASANT, NO-FUSS WAY, AND IT CAN ACCOMPANY PRACTICALLY ANYTHING IN THE WAY OF MEAT. ALSO, IT IS JUST PLAIN DELICIOUS. IF YOU CAN FIND ONLY THE MEDIUM GRADE OF CRACKED BULGUR, IT CAN BE BOILED FOR A FEW MINUTES BEFORE SOAKING TO MAKE IT TENDER.

Tabbouleh Salad

SERVES 4–6

1 *cup fine cracked wheat*
3 *tomatoes, peeled and chopped*
1 *cucumber, peeled, seeded, and chopped*
½ *cup thinly sliced radishes*
½ *cup chopped green onions with part of tops*
¼ *cup minced parsley*
2 *tablespoons minced fresh mint* (or 1 tablespoon dried)
juice of 1 lemon
½ *cup olive oil*
salt and freshly ground pepper

Pour boiling water over wheat—just enough to come to the top. Cover pan and let sit 1 hour. It should absorb all the water, but if not drain it well. Mix in vegetables and herbs, then toss with lemon juice, olive oil, and salt and pepper to taste.

Ratatouille & Co.

This would be the sign on my roadside produce stand, if ever I had one. Nothing can equal that marriage of vegetable cousins—purple eggplant, scarlet tomato, green and ivory zucchini, green or red or yellow peppers, white onion and garlic—lept from ground to table through slow fire, fine oil and herbs. Consumed with neighbor wines, broken breads, a proper ratatouille becomes a friend for life. Even without a garden or roadside and farmer's market, the convinced will find the gleaning of a refrigerator bin has the makings of a feast about it. Everything goes.

Well, almost everything. A good rule of thumb is never toss together root vegetables with those grown above ground (aside from onions and tomatoes, which go with everything). A prime example is the institutional combination of peas and little cubed carrots, which does nothing for either, however colorful. But spiced and tossed and cosseted in general over a low flame or in a moderate oven, friendly and even humble vegetables may stand up on their own as A Dish, better through company than alone.

This can be a simple refrigerator inspection resulting in a few green onions stewed in butter, along with some scraped ears of lost corn and green pepper gone soft in a spot, later a splash of water and slices of a zucchini and a yellow squash tossed through until just done. A squeeze of lemon, minced fresh basil, salt and pepper to taste, swift to table. In effect, what our ancestors called a "succotash." But first let us examine the veritable ancestor.

Ratatouille

SERVES 6

1–2 *onions, sliced*
3–4 *cloves garlic, minced*
  ½ *cup olive oil*
  2 *green (or red) peppers, seeded and cut in strips*
  1 *large eggplant, diced (with or without skin)*
4–5 *small zucchini, cut in slices*
2–3 *cups peeled, diced tomatoes (fresh or canned)*
  2 *tablespoons chopped fresh basil (or 2 teaspoons dried basil chopped with some parsley)*
salt and freshly ground pepper

Sauté onions and garlic in olive oil in a large saucepan. When onions soften, add peppers, eggplant, and zucchini, tossing to coat all with oil. Reduce heat, cover pan, and simmer 10–15 minutes. Add tomatoes, basil, and salt and pepper to taste. Cover pan and cook another 10–15 minutes. Uncover pan and cook 1 hour, stirring now and again to distribute flavor. The vegetables should be soft but not mushy when done. Taste for seasoning. Serve at room temperature or cold. If cold, sprinkle with a little red wine vinegar or lemon juice before serving.

These are the bare bones of the recipe, fleshed as you will. Acceptable additions are a little white wine, thyme, a bay leaf, or capers added toward the end. It is fine to use green tomatoes for some of the red, as they do in the Midwest, or okra, as they do in the South. If your basil is fresh I see no reason for other herbs, but I do agree that the wine or capers add a necessary fillip of acidity.

One of the best things about a ratatouille is that it is at its best after 2 or 3 days, served either chilled or reheated. And versatility is the chief of its virtues. It can be served as a first course or partnered with grilled or roast meats. With cheese, and bread to sop up the juices, it can make lunch an event. For a supper dish, perhaps spooned in a ramekin with an egg dropped on top and then a sprinkle of cheese, it can be baked in a hot oven until the egg sets and the cheese melts. To me, even with a brimming summer garden, it would never come to be boring.

For this reason I like to make as much as possible and bake it in a lasagna pan covered with foil, as in the method of the recipe for Eggplant Vals that I have used for years. I don't know where it came from, but it is definitely one of the "cousins" that ring the Mediterranean. It really doesn't need measurements since it depends on what kind of pot or pan you have at hand and how many eager mouths you have to feed.

To try the versatility of the far-flung clan, you should also cook an elaborate Turkish version (Imam Bayildi) and a thrifty Greek version (Briami).

Eggplant Vals

THE RECIPE ADDS THAT THIS METHOD COULD BE USED FOR LEEKS, ARTICHOKES, SQUASH, CUCUMBERS, OR ONIONS (AND PRESUMABLY ANY MEDLEY THEREOF). YOU CAN SEE WHAT A USEFUL DISH THIS COULD BE, PARTICULARLY WHEN LUSCIOUS RIPE BEEFSTEAK TOMATOES ARE AVAILABLE TO DROP THEIR JUICES SLOWLY INTO THE SNUGGLED VEGETABLES. IN *WITH BOLD KNIFE & FORK*, M. F. K. FISHER RECORDS ANOTHER MEMBER OF THE FAMILY SHE CALLS "MINORCAN STEW," WHICH IS BASICALLY THE INGREDIENTS OF A RATATOUILLE COOKED, AS THIS IS, WITH A TOP LAYER OF TOMATOES.

Peel eggplants and cut into 1-inch cubes. Drop in a pot of boiling salted water and cook 10 minutes. Drain well in a colander. Place in a baking dish well coated with olive oil. Stir in salt and pepper to taste, 1 or 2 chopped onions, a couple of cloves, and strew with thyme and minced parsley. Cover with a thick layer of peeled and sliced garden tomatoes (or, lacking those, canned are fine). Douse well with olive oil, more salt and pepper, and cook, covered, in a 325° oven 1½–2 hours. Remove cover and sprinkle lightly with wine vinegar, then replace in oven 10–15 minutes. Remove and let come to room temperature, or chill.

Imam Bayildi

IN ENGLISH, IMAM BAYILDI, MEANS "THE IMAM SWOONED." MOST COOKBOOKS WILL TELL YOU THIS WAS FROM SHEER PLEASURE, BUT SINCE IT IS USUALLY SERVED LITERALLY SWIMMING IN OIL, I RECKON IT WAS MORE LIKE ACUTE INDIGESTION. THOUGH COOKBOOKS, EVEN GOOD TURKISH ONES, DISAGREE ON SOME INGREDIENTS, ORIGINALLY THE EGGPLANTS WERE SLICED NOT QUITE THROUGH AND OPENED RATHER LIKE A BOOK. A STUFFING OF TOMATOES, ONIONS, GARLIC, PARSLEY, AND SO FORTH, WAS PLACED BETWEEN THE PAGES, AND THEN IT WAS COOKED IN A BATH OF OLIVE OIL. AS EGGPLANT IS PERHAPS THE MOST ABSORBENT VEGETABLE AROUND (PARTICULARLY NEAR OIL), I PREFER TO USE THIS METHOD SUGGESTED BY THE LATE JAMES BEARD. TRY IT. IF IT CAN SATIATE SULTANS, WHAT MIGHT IT NOT DO TO YOUR GUESTS AT AN OUTDOOR BARBECUE?

SERVES 4

2 *large eggplants*
salt and freshly ground
   pepper
7 *tablespoons olive oil*
2 *medium onions, finely*
   chopped
1 *large clove garlic, minced*
1 *cup chopped tomatoes*
   (*fresh or canned*)
¼ *teaspoon ground*
   cinnamon
pinch of ground allspice
1 *bay leaf*
½ *teaspoon sugar*
2 *tablespoons minced*
   parsley
2 *tablespoons currants* (*or*
   chopped raisins)
   (*optional*)

Preheat oven to 350°. Cut green ends off eggplants. Drop whole in a large pot of boiling water, cover, and cook 10 minutes. Drain and put into cold water 5 minutes. Cut in half lengthwise and scoop out flesh, leaving ½ inch for a shell. Place shells in a baking dish, salt and pepper lightly, and place 1 tablespoon of olive oil in each—brushing shells all over. Bake, uncovered, 30 minutes.

Heat remaining oil in a saucepan and sauté onions and garlic until softened. Add tomatoes, cinnamon, allspice, bay leaf, sugar, and parsley. Add salt and pepper to taste and simmer, uncovered, 15 minutes. Stir now and again as it cooks. Chop eggplant flesh well and add to the pan, along with currants if you use them, and cook another 15 minutes over low heat. Fish out the bay leaf. Remove shells from the oven and stuff them with the mixture. Serve warm or cold.

A GRACIOUS, HEARTY DISH FLAVORED, AS YOU SEE, WITH DILL
RATHER THAN THE UBIQUITOUS BASIL. THOSE WHO DON'T ADMIRE
OKRA MAY SUBSTITUTE GREEN PEPPER STRIPS.

Briami

SERVES 8

1 *large eggplant*
¾ *pound okra, trimmed*
1 *tablespoon vinegar*
1½ *pounds zucchini, sliced*
1 *pound tomatoes (fresh*
   or canned), chopped
½ *cup minced parsley*
¼ *cup minced fresh dill*
   (or 1 tablespoon dried)
salt and freshly ground
   pepper
½ *cup olive oil*
2 *medium onions,*
   chopped
3 *cloves garlic, minced*
bread crumbs

Peel and slice eggplant. Salt it liberally and place in a
colander to drain 1 hour. Put okra in a bowl and sprinkle
with vinegar. Preheat oven to 350°. Pat eggplant dry with
paper towels and rinse okra.

In a large oiled casserole make alternate layers of
vegetables, sprinkling as you go with herbs and a little salt
and pepper. Use only half the tomatoes. Place olive oil in a
saucepan and sauté onions and garlic until translucent.
Add remaining tomatoes and simmer 10 minutes, then
spoon over vegetables. Dust top with bread crumbs and
bake, uncovered, 1 hour. Serve at room temperature or
cold.

THESE ARE LOVELY BAKED ALONG WITH MEATS, BUT THEY SEEM PARTICULARLY FINE TO BAKE AHEAD AND THEN WARM ON THE GRILL WHEN BARBECUING.

Rosemary Onions

SERVES 4

4 *medium onions, peeled*
2 *tablespoons butter*
4 *sprigs of fresh rosemary*
   (*or 1 teaspoon dried*)
salt and freshly ground
   pepper

Preheat oven to 375°. Remove a little of the center of each onion with an apple corer. Divide butter and place some in each cavity, along with rosemary.

Place onions on a 6-inch square of foil, sprinkle well with salt and pepper, and seal up. Place in a baking dish and cook 45–50 minutes. Squeeze to make sure they are soft, then serve either still wrapped or unwrapped.

SIMPLE AND UTTERLY DELIGHTFUL! ALSO, IF YOU KEEP A SHELF OF
FLAVORED OR HERBED VINEGARS ON HAND, TRY ANY ONE OF
THEM—WHITE WINE VINEGAR WITH TARRAGON IS PARTICULARLY
FINE WITH FISH OR CHICKEN.

Onions Baked with Red Wine Vinegar

SERVES 4

4 *medium onions*
water
salt
butter
2 *tablespoons red wine
  vinegar*
1 *tablespoon sugar*
freshly ground pepper

Preheat oven to 350°. Peel onions carefully, being sure to keep root ends trimmed but intact. Drop them in a pot of boiling salted water and cook 10 minutes. Drain, and when cool enough to handle, cut each in half vertically. Place in a buttered baking dish, cut side down.

Put wine vinegar, sugar, 1 tablespoon of butter, and ¼ cup of water in a small saucepan and stir over medium heat just until sugar dissolves. Pour over onions, salt and pepper lightly, and place in the oven. Bake 30–40 minutes, basting every now and again. The onions are done when a small knife slips into them easily.

THIS IS VERY SIMPLE-SOUNDING PURITAN FOOD, BUT THESE ONIONS MAKE A LOVELY, SOOTHING ACCOMPANIMENT TO ROAST CHICKEN, LAMB, OR BEEF, IN PLACE OF THE USUAL POTATO. A SQUIRT OF DRY SHERRY OR MADEIRA, IF YOU HAVE SOME ON THE SHELF,

Massachusetts Hashed Onions

SERVES 4

TAKES SOME OF THE PURITAN STARCH OUT OF THEM.

3 *large white onions*
½ *cup milk*
1½ *cups water*
2 *tablespoons butter*
¼ *cup heavy cream*
salt and freshly ground pepper
freshly grated nutmeg

Peel onions and cut in quarters vertically. Place in a saucepan and cover with milk and water. Bring to a boil and simmer, covered, 15 minutes.

Drain and chop onions coarsely. Return to the pan, add butter, cream, and seasonings to taste. Cook, uncovered, 10 minutes over low heat, or until soft and tasty.

THESE ARE GREAT FOR A BUFFET PARTY, A HOLIDAY FEAST, OR WITH AN OUTDOOR BARBECUE. THERE ARE A LOT OF RECIPES FOR VEGETABLES A LA GRECQUE, BUT THIS IS ONE APART.

Onions à la Grecque

SERVES 6–8

36 *small pickling onions*
 1 *cup water*
 1 *cup beef stock*
½ *cup olive oil (or
    vegetable oil)*
½ *cup dry white wine*
 1 *teaspoon dried tarragon*
 1 *teaspoon dry mustard*
 1 *teaspoon mustard seeds*
 4 *whole cloves*
*salt and freshly ground
    pepper*
½ *cup raisins*
 1 *teaspoon sugar*
¼ *cup minced parsley*

Drop onions in a pot of boiling water and drain after 30 seconds, then slip off their skins. Place back in the pot with all ingredients up through salt and pepper to taste. Simmer, uncovered, about 20 minutes, until just tender. Add raisins and sugar, and cool to room temperature. Chill in refrigerator. Serve sprinkled with parsley.

THESE ARE ESSENTIALLY DUCHESS POTATOES, TURNED OUT ON EVERY INTERNATIONAL PLATTER, WHETHER YOU WANT THEM OR NOT. BUT THIS VERSION ADDS THE DIFFERENCE OF GARLIC AND PARSLEY. LIKE DUCHESS POTATOES, THEY CAN BE PIPED IN SWIRLS AROUND THE MEAT, BUT THEY'RE FINE AS IS.

Alsace Potato Puffs

SERVES 4–6

1½ *pounds potatoes*
⅓ *cup milk, heated*
2 *tablespoons butter*
4 *teaspoons flour*
1 *clove garlic, minced*
2 *tablespoons minced parsley*
2 *eggs, well beaten*
freshly grated nutmeg
salt and freshly ground pepper
2 *tablespoons melted butter*

Boil potatoes—2 large baking potatoes or about 5 regular potatoes should do—in salted water until they can be pierced by a fork. Drain, put a double paper towel over the pot, and let sit with the lid on 5–10 minutes to dry out. Peel and put them through a ricer or sieve. Measure 3 cups (not packed down) and place in a bowl.

Stir in hot milk, butter, flour, garlic, parsley, eggs, and enough nutmeg, salt, and pepper to give the mixture savor. Scoop into oval mounds of about 2 tablespoons each and place on a lightly buttered baking sheet. These can sit for a while covered with plastic wrap, if necessary.

Heat oven to 325°. Bake puffs 10–12 minutes, or until they feel set on top. Brush with melted butter, then broil briefly until they start to sputter and turn golden.

Nebraska Potatoes

TRUSTY, CRUSTY, AND FLAVORED THROUGH WITH JUST A HINT OF THYME, THESE MIDWESTERN DELIGHTS CAN BE SUBTLY VARIED ACCORDING TO THE MEAL. I SOMETIMES USE A STREW OF WHAT THE FRENCH CALL *FINES HERBES* OR SOME FRESH TARRAGON ON THOSE DESTINED FOR A PLATE OF LEMONY FISH. PARMESAN AND GARLIC MIXED WITH THE BREAD CRUMBS WORKS, TOO. IF YOU DON'T HAVE SMALL POTATOES, QUARTERED LARGE ONES WILL DO.

SERVES 4

8 *2-inch red potatoes, peeled*
4 *tablespoons butter, melted*
⅓ *cup bread crumbs*
⅛ *teaspoon dried thyme*
salt and freshly ground pepper

Preheat oven to 350°. Roll potatoes in melted butter. Mix bread crumbs, thyme, and salt and pepper to taste in a small bowl. Dip potatoes in this one by one, and place in a casserole that has a cover. Dribble leftover melted butter on the tops of potatoes and bake, covered, 50–60 minutes, or until golden and a fork will gently pierce them.

As you can see from all those "optionals," this, too, is a versatile recipe according to what you serve with the potatoes. It can also be cooked at a higher temperature, along with some meat, but cut down on the cooking time.

My Oven-Roasted Potatoes

SERVES 4

4 *medium potatoes*
¼ *cup olive oil (or vegetable oil)*
¼ *cup minced parsley*
1 *teaspoon favorite dried herb (optional)*
1 *clove garlic, minced (optional)*
salt and freshly ground pepper
freshly grated nutmeg (optional)

Preheat oven to 325°. Pare potatoes and cut into ⅛-inch slices. Drop in a bowl of water so they won't discolor. Drain, pat dry with paper towels, and toss with all ingredients—I like to do this right in the baking pan or pans. You want one that will hold the potato slices in about 3 layers. For instance, 2 pie plates are fine here.

Bake 1 hour, or until crisp and starting to turn golden. Serve hot, cut into serving portions.

Potatoes in Milk

ITALIANS DO COOK POTATOES, AS THIS EXCELLENT AND SIMPLE RECIPE ATTESTS. NOT ONLY DO THEY HAVE A FINE TASTE AND TEXTURE, IT IS PROBABLY THE ONLY WAY EVER DEVISED TO COOK A POTATO WITHOUT ANY OIL, BUTTER, OR CREAM. HENCE, THEY ARE A DIETER'S DELIGHT, SINCE MOST OF THE POTATO'S CALORIES COME FROM ADDED FATS RATHER THAN THE INNOCENT VEGETABLE. A FRIEND ONCE MENTIONED THE IDEA OF COOKING POTATOES IN LEFTOVER ARTICHOKE COOKING WATER. THAT IS A SECRET ONE LONGS TO HEAR, AND CERTAINLY IT RESULTS IN A DELICATELY PERFUMED POTATO, COOKED JUST AS THESE ARE, THOUGH I THINK WITH A LITTLE BUTTER.

SERVES 4

4 *medium potatoes*
milk
salt and freshly ground
  pepper
freshly grated nutmeg
minced parsley (or fresh
  herbs)

Peel potatoes and slice in ½-inch rounds. Place in a saucepan and add milk to cover. Simmer 15–20 minutes, until just tender. Drain, reserving milk. Heat oven to 350°.

Place potatoes in a shallow pan large enough to hold them in a single overlapping layer. Sprinkle with salt and pepper to taste and a whisper of nutmeg, then strew with parsley. Finally, sprinkle with a little of the cooking milk, just enough to moisten slightly. Bake about 5 minutes to warm through and dry out slightly. Serve hot.

DELIGHTFUL CRISPY MOUTHFULS TO SERVE WITH PORK OR OTHER MEATS. YAMS ARE MORE RICH AND DELICATE, BUT SWEET POTATOES DO VERY NICELY.

Sweet Potato Cakes

SERVES 4

1 *large (9–10-ounce) sweet potato (or red-fleshed yam)*
1 *small onion*
2 *eggs*
2 *tablespoons flour*
⅛ *teaspoon ground mace*
salt and freshly ground pepper
3–4 *tablespoons vegetable oil*

Peel potato and onion, then grate both coarsely into a colander. Push down with a paper towel to extract as much moisture as possible. Place in a bowl and mix in eggs, flour, mace, and salt and pepper to taste.

Heat vegetable oil in a frying pan and cook in cakes of about 2 tablespoons until browned on both sides. It will take about 1½ minutes per side. Serve hot.

Cuban-styled Yams

Have you ever wondered why there are so few recipes for sweet potatoes and yams, and the ones you find are all sugared and pineappled and marshmallowed and spiked with slugs of booze? I have. Sweet potatoes are sweet already, and yams especially have a beautiful flavor and texture, splendid indeed when simply baked and slathered with butter. This particular dish has an exotic flavor excellent with pork or turkey.

SERVES 4

1½ *pounds red-fleshed yams*
 1 *ripe banana*
 1 *tablespoon lime juice (or lemon)*
 2 *tablespoons minced fresh coriander leaves*
 ¼ *teaspoon ground cumin*
pinch of ground mace
salt
 1 *tablespoon butter, melted*

Heat oven to any convenient temperature and bake potatoes until quite soft. These may be made at any time and reserved.

When ready to prepare dish, heat oven to 350°. Scoop flesh out of potatoes and discard peel. Mash well with banana or put through a food mill. Add lime juice, coriander, the spices, and salt to taste.

Grease a pie plate with some of the butter, smooth the mixture in, and dribble with remaining butter. Bake 20–25 minutes, or until yams start to take color on top.

THIS GIVES A ZING TO ORDINARY RICE THAT IS HARD TO RESIST WITH SOMETHING LIKE LAMB OR A HEARTY CHICKEN DISH.

Cumin Rice

SERVES 4

½ teaspoon cumin seeds
1⅓ cups water
salt
⅔ cup long-grain rice
2 strips lemon peel
2 tablespoons butter
freshly ground pepper

Place seeds in a dry frying pan and shake over medium heat until they begin to turn color slightly and give off a fragrant aroma. Place in a saucepan, pour water over, add salt to taste, and bring to a boil. Pour in rice, add lemon peel, and when it returns to a boil, lower heat. Cover and simmer 20 minutes. Fish out peel and stir in butter and a grind or two of pepper.

PERFECT WITH FISH OR ROAST CHICKEN JUST AS IS, THIS RICE CAN ALSO BE SPRINKLED WITH SESAME SEEDS THAT HAVE BEEN STIRRED AND TOASTED UNTIL GOLDEN IN A DRY FRYING PAN. SLIVERS OF SNOW PEAS MAY BE PUT IN TO COOK DURING THE LAST MINUTES, FOR FURTHER SLEIGHTS OF HAND.

Lemon-scented Rice

SERVES 4

1⅓ *cups water*
salt
　⅔ *cups long-grain rice*
　½ *lemon*
　3 *tablespoons butter*

Bring water to boil in a saucepan, add a sprinkle of salt, then rice. Let come to a boil, lower heat, cover, and simmer 20 minutes. Uncover and stir in grated rind and juice from lemon half, along with butter.

TURMERIC GIVES THE SAME GLOWING COLOR TO RICE AS SAFFRON AND IMPARTS A SUBTLE NUTTY FLAVOR ALL ITS OWN, DELICIOUS WITH LAMB, CHICKEN, OR EVEN FISH. IF YOU CAN'T FIND THE RICE-SHAPED

Turmeric Rice and Orzo Pilaf

PASTA ORZO, DON'T WORRY—JUST SUBSTITUTE ONE CUP OF RICE INITIALLY. I USE IT HERE BECAUSE IT ADDS A SLIGHTLY DIFFERENT TEXTURE TO THE PILAF.

SERVES 4

2 tablespoons butter
¼ cup finely chopped onion
⅔ cup long-grain rice
½ teaspoon ground turmeric
salt and freshly ground pepper
2 cups chicken stock
⅓ cup orzo

Melt butter in a saucepan and when it bubbles add onion. Sauté 3–4 minutes, then stir in rice until all grains are coated. When the rice starts to turn opaque, stir in turmeric and cook 2 minutes. Add salt and pepper to taste and chicken stock. When the stock bubbles, add orzo, cover the pan, turn heat low, and simmer 20 minutes.

EVERYONE KNOWS AND SERVES POTATO SALAD, MACARONI SALAD, AND EVEN SALADS WITH SEVERAL BEANS, DRIED AND NOT, BUT I SELDOM SEE OR TASTE RICE SALAD. IT IS PARTICULARLY FINE TO ACCOMPANY SUMMER MEATS, PERHAPS ON A LETTUCE LEAF, OR TO TAKE ON A PICNIC. OTHER BITS CAN BE ADDED SUCH AS CHOPPED OLIVES OR PEPPERS (GREEN OR RED), AND THE FRENCH DOTE ON A SCATTERING OF SHRIMPLETS. THE SALAD CAN ALSO BE GARNISHED WITH RADISH ROSES OR SLICES OF HARD-BOILED EGGS, BUT THESE ARE ONLY GILDINGS TO A VERY FINE LILY.

French Rice Salad

SERVES 4–6

  1 *cup long-grain rice*
  ¼ *cup olive oil (or*
     vegetable oil)
1½ *tablespoons white wine*
     vinegar
salt and freshly ground
     pepper
  4 *green onions, minced*
  2 *tablespoons parsley*
  1 *teaspoon fresh tarragon*
     (or ½ teaspoon dried)

Put rice to boil in rather a lot of salted water and simmer, uncovered, 17–18 minutes. The rice should still have a little bite to it. Drain well in a colander and place in a bowl. Stir together olive oil, wine vinegar, and salt and pepper to taste. Add to the bowl and toss well to coat the rice. Add onions, mince parsley and tarragon together, then add to mixture and toss. The salad can be served at room temperature or chilled.

THESE ARE A VERY LIGHT, FLUFFY CAKE WITH A CONTRAST IN TEXTURE FROM THE RICE AND CORNMEAL. THIS IS A FINE WAY TO USE LEFTOVER RICE, AND THOUGH THE CAKES CAN BE EATEN WITH SYRUP LIKE ANY PANCAKE, I REALLY LIKE THEM AS THEY ARE FOR AN ACCOMPANIMENT TO MEATS RATHER THAN THE USUAL POTATO, RICE, OR NOODLE.

Rice Cornmeal Cakes

MAKES 12 4-INCH CAKES

½ *cup flour*
1 *teaspoon salt*
¼ *teaspoon sugar*
½ *cup cornmeal (preferably stone-ground)*
1 *cup cold cooked long-grain rice*
2 *cups buttermilk*
½ *teaspoon baking soda*
2 *tablespoons vegetable oil*
2 *eggs, separated*

Sift flour, salt, and sugar into a bowl. Mix in cornmeal and rice. Stir buttermilk and baking soda together, then combine it with vegetable oil and egg yolks, beating well. Stir gently into dry mixture with a few quick strokes. Beat egg whites until they hold soft peaks, then fold in. Fry as you would pancakes.

A classic Greek dish that makes a fine starch and vegetable combination to accompany almost any meat. Unlike most Greek dishes, this should be served hot rather than at room temperature. You could probably use frozen spinach leaves, but fresh is definitely best here.

Greek Spinach Pilaf

SERVES 4

1 *pound fresh spinach*
2 *tablespoons olive oil*
⅔ *cup long-grain rice*
2 *tablespoons minced onion*
2 *tablespoons tomato paste*
1⅓ *cups water*
salt and freshly ground pepper
freshly grated nutmeg
¼ *teaspoon dried mint (or ½ teaspoon fresh)*

Wash spinach in several waters and strip leaves from stems. Place leaves in a bowl with water that clings to them.

Put olive oil in a large saucepan. Stir rice over medium heat until it turns opaque, then add onion and sauté until it turns limp. Add spinach and cover pan until it wilts—a minute or so only. (If you don't have a saucepan large enough, do this step in batches.)

Dissolve tomato paste in water and add to the pan with salt, pepper, and nutmeg to taste, then mint. Stir well, turn heat low, and simmer, covered, 20 minutes.

Rice with Zucchini

SERVES 4

2/3 cup long-grain rice
1 1/3 cups water
salt
2 medium zucchini,
   trimmed and coarsely
   grated
freshly ground pepper
2 tablespoons butter

PROPERLY DONE, WITH THE RICE AND ZUCCHINI STILL RETAINING A LITTLE BITE TO THEM, THIS MAKES A SIMPLE BUT DELICIOUS DISH, USEFUL ON MANY OCCASIONS. IT HAS THE MERIT OF EASILY COMBINING BOTH STARCH AND VEGETABLE, EQUALLY GOOD WITH FISH, CHICKEN, OR MEATS. I LIKE TO PAIR IT WITH ANOTHER EASY VEGETABLE, CARROTS WITH GARLIC (PAGE 279), FOR COLOR CONTRAST.

Drop rice in a saucepan of boiling salted water. Cover, turn heat low, and simmer 16–17 minutes. Uncover, add zucchini and some pepper, and top with butter. Cover and cook another 2–3 minutes. Gently stir the mixture together and serve immediately.

THIS IS A LITTLE MORE COMPLICATED THAN THE PRECEDING RECIPE FOR RICE WITH ZUCCHINI, BUT IT LOOKS VERY PRETTY, AND SINCE IT IS SERVED AT ROOM TEMPERATURE, IT MAKES A FINE PRESENTATION FOR A BUFFET, OR TO BE SLICED AT TABLE FOR A PARTY DINNER.

Rice and Zucchini "Gateau"

SERVES 4

3 *medium zucchini, thinly sliced*
salt
1 *tablespoon butter*
1 *tablespoon olive oil (or vegetable oil)*
1 *small onion, chopped*
1 *clove garlic, minced*
freshly ground pepper
1 *cup drained and chopped canned tomatoes*
½ *cup cooked long-grain rice*
1 *tablespoon minced parsley*
¼ *cup grated Parmesan cheese*

Put zucchini in a colander and toss with salt. Let sit 30 minutes to drain, then pat dry with paper towels.

Preheat oven to 425°. Put butter and oil in a frying pan over medium heat. Sauté onion and garlic several minutes, or until onion wilts. Add zucchini and cook 2–3 minutes, then add pepper to taste and tomatoes. Simmer a few more minutes, then add rice, parsley, and half the Parmesan cheese.

Place in a lightly oiled 7-inch soufflé dish and press down gently, smoothing the top. Sprinkle remaining Parmesan cheese on top and bake 30 minutes. Remove from oven and let cool to room temperature. Unmold onto a serving plate. Serve cut into pie-shaped wedges.

Zucchini with Rosemary Cream

THIS IS BASED ON A SUGGESTION IN JANE GRIGSON'S LOVELY *VEGETABLE BOOK*. SHE IS PERHAPS THE BEST FOOD WRITER IN ENGLAND SINCE ELIZABETH DAVID, AND I HIGHLY RECOMMEND ALL HER BOOKS NOW THAT MOST OF THEM CAN BE FOUND IN PAPERBACK. SHE SAYS THIS METHOD MAY USE MOST ANY HERB, BUT THAT ROSEMARY IS BEST. I THINK YOU'LL DECIDE IT IS, TOO.

SERVES 4

4 *6-inch zucchini*
2 *tablespoons butter*
1 *2-inch sprig of fresh rosemary (or 1 teaspoon dried)*
salt and freshly ground pepper
½ *cup heavy cream*

Wash and trim zucchini, then slice diagonally in ½-inch pieces. Heat butter in a saucepan, then add zucchini, rosemary, and salt and pepper to taste. Cover pan and cook 4–5 minutes over medium heat, or until almost done. Add cream and cook another 3–4 minutes over high heat, or until cream thickens slightly. If you used a fresh sprig of rosemary, remove it before serving.

I ONCE SET OUT TO FIND THE BEST POSSIBLE SHAPE FOR DEEP-FRYING ZUCCHINI, AND I HAD CUT WEDGES, STRIPS, AND ROUNDS, BUT THEN I HAD ONE LEFT OVER AND THOUGHT MAYBE THEY WOULD CURL IN WATER IF THINLY CUT. THESE WERE THE LAST BATCH TO TRY, AND I KNEW I HAD A RECIPE THE LIKE OF WHICH THE WORLD HAD NOT SEEN BEFORE (OR I'D NEVER HEARD OR READ OF, ANYWAY). THEY PUFF UP LIKE *POMMES SOUFFLÉS*, SO CRISPLY DELICATE THAT I CERTAINLY DON'T THINK ABOUT OTHER SHAPES THESE DAYS. I HAVE NOT INCLUDED MANY DEEP-FRIED DISHES IN THIS BOOK BECAUSE THEY ARE NOT ECONOMICAL IF YOU HAVE TO DISCARD THE OIL AFTERWARD. BUT IF YOU FRY FOODS WITHOUT A STRONG TASTE, SUCH AS THESE, THE OIL CAN BE PUT THROUGH A FINE STRAINER AND REFRIGERATED FOR USE AGAIN. ONLY ADD A LITTLE FRESH OIL FOR THE NEXT BATCH.

My Zucchini Puffs

SERVES 4

3 *6-inch zucchini*
salt
vegetable oil
flour
freshly ground pepper
freshly grated nutmeg

Wash and trim zucchini. With a swivel vegetable peeler cut strips the length and width of zucchini, discarding first and last strips that are all peel. Cut strips in half so you have 3-inch pieces and place in a bowl of salted ice water. Cover and refrigerate 1 hour or more, or until they curl.

Heat 1 inch or more of vegetable oil in a cast-iron frying pan or deep-fat fryer until it starts to shimmer (about 370°–375°). Drain zucchini, pat lightly with paper towels, and shake in a bag of flour seasoned with salt, pepper, and a little nutmeg. Shake off any excess flour and fry in batches until they puff up and color lightly. Remove with a slotted spoon to paper towels. (I don't think these need salt, but taste one and see.) Serve immediately.

Zucchini Josephine

THOUGH I PREPARE THESE A LITTLE DIFFERENTLY, THIS RECIPE CAME ORIGINALLY FROM JOSEPHINE ARALDO'S *COOKING WITH JOSEPHINE*, A CHARMING BOOK TO HAVE ON THE SHELF, AS CHARMING AS JOSEPHINE HERSELF. A CORDON BLEU-TRAINED CHEF, SHE MOVED LONG AGO TO SAN FRANCISCO, WHERE SHE STILL REIGNS AS COOK, TEACHER, AND WRITER—THE ONLY EIGHTY-YEAR-OLD I'VE EVER MET WHO COULD BE DESCRIBED AS *GAMINE*. HER DISH IS NOT ONLY DELICIOUS, IT IS ADJUSTABLE. YOU DON'T NEED FRESH HERBS OTHER THAN PARSLEY, AND YOU CAN USE ALMOST ANY HERB YOU FANCY. A COMBINATION OF PARSLEY, GARLIC, AND DRIED BASIL, FOR INSTANCE, IS LOVELY, IF NOT QUITE AS DELICATE AS HER *FINES HERBES*. THESE ZUCCHINI ARE TASTY ACCOMPANIMENTS FOR SUMMER BARBECUES OR EVEN PICNICS SINCE THEY MAY BE EATEN OUT OF HAND IF NECESSARY. A PLATTER OF THEM NESTLED AMONG LETTUCE LEAVES MAKES AN EASY SHOW FOR A BUFFET PARTY. I LIKE THEM ANYTIME IN PLACE OF SALAD, PART OF AN ANTIPASTO, OR SIMPLY AS A FIRST COURSE WITH BREAD AND A GLASS OF WINE.

SERVES 4

6 *medium zucchini*
3 *tablespoons mixed, minced parsley, chives, and tarragon*
3 *tablespoons butter*
3 *tablespoons olive oil (or vegetable oil)*
1 *tablespoon white wine vinegar*
1 *teaspoon Dijon-style mustard*
salt and freshly ground pepper

Wash zucchini, cut off tips, and cut in half lengthwise. With a small spoon scrape out flesh so you have shells about ⅛ inch thick. Parboil shells 5 minutes in boiling salted water, then drain.

Mince scooped-out flesh with herbs and sauté in butter about 3 minutes. In a small bowl combine olive oil, vinegar, mustard, and salt and pepper to taste. Remove zucchini mixture from heat, add dressing, and stir to combine. Stuff shells with mixture and chill thoroughly.

BOTH HERBY AND TASTY, THESE ARE ALSO VERY ATTRACTIVE. IF NECESSARY, THEY CAN BE COOKED A BIT AHEAD AND BROILED AT THE LAST MINUTE.

Zucchini Fans

SERVES 4

4 *medium zucchini*
½ *teaspoon dried basil*
2 *tablespoons minced*
  parsley
6 *tablespoons butter, at*
  room temperature
vegetable oil
¼ *cup water*
1 *tablespoon bread crumbs*
2 *tablespoons grated*
  Parmesan cheese

Preheat oven to 400°. Being careful not to cut through stem end, slice each zucchini lengthwise into 4 slices. Chop together basil and parsley, and mix with butter. Spread mixture between zucchini leaves and press together lightly.

Oil a large baking pan and put water in. Separate zucchinis slightly so they fan out from the stem and place in the pan. Bake 18–20 minutes, or just until tender.

Sprinkle the fans with bread crumbs mixed with Parmesan cheese and broil 1–2 minutes, or until golden.

"*Anything Edible . . . May be Curried*"

Hermione Gingold's quip about British cookery is almost true, for a curry extends leftovers in a lively, creamy, spicy way most everyone approves, and though we don't ordinarily curry pork, ham, or corned beef, we feel comfortable that we might curry anything else. The Shakers even lightly curry cabbage for an ineffable dish, and Southerners add hints of curry powder to many dishes not strictly called curries.

One hardly feels the need of a recipe, even. You should certainly sauté in butter a good bit of chopped onion—never be stingy with onions in a curry—until soft and golden, and then stir in your meat, or fish, with at least a heaping tablespoon of good fresh curry powder. This should be at your seasoned judgment, for it's not as good to add it later. For variety you might also throw in a little ground coriander, some cardamom, cumin that has been shaken in a hot dry skillet, cayenne pepper, a scrap of garlic, a *soupçon* of fresh ginger. Also stir in a heaping tablespoon of flour, then add enough water or light stock so you have a good medium gravy—not a thick goo.

This, everybody knows. From here I go my own way with several simple tricks. I grate in a cucumber and apple, and a handful of raisins before cooking the curry about thirty minutes over a low heat. I taste and sample now and again for salt and hotness. I shoot in a good squirt of Tabasco for good measure. If there's time, a curry improves when it sits for a while to mellow. As the rice cooks, I warm the pot and let it bubble lightly, and then I stir in some cream for smoothness and a few drops of lemon juice to give it zing. Now it tastes just right!

Not so many years ago as we would like to think a curry was served in an American household with odd bowls of this and that to sprinkle and spoon over the dish, which even to my untutored tastes seemed not quite the right bowls. There were raisins, peanuts, chopped eggs, crumbled bacon bits, along with whatever else the cook could dream up to clean out the refrigerator and if you were lucky a small jar of Major Grey's Chutney bought especially at the store.

Of these, I throw all but the chutney to the winds. And though Major Grey, still expensive from the store, remains a friend, I put up my own chutnies every year from autumn bounty, as they do down South, for they are useful and charming on many occasions without the ghost of a curry in tow. Here are the accompaniments I finally settled on so there will be dollops of creaminess, tartness, sweetness, spiciness, and crispness to glorify a curry with every bite and make any fit for guests.

These are in amounts that serve 6, but they can be adjusted easily for any number—even yourself alone at table.

Raita

Put 2 cups of plain unsweetened yogurt in a bowl. Peel a cucumber, cut it in half lengthwise, and scoop out seeds, then grate it coarsely into the bowl. Add a minced clove of garlic and salt, pepper, and lemon juice to taste—it should be a shade tart. Add 1 tablespoon or so of freshly chopped mint (or dried mint chopped with parsley or some fresh coriander leaves). Stir all together, cover with plastic wrap, and let sit in refrigerator 1 hour or more to gather flavor.

Clove Bananas

Take 3 ripe but not soft bananas and peel them, then cut in ⅓-inch slices. Heat 3 tablespoons of butter in a frying pan and sauté slices lightly on each side, sprinkling with a little ground cloves as you go. When they are heated through, remove from the pan and keep warm.

Toasted Almonds

Drop ⅔ cup of shelled almonds in a pan of boiling water. Cook only 1–2 minutes, or until their skins shrivel, then drain and slip off skins. Cut lengthwise in small slivers. Heat 1 tablespoon of butter with 2 tablespoons of vegetable oil, and when it sizzles stir in almonds. Stir slowly over medium heat until almonds are evenly golden. Drain on paper towels.

Sweet Nothings

Y ou don't need them every day, but everybody seems to like desserts. And neither do they have to be all raspberry with chocolate and swirls of whipped cream— they can be simple yet spectacular. Gathered here, somewhat in a bouquet, are really those old all-purpose desserts called by the British and early Americans just "pudding." Meant for any family or elect company, most are thrifty, easy, adaptable, turned out with basic pans and skills. Though jewels, certainly none should be kept a secret.

The fine thing about puddings is they often settle into being good next day, and the next. Or even better— these are the ones I'm on the lookout for always. This is the cream of my crop, most so luscious they don't even need the cream. My father, who whispered to me aside from my mother that he "lives for desserts," has sampled most all of them.

I DON'T KNOW ABOUT QUEEN OF PUDDINGS, BUT THIS IS CERTAINLY
ONE OF THE MOST DELICIOUS BREAD PUDDINGS IN THE WORLD. IT IS
AN HEIRLOOM CHARLESTON RECIPE, BUT ITS ROOTS WOULD SEEM TO
BE PURE MRS. BEETON.

Queen of Puddings

SERVES 9

1   *quart milk*
2   *cups fresh breadcrumbs*
4   *eggs, separated*
1¼ *cups sugar*
1½ *tablespoons butter,*
    melted
1   *lemon*
¾   *cup jelly (or jam)*

Preheat oven to 350°. Place milk, bread crumbs, egg yolks, 1 cup of sugar, and melted butter in a bowl. Grate lemon rind and add to bowl with half of lemon juice. Beat well to combine and pour into a buttered 8-inch-square baking dish. Bake 50 minutes to 1 hour, or until the pudding is set.

Spread the jelly or jam over top of the pudding. Beat egg whites until stiff, then beat in remaining ¼ cup sugar and remaining lemon juice. Spread over the pudding and whirl a fork through topping so it makes little peaks. Return to the oven another 15 minutes, or until the meringue starts to brown lightly.

I learned this pudding from one of the best simple home cooks I've ever known. She also taught me her Summer Pudding, fresh currants or raspberries sugared and put in a bowl lined with bread, served after it had steeped well with a cloud of clotted cream—bliss. Most bread puddings cook up as a kind of bready mass, but this one is distinguished by a beautiful custard floating buttery crisp bread. Try it.

English Bread and Butter Pudding

SERVES 6

2 *cups milk*
4 *eggs*
¾ *cup sugar*
pinch of salt
½ *teaspoon vanilla extract*
4 *slices bread (white or wheat)*
4 *tablespoons butter, melted*
½ *cup raisins*

Preheat oven to 350°. Heat milk in a saucepan until bubbles appear around the edge. In a separate bowl, beat eggs with sugar and salt until light and frothy, then slowly beat in hot milk bit by bit. Add vanilla extract.

Cut bread (trimmed of crusts or not) into ½-inch cubes and place in an 8-inch-square baking pan. Add butter to cubes and toss to coat evenly. Add raisins and pour egg-milk mixture over. Stir briefly—the raisins will drop to the bottom and the bread will float on top.

Place whole pan in a larger baking pan with about 1 inch of hot water in it and bake 45 minutes, or until custard is set and the top begins to turn golden.

Jefferson Rice Pudding

On the whole, rice puddings are dreary affairs, leaden from too much rice, but Thomas Jefferson's favorite is perfect: light and creamy, with a great rum-flavored sauce to pour over and around. Don't hesitate to serve it to best company.

SERVES 6

4 *cups milk*
⅓ *cup long-grain rice*
3 *egg yolks*
1 *cup sugar*
1 *tablespoon rum*
1½ *teaspoons vanilla*
   extract
4 *eggs, separated*
2 *teaspoons grated lemon*
   rind

Put 3 cups of milk and the rice in a saucepan and cook 1 hour and 20 minutes over very low heat. The milk should not boil but just shimmer.

Meanwhile, make the sauce: scald remaining cup of milk. In a separate bowl, beat 3 egg yolks with ½ cup of sugar until light. Beat in a little of the hot milk to combine, then whisk all together. Cook over simmering water in a double boiler until slightly thickened and it coats a wooden spoon. Remove from heat and stir in rum and ½ teaspoon of vanilla extract. Let cool to room temperature, stir, then cover with plastic and refrigerate.

Preheat oven to 350°. Lightly butter a 1½-quart soufflé dish or casserole, and dust it with sugar. Beat yolks from the 4 separated eggs with the remaining ½ cup of sugar until light. Stir in lemon rind and remaining teaspoon of vanilla extract. Whisk in some of rice-milk mixture, then add the rest. Cook in the top of a double boiler until slightly thickened. Beat 4 egg whites until stiff but not dry, then fold into rice custard.

Pour into prepared dish, place in a larger pan, and add about 1 inch of hot water to pan. Bake 25–30 minutes, or until set. Serve pudding warm with cold sauce.

THIS PUDDING IS AN OLD-FASHIONED DELIGHT ADAPTED FROM A RECIPE OF FOOD WRITER RICHARD SAX. IT TAKES A HOMELY THING LIKE TAPIOCA PUDDING AND TREATS IT AS IF IT WERE ROYALTY.

Tapioca Flan

SERVES 4–6

⅔ cup plus 3 tablespoons
    sugar
1½ cups milk
⅓ cup quick-cooking
    tapioca
2 eggs, separated
2 tablespoons butter
1 teaspoon vanilla extract

Preheat oven to 325°. Put ⅔ cup of sugar in a small saucepan and let it caramelize over medium heat until amber-colored. There is no need to stir it until well toward the end, to make sure all sugar has melted. Quickly pour into a pie plate and tilt around so caramel coats the plate.

Put milk in a clean saucepan, stir in 3 tablespoons of sugar and tapioca, and bring to a boil over medium heat, stirring almost constantly so tapioca doesn't burn on the bottom. As it starts to thicken, it's a good idea to turn heat down low to make sure this doesn't happen. Remove from heat when it starts to bubble and stir in egg yolks, butter, and vanilla extract.

Beat egg whites until stiff but not dry and fold gently into pudding mixture. Scoop into pie plate. Place plate in a larger pan and pour hot water in pan to come up about halfway around plate. Bake 20–25 minutes, or until pudding is slightly firm to the touch and doesn't jiggle in the middle.

Remove pudding from oven and cool at least 15 minutes before serving. It is best warm, I think, rather than at room temperature or cold, but it's superb any way. To serve, run a knife around pudding and invert on a platter so syrup runs around it.

Woodford Pudding

SERVES 8–10

THE *LOS ANGELES TIMES* MENTIONED RECENTLY IN THEIR COOKING PAGES THAT THIS WAS ONE OF THE MOST REQUESTED RECIPES THEY HAD EVER PUBLISHED. I CAN WELL IMAGINE, FOR IT IS A DESSERT ANYONE WOULD LONG TO SERVE. AFTER A LITTLE RESEARCH I DISCOVERED FROM A FRIEND IN THE SOUTH THAT IT IS A COMMON RECIPE PASSED FROM HAND TO HAND THERE, IN BLACKBERRY COUNTRY.

¾ *cup butter*
1 *cup sugar*
3 *eggs, beaten*
1¼ *cups flour*
1 *teaspoon cinnamon*
1 *teaspoon baking soda*
½ *cup buttermilk*
1 *cup blackberry jam*
1½ *cups dark brown sugar*
1 *cup boiling water*
salt
2 *tablespoons heavy*
   cream
½ *teaspoon vanilla extract*

Preheat oven to 325°. Cream ½ cup of butter and sugar until light. Add eggs and beat well. Sift 1 cup of flour with cinnamon. Dissolve baking soda in buttermilk. Beat flour and buttermilk in alternately. Stir in jam. Grease a 12-inch by 7-inch baking dish (or 2 9-inch-round cake pans) and put in mixture. Bake 40–45 minutes, or until a toothpick inserted in the center comes out clean.

To make the sauce, mix brown sugar with remaining ¼ cup of flour. Pour boiling water into it and add a pinch of salt. Cook in a saucepan, stirring, about 8 minues. It should be smooth and thick. If too thick, add a bit more boiling water. Remove from heat and stir in remaining ¼ cup of butter, cream, and vanilla extract.

The pudding can be warm or cold, but the sauce ladled over the slices should be hot.

AS YOU SEE, THIS IS AS VERSATILE A PUDDING AS ANYONE COULD ASK FOR, ACCORDING TO WHAT'S IN SEASON OR WHAT YOU HAVE ON HAND. I LIKE TO USE AT LEAST TWO FRUITS, SUCH AS RHUBARB AND PEACHES, OR BERRIES AND APPLES, BUT THIS IS NOT NECESSARY. IF YOU KEEP A COUPLE OF CANS OF FRUIT ON HAND, THE PUDDING CAN BE MADE AT THE DROP OF A HAT, USING THE JUICES FROM THE CANS FOR THE TOPPING. THE ONLY THING ABOUT THIS DESSERT THAT IS NOT FINE IS THAT IT DOESN'T CHILL WELL AND SO SHOULD BE EATEN WHEN JUST COOKED.

Old-Fashioned Floating Fruit Pudding

SERVES 6

4 *tablespoons butter*
2 *cups fruit (fresh, canned, or thawed frozen)*
1 *tablespoon lemon juice*
1 *cup sugar*
1 *cup flour*
1 *teaspoon baking powder*
pinch of salt
⅛ *teaspoon freshly grated nutmeg*
½ *cup milk*
1 *tablespoon cornstarch*
1 *cup any fruit juice, heated*

Preheat oven to 375°. Use 1 tablespoon of butter to grease an 8-inch-square baking dish. Add fruit and sprinkle with lemon juice. (If using fresh fruit, peel, seed, and dice it. Canned fruit must be drained, frozen fruit need only be thawed.)

Beat remaining 3 tablespoons of butter with ¾ cup of sugar. Sift flour with baking powder, salt, and nutmeg, and add it alternately with milk to butter-sugar mixture until you have a batter. Spread this over fruit. Mix cornstarch and remaining ¼ cup of sugar and sprinkle over batter, then pour fruit juice on top.

Bake 1 hour, or until crusty and bubbly. Serve warm.

Lemon (or Orange) Sponge Custard

A GLORIOUS, COMFORTING OLD-TIME SWEET THAT MAKES A DELICATE SPONGE CAKE TOPPING WITH CUSTARD BENEATH FOR SAUCE. IT REALLY NEEDS NOTHING, BUT A DOLLOP OF UNSWEETENED WHIPPED CREAM WON'T HURT AT ALL. IT CAN EVEN BE MADE WITH LIMES, AND FOR THAT I LIKE TO ADD ONE TABLESPOON OF LIGHT RUM.

SERVES 4

1 *cup sugar*
½ *cup flour*
½ *teaspoon baking powder*
pinch of salt
3 *eggs, separated*
2 *teaspoons grated lemon (or orange) rind*
¼ *cup lemon juice (or ⅓ cup orange juice)*
2 *tablespoons melted butter*
1½ *cups milk*

Preheat oven to 350°. Lightly butter a 2-quart baking dish or 6 custard cups. Sift ¾ cup of sugar with flour, baking powder, and salt. Beat in egg yolks, rind, juice, butter, and milk. In a separate bowl, beat egg whites until stiff but not dry, and then beat in remaining ¼ cup of sugar to make a meringue. Fold this into the pudding mixture until no white flecks show.

Spoon into baking dish or cups. Place in a pan of hot water 1 inch deep. Bake 45 minutes, or until golden on top. Serve chilled.

I'M A GREAT FAN OF RICH CAKES OOZING WITH WHISKEYS OF ONE
KIND OR ANOTHER, BUT I TASTED THIS (JUST AS OOZING BUT MUCH
MORE ECONOMICAL) ONE DAY AT A FRIEND'S HOUSE AND RAN HOME
TO MAKE MY OWN. IT GETS BETTER AND BETTER
OVER SEVERAL DAYS IF YOU CAN KEEP YOUR
FAMILY AWAY FROM IT.

Coffee Syrup Cake

SERVES 9–12

- 3 *eggs*
- 3 *cups sugar*
- 1½ *tablespoons lemon juice*
- ½ *teaspoon grated lemon peel*
- ¾ *cup milk*
- 2 *tablespoons butter*
- 1½ *cups flour*
- 1½ *teaspoons baking powder*
- ¼ *teaspoon salt*
- 1½ *cups strong coffee*
- 2 *tablespoons rum (optional)*
- 1 *cup apricot jam*

Preheat oven to 350°. Beat eggs in a bowl until light colored and thick. Beat in 1½ cups of the sugar, lemon juice, and peel. Place milk in a saucepan with butter and heat until butter melts. Beat this into the egg mixture. Sift together flour, baking powder, and salt, then add to the liquid, mixing well. Place in a greased and floured 8-inch-square baking pan. Bake 35–40 minutes, or until a toothpick inserted in the center comes out clean.

While cake bakes, combine coffee and remaining 1½ cups of sugar in a saucepan. Bring to a boil, turn heat down, and let cook 3 minutes to make a syrup. Add rum if you use it. While the cake is still hot, ladle syrup over it—it seems like a lot, but the cake will absorb it like a sponge. Cool the cake in its pan. When cooled, spread with heated apricot jam.

Caramel Apple Cake

A LUSCIOUS CROSS BETWEEN A RICH PUDDING AND A CAKE, WITH THE WHOLE LAYER OF APPLES SWIMMING IN A BUTTERY CARAMEL AND ONLY A LIGHT CAKE MASKING THE TOP. YOU COULD SERVE IT WITH A LITTLE CREAM FROM A PITCHER, BUT IT REALLY DOESN'T NEED ANYTHING.

SERVES 9

10 *tablespoons butter, at room temperature*
 1 *cup light brown sugar, packed*
 5 *medium Golden Delicious apples, peeled, cored, and thinly sliced in wedges*
¾ *teaspoon cinnamon*
½ *cup milk*
 1 *egg*
 1 *teaspoon vanilla extract*
¼ *teaspoon salt*
 1 *cup flour*
½ *teaspoon baking soda*
½ *cup chopped walnuts (optional)*

Preheat oven to 350°. Spread 6 tablespoons of butter evenly over bottom of an 8-inch-square baking pan. Sprinkle with ½ cup of brown sugar. Stand apple slices upright in 3 rows with the curved side down, then use remaining slices to fit in between them, with the pointed side down. Sprinkle with cinnamon.

Cream remaining 4 tablespoons of butter with remaining ½ cup of brown sugar, then beat in milk, egg, vanilla extract, salt, flour, and baking soda. Add walnuts if you use them. Spread batter over the apples and bake 45–50 minutes. Let cake stand at least 10 minutes before cutting.

A DELIGHTFUL SPICY MOIST CAKE, MADE EVEN MOISTER WITH THE
SAUCE POURED OVER. DON'T WORRY IF YOU HAVE A SMALL FAMILY
BECAUSE THIS LASTS SEVERAL DAYS, GETTING EVEN BETTER. IT'S SO
GOOD, THIS SHAKER DELICACY, I NOTICE EVEN
SO-CALLED PRUNE HATERS GOBBLE IT UP.

Shaker Prune Cake

SERVES 12

3 *eggs*
1 *cup vegetable oil*
2½ *cups sugar*
2 *teaspoons baking soda*
1½ *cups buttermilk*
1 *teaspoon cinnamon*
1 *teaspoon allspice*
½ *teaspoon nutmeg*
2 *teaspoons vanilla
   extract*
2 *cups flour*
1 *cup coarsely chopped
   cooked prunes*
1 *cup chopped pecans (or
   walnuts)*
1 *tablespoon light corn
   syrup*
6 *tablespoons butter*

Preheat oven to 300°. Beat eggs lightly, then stir in vegetable oil and 1½ cups of sugar. In a separate bowl, stir 1½ teaspoons of baking soda into 1 cup of buttermilk and let it puff up. Add it to egg and sugar mixture along with spices, 1 teaspoon of vanilla extract, flour, prunes, and nuts. Grease 2 9-inch-round cake pans and flour them. Divide batter between pans and bake 40–45 minutes, or until cakes start to come away from the pan edge and a toothpick inserted in the center comes out clean. Remove from oven and set on a cake rack.

Immediately combine remaining 1 cup of sugar, ½ teaspoon of baking soda, ½ cup of buttermilk, corn syrup, and butter. (Use a rather large saucepan because this sauce boils up rather alarmingly.) Bring to a boil over high heat and let boil up as you stir. In 2 or 3 minutes the sauce will start to darken slightly. Remove from heat and let cool a little bit before stirring in remaining teaspoon of vanilla extract.

While the cakes are still warm, poke holes in them with a toothpick and spoon sauce over them. Serve when cool and all sauce has been absorbed.

THIS QUICK AND EASY CAKE IS A JOY TO HAVE ON HAND. WHAT THE
RECIPE DOESN'T SHOW IS HOW PRETTY THE BANANAS ARE HERE.
EVEN BEFORE BEING GLAZED THEY TAKE ON DELICATE COLORINGS AS
LOVELY AS ANY KIWI FRUIT.

Banana Upside-Down Cake

SERVES 6

1 *tablespoon butter*
½ *cup plus 2 tablespoons sugar*
3 *medium bananas*
3 *tablespoons melted butter*
1 *egg*
¾ *cup flour*
½ *teaspoon baking powder*
3 *tablespoons buttermilk*
¼ *teaspoon baking soda*
½ *teaspoon vanilla extract*
pinch of salt
½ *cup chopped walnuts (or pecans) (optional)*
2 *tablespoons currant jelly*
1 *tablespoon water*

Preheat oven to 350°. Butter a regular pie plate and sprinkle with 2 tablespoons of sugar. Slice enough bananas about ⅛ inch thick to decoratively cover bottom and sides of the pie plate. Mash remaining bananas to measure ½ cup. Put in a bowl and mix in remaining ½ cup of sugar, melted butter, and egg. In a small bowl, sift flour and baking powder together. In another bowl, stir buttermilk and baking soda together. Beat them into batter alternately, then add vanilla extract, salt, and nuts if you use them. Spoon over the banana-lined pan.

Bake 30 minutes, or until an even brown on top. Remove from oven and let cool to room temperature. To serve, run a knife around the pan and invert on a plate. Melt jelly with water over low heat, stirring until all lumps are gone. Glaze cake with this and serve.

THIS IS A WONDERFUL CAKE, MOIST, YET CRUNCHY FROM THE SUGAR TOPPING, AND WITH LOVELY TART POCKETS OF RHUBARB. IT IS SUPERB JUST AS IS, BUT FOR COMPANY I LIKE TO STACK IT UP WITH A LEMON FILLING BETWEEN THE LAYERS.

Rhubarb Sour Cream Cake

SERVES 12

¼ *cup butter*
1½ *cups brown sugar*
1 *egg*
1 *teaspoon vanilla extract*
2⅓ *cups flour*
1 *teaspoon baking soda*
½ *teaspoon salt*
1 *cup sour cream*
4 *cups ¼-inch-sliced rhubarb*
⅔ *cup sugar*
½ *teaspoon freshly grated nutmeg*

LEMON FILLING (optional)

2 *tablespoons cornstarch*
⅓ *cup sugar*
pinch of salt
⅓ *cup water*
2 *tablespoons lemon juice*
½ *teaspoon grated lemon rind*
1 *tablespoon butter*
2 *egg yolks, slightly beaten*

Preheat oven to 350°. Beat butter until light and creamy, then beat in brown sugar bit by bit. Beat in egg and vanilla extract. Sift flour with baking soda and salt, and beat it in alternately with sour cream. Finally, fold in the rhubarb. Divide batter between 2 9-inch-round cake pans that have been buttered and then floured. Smooth batter to the edges. Sprinkle with sugar mixed with nutmeg. Bake 40–45 minutes, or until springy on top. Cook on cake racks.

For the lemon filling: Stir cornstarch with sugar and salt. Stir in water, lemon juice, lemon rind, and butter. Cook in the top of a double boiler about 10 minutes, until thick. Off the heat, stir in egg yolks. Let cook another 2–3 minutes. Let cool a bit before filling cake layers.

French Pear Tart

THIS IS BASED ON A RECIPE OF JANE GRIGSON'S CALLED TARTE DE COMBRAI THAT I HAD FOUND IN A MAGAZINE, COMPUTED AMERICAN MEASURES FOR, AND COOKED WITH GREAT SUCCESS. WHEN I GOT READY TO MAKE IT AGAIN, I'D LOST THE RECIPE SO I CAME UP WITH THIS RICH AND CRUSTY VERSION.

SERVES 6

    4 *large ripe pears*
    2 *teaspoons lemon juice*
   ⅓ *cup flour*
   ½ *teaspoon baking powder*
   ⅛ *teaspoon powdered*
       ginger
pinch of salt
   ⅔ *cup sugar*
   ⅓ *cup milk*
    1 *egg*
    5 *tablespoons butter,*
       melted

Preheat oven to 400°. Peel and cut pears in quarters, then cut out cores. Cut each quarter in 3 slices and place in a bowl. When all are done, toss with lemon juice. Beat dry ingredients with ⅓ cup of sugar, milk, and egg, to make a batter. Add 1 tablespoon of butter to the batter and use some more to grease a pie plate. Lay pears in a wheel, pointed tips toward the center. Sprinkle with some of remaining sugar, pour batter over, then sprinkle with the last of the sugar. Pour remaining butter over and place pie plate in oven.

Bake 40 minutes, or until top is crusty and golden with pears showing through. Serve warm, cut in slices.

Emperor's Omelet

THIS HAS REALLY TOO MUCH FLOUR TO BE A PROPER OMELET, IT IS MORE A LIGHT PUDDING. BUT IT IS A LOVELY VIENNESE SWEET EASILY PUT TOGETHER AND A DELIGHT FOR COMMONERS AS WELL AS KAISERS. BECAUSE THERE IS NO DANGER THAT IT WILL FALL, IT CAN BE BAKED BEFORE DINNER AND ALLOWED TO SIT UNTIL YOU ARE READY TO TOSS IT WITH THE BUTTER AND SUGAR.

SERVES 3–4

⅓ *cup raisins*
2 *tablespoons rum (or brandy)*
2 *eggs, separated (at room temperature)*
½ *cup plus 1 tablespoon heavy cream*
¼ *cup plus 1 tablespoon sugar*
¾ *cup flour*
pinch of salt
2 *tablespoons butter*

Preheat oven to 350°. Put raisins in a small saucepan with rum or brandy. Cover pot, bring to a boil, turn off heat, and let soak 15–20 minutes to puff up.

Beat egg yolks in a bowl with cream. Beat in ¼ cup of the sugar, flour, and salt. Whip egg whites until they hold stiff peaks but are not dry, and fold them gently into yolk mixture. Place in a buttered soufflé dish and bake 25–30 minutes—or until puffed and golden. Remove from oven.

Melt butter and 1 tablespoon of sugar in a large frying pan over medium heat. Loosen edges of the pudding and lift it into the pan. Tear it gently with 2 forks into bite-size pieces. Add raisins and sauté quickly in butter-sugar mixture until each piece is lightly coated. Serve at once on warm plates.

Variations: 1. For an Orange Emperor's Omelet, use orange juice for about half the cream, and substitute candied strips of orange peel for the raisins. 2. For a Spanish Emperor's Omelet, add ¼ teaspoon of ground cinnamon to the butter-sugar mixture and serve a vanilla custard sauce as in the recipe for Caramel Meringue (page 340).

ALICE TOKLAS GOT IN TROUBLE ASKING FRIENDS FOR FAVORITE RECIPES. THIS IS NOT "HASCHICH FUDGE," BUT I THINK I RATHER STICK MY NECK OUT TO OFFER BRITISH ACTOR PETER BROMILOW'S RECIPE. AS HE ADMITS, "IT LOOKS TERRIBLE," HENCE ITS NAME. BUT I LIKE HIS HISTORY: "ORIGINALLY A NURSERY PUDDING INVENTED BY LADY BAMFIELD, BUT IMPROVED UPON BY MYSELF BY THE ADDITION OF RUM OR BRANDY, WHICH GLORIFIES IT AND BRINGS IT DOWN FROM THE NURSERY TO THE DINING ROOM." (ALL THIS IN AN OROTUND VOICE AUDIBLE TO THE FARTHEST BALCONY.) I FIRST TASTED IT AT A CHRISTMAS FEAST, AFTER WHICH PETER ENTERTAINED THE COMPANY WITH IMPROVISED IMPROPER CAROLS. DESPITE THIS PUDDING'S REPUTATION, IN THAT COMPANY IT TASTED DELICIOUS.

Mincemeat Moose (or Mouse)

SERVES 8

1 *envelope plain gelatin*
½ *cup water*
½ *cup rum (or brandy or mixture)*
1½ *cups mincemeat*
4 *egg whites*
⅓ *cup sugar*
1 *cup heavy cream*

Sprinkle gelatin on water, stir in, and let soften for 3 minutes or so. Stir in rum, or brandy, then stir mixture into mincemeat. Cover with plastic wrap and chill in refrigerator until consistency of egg whites.

Beat egg whites stiff, adding sugar bit by bit. Fold into mincemeat. Whip cream until it holds soft peaks, then fold into mincemeat. Place in an oiled 10-inch ring mold and chill several hours. Turn out on a serving plate and garnish judiciously.

I DON'T LIKE TO BANDY ABOUT THE WORD FABULOUS, BUT HERE IT FITS.

Caramel Meringue

SERVES 4–6

5 *eggs, separated*
sugar
salt
2 *cups milk, heated*
1 *teaspoon vanilla extract*
   (or 2 tablespoons rum)
1 *tablespoon water*
cream of tartar
toasted slivered almonds
   (optional)

Early in the day make the custard sauce: beat yolks with ¼ cup of sugar and a pinch of salt. Beat a bit of heated milk into them, then some more, then beat all together. Cook in the top of a double boiler over simmering water, stirring until custard thickens slightly and coats a wooden spoon. Remove from heat, cool to room temperature, then add vanilla extract or rum. Refrigerate, covered in plastic wrap.

Preheat oven to 400° about a half hour before serving. Place ¼ cup of sugar, water, and a pinch of cream of tartar in a small saucepan. Cook over medium heat until mixture turns deep golden. As it cooks, beat egg whites with ¼ teaspoon of cream of tartar and a pinch of salt until they hold glossy peaks. Beat in ⅓ cup of sugar bit by bit, then add caramelized sugar in a stream, beating at high speed. (If you don't have a mixer, have a partner—one to beat and one to pour.)

Butter an 8 cup soufflé dish, and dust with sugar. Carefully scoop in meringue. Bake 5 minutes, then turn off heat and let sit in unopened oven 15 minutes. Serve portions of the meringue in a pool of custard sauce, sprinkled with almonds if you use them.

Still Life, with Bowl of Fruits

Across the great museum corridors of Europe, masterpiece after masterpiece, I begin always to long for that seat in a faraway corner dedicated to ruddy, rounded peaches, pomegranates split among burnished apples, cloudy purpled grapes dangling a platter's edge, or cherries in a ribboned basket. There will be, I trust, a familiar glinting knife laid so any might see it had just cut half a lemon's peel in spiral, nuts to crack will lie alongside a slab of veined and mottled cheese, a sparkling glass of wine will beckon. . . . An idea, this, no fair dining lives up to, or seldom outside palaces.

Thus restored, the cook in all of us stirs and itches for the kitchen. Might that forever unplucked plum, that orange or red apple, be chosen from cornucopia to tease and test the home palate? Can there be a pear edible beyond the pear a painter has to show?

ONE OF THE TREASURES OF MY FILES: DON'T GO LOOKING GIFT
APPLES IN THE MOUTH HERE, THEY CAN TURN TO MUSH IN A
TWINKLING. STICK WITH THE UBIQUITOUS GOLDEN DELICIOUS.

Custard Apples

SERVES 4

4 *small Golden Delicious apples*
1 *egg*
⅓ *cup sugar*
¼ *cup milk*
1 *lemon*
3 *tablespoons butter, melted*

Preheat oven to 350°. Core apples and peel about ⅓ of the way down from the top. Place in a small baking dish, just the size to hold them all, cover with foil, then place a lid over. (I use a soufflé dish for this, with a lid from another pot.) Bake 30–40 minutes, or just until soft but not falling apart. Check after 30 minutes to make sure.

Beat egg, sugar, milk, grated lemon rind, and 1 tablespoon of lemon juice together. Beat in butter, and add any juice that has come from the apples and pour over and around apples. Bake, uncovered, another 15 minutes. Serve warm.

OKAY, THIS IS NOT SO SIMPLE, BUT IT WILL MAKE YOUR REPUTATION AS A COOK! IT'S ALSO POSSIBLE TO SHARE THE PRAISE, IF YOU ARE IN CHARGE OF MAKING AND ROLLING OUT THE CRUST, WHILE THE KIDS CREATE THE SYRUP, PEEL AND CORE THE APPLES. YOU CAN ALL THEN STUFF AND WRAP AND POUR AND SPRINKLE AND BAKE TOGETHER, A FINE FAMILY AFFAIR.

Old-Fashioned Apple Dumplings

SERVES 6

2¼ cups flour
¼ teaspoon salt
¾ cup cold lard (or vegetable shortening)
6 tablespoons ice water
1 cup brown sugar
2 cups water
butter
1 teaspoon vanilla extract
6 medium apples (Golden Delicious, preferably)
sugar
cinnamon
heavy cream

Place flour and salt in a bowl and cut in lard until no piece is larger than a small pea. Sprinkle ice water on as you mix with a fork, distributing water as well as possible. Put the mixture in plastic wrap or waxed paper, press to make a compact ball, and refrigerate at least 1 hour to let water permeate.

Preheat oven to 450°. Divide dough into 6 portions and roll out each portion as for a pie crust. Cut each into a 7-inch square and set aside.

Put brown sugar, water, and 3 tablespoons of butter in a saucepan and bring to a boil. Cook 3 minutes, then turn off heat and stir in vanilla extract.

Pare and core the apples. Fill cavities almost to the top with sugar, give a good sprinkle of cinnamon, and stuff each with about ½ tablespoon of butter.

Moisten edges of pastries slightly. Place an apple on each pastry and bring opposite corners up over the apple, sealing tops with a pinch. Fold corners gently all in the same direction around the apple.

Place apples in a shallow baking pan large enough to hold them all about 1 inch apart. Sprinkle lightly with sugar and a little more cinnamon. Pour brown sugar syrup around (not over) them.

Bake 10 minutes, then lower heat to 350°. Bake another 30 minutes, or until nicely browned and the apples are soft when you test with a small knife. Remove from oven and serve warm. They're so juicy you really don't need cream, but I serve them with cream from a small pitcher anyway.

THESE COOK LONGER THAN MOST BAKED BANANAS, BUT WHAT A DIFFERENCE IT MAKES! THERE IS AN EXOTIC HINT OF EDEN ALWAYS, I THINK, IN THE MIX OF ACID ORANGE AND BLAND SWEET BANANA—PERFECT PARTNERS

Orange Candied Bananas

SERVES 4

4 *bananas*
2 *tablespoons butter*
½ *cup orange juice*
½ *teaspoon grated orange peel*
¼ *cup brown sugar*
whipped cream

Preheat oven to 375°. Choose bananas that are ripe but not yet begun to speckle. Peel them, cut lengthwise in half, and lay cut side up in a baking dish large enough to hold them in a single layer.

Put all ingredients, except whipped cream, in a saucepan and stir over medium heat until sugar dissolves and the mixture begins to boil. Pour over bananas, place in the oven, and bake 30 minutes, spooning the orange syrup over them 3 or 4 times as they cook. When done, the juices will have become thickened and the bananas will start to candy.

Serve hot or at room temperature, with a dollop of unsweetened whipped cream.

THIS RECIPE HAS BEEN IN EVERY COOKBOOK I'VE EVER WRITTEN, AND I'M NOT GOING TO LEAVE IT OUT NOW FOR FIFTY CENTS' WORTH OF RUM. IT CAN BE SERVED WITH A LITTLE WHIPPED CREAM OR *CRÈME FRAÎCHE*, BUT IT REALLY DOESN'T NEED IT.

Bananas in Rum

SERVES 4

4 *bananas*
2 *tablespoons butter*
⅓ *cup sugar*
⅓ *cup rum*

Peel bananas, slice lengthwise, then cut slices in the middle to make 16 finger-shaped slices. Melt butter in a large frying pan over medium heat. Fry bananas 3 minutes per side and lift out to a shallow dish large enough to hold them all in a single layer.

Add sugar and rum to frying pan and cook, stirring, until the sugar dissolves and bubbles. Pour over bananas, cover, and refrigerate several hours.

To serve, place bananas in a fan on serving plates. Pour sauce into a saucepan and heat it, then pour over cold fruit.

WHAT COULD BE SIMPLER—OR MORE SENSUOUS?

Italian Glazed Oranges

SERVES 4

4 *oranges*
⅔ *cup sugar*
½ *cup water*

Pare strips of peel from 2 of the oranges with a vegetable peeler. Stack them up in batches and cut into matchstick lengths. Place these in a pot of boiling water and cook 3–4 minutes, then drain and reserve.

Peel all oranges with a sharp knife so every bit of pith is removed. Bring sugar and water to boil in a saucepan and cook over high heat until it makes a thick syrup. Remove from heat and roll oranges in the syrup until glazed all over. Place them in serving dishes.

Add peel to the syrup and cook over medium heat until transparent. Scoop out with a slotted spoon and arrange piles of peel on each orange. Serve chilled.

WHO FIRST TOLD ME A WHISPER OF CARDAMOM WITH PEARS WAS INEFFABLE? I DO NOT REMEMBER, BUT I KEEP THIS RECIPE IN MY PERMANENT BAGGAGE, READY TO SHIP OUT AND COOK WITH THE BEST.

Pears Poached with Lemon and Cardamom

SERVES 4

1 *lemon*
4 *pears, firm but ripe*
1 *cup sugar*
2 *cups water*
4 *cardamom pods*

Peel lemon with a vegetable peeler. Stack strips of peel in batches and cut into matchstick strips. Reserve. Put half the lemon juice in a bowl of water (this will keep the pears from turning brown). Peel pears, cut in half, and core them. Drop into lemon water.

Put sugar, water, and remaining half of lemon juice in a large saucepan. Crush cardamom pods lightly with a knife and extract seeds. Add them to the saucepan and bring to a boil. Simmer pears in this syrup until tender—about 15 minutes, depending on the fruit.

Scoop out pears with a slotted spoon and place in a bowl. Boil syrup down 5 minutes over high heat. Drop lemon peel into pan and boil until transparent, a matter of 3–4 minutes. Test one to see if it is tender. Strain syrup onto the pears, then pick out cardamom seeds and lemon peel and reserve peel.

Refrigerate for 1 hour or more. To serve, lift pears out onto plates, sprinkle with some syrup, and top with candied lemon strips.

FRENCH WRITER COLETTE THOUGHT THIS HER FAVORITE SWEET, BUT COMPLAINED SHE HAD TO MAKE A DOUBLE RECIPE, HER CATS LIKED IT SO. SO WILL YOU.

Pears Colette

SERVES 4

4 *pears*
½ *cup light brown sugar*
2 *tablespoons butter, melted*
⅓ *cup cream*
¼ *teaspoon vanilla extract*

Preheat oven to 350°. Peel pears and cut each in half, then scoop out cores with a small spoon. Drop immediately into a bowl of water with a little lemon juice in it so they won't discolor.

Place pears cut side down in a baking dish large enough to hold all in a single layer. Sprinkle sugar over, then dribble on butter. Bake 30–45 minutes depending on ripeness of pears, basting several times during cooking to ensure a glaze on the pears.

Remove from oven, pour the caramel syrup into a saucepan, and add cream. Cook over high heat until slightly thick, then pour over pears. Chill in the refrigerator for 1 hour or more before serving.

Snow Ice Cream

Enough just to drift and heap, before the first footstep or sled even, new fallen snow is a crop few harvest now. Our two festivals, growing up in Kansas—equivalent to stomping grapes in other climes—were the whole family soaping up in swimsuits out under the first summer downpour, and scooping up bowls for Snow Ice Cream—nothing more cold, more clear—only a few breathless minutes from backyard to kitchen table.

Everyone, no matter what age, seems to like catching snowflakes on the tongue, to throw snowballs, sculpt snowmen, and even to lie on it thrashing arms up and down to make imprints of "angels." But the art of making ice cream from that frosted bounty, surely one of my most sharp culinary memories, seems near lost as the skies grow grim. My last outpost back East writes that you can figure the first six inches clears the atmosphere, and if the top crust is suspect, the inner layer remains edible.

From there, granted your snowfall, this still exists as one of the superb family participation events, comparable to helping knead bread or decorating a Christmas tree. In New England, they loop out thick maple syrup onto snow, to pick up and chew with sour pickles and hot coffee—an unimaginable feast for those not brought up on it. The rest of the snowbelt sends out family runners to fill a huge bowl, meanwhile whisking cream with sugar and plenty of vanilla. Snow is folded into the mixture until you have a mount, and is then spooned up so cold as to make the forehead ache if the mouth is overeager.

A delight is that there can be no final recipe here, for snows are as unlike as each individual flake. Whoever is the principal whisker should, however, be the taster and spooner. The mixture should be of light (not heavy) cream, dissolved sugar, and vanilla. It should taste sweeter than you imagined and sharply of vanilla, for snow is a huge blotter of flavor. If you've planned the foray, use regular granulated sugar, if not, sift some powdered. For four, this would be about a cup of light cream, a cup and a half sugar, then a tablespoon and a good splash of pure vanilla extract.

Add first a good heap of snow, stir in deftly, then add scoop by scoop enough to make a creamy mass that holds a peak. If too soft, add snow, if too thick, more cream. Spoon into bowls held out by family. Though this is a dish of pure spontaneity, no one would object here to oven-warm cookies, but leave the cream simple—no fruits or chocolate fuss—only friends and family merry yet under the darkening skies, before the fire.

Index

About the Author

RONALD JOHNSON was born in Kansas and received his bachelor's degree from Columbia University. Primarily a poet, he wrote his first cookbook in 1968 and has continued to work in the culinary world, opening a successful San Francisco restaurant in 1976, and assisting for several years with one of the city's top caterers. For the last ten years he has been at work on a long poem entitled ARK which has been compared to Ezra Pound's *Cantos,* and critic Guy Davenport has said, recently, "Ronald Johnson is America's greatest living poet."